WHO WAS ARTHUR ZIMMERMANN
AND
WHAT WAS THE ZIMMERMANN TELEGRAM?

ARTHUR ZIMMERMANN—Crafty German Foreign Minister, he gambled with the fate of his warring nation. The stakes: total victory and world domination for Germany.

THE TELEGRAM—Sent by Zimmermann in German code, it offered Mexico and Japan a return to their former glory. The price they had to pay: declaration of war against the United States.

1917—a flaming world at war brought vividly to life by Barbara W. Tuchman, distinguished author of **The Guns of August** and **The Proud Tower.**

Bantam Books by Barbara W. Tuchman

THE PROUD TOWER
THE ZIMMERMANN TELEGRAM

The Zimmermann Telegram

by Barbara W. Tuchman

BANTAM BOOKS · TORONTO · LONDON · NEW YORK

A NATIONAL GENERAL COMPANY

*This low-priced Bantam Book
has been completely reset in a type face
designed for easy reading, and was printed
from new plates. It contains the complete
text of the original hard-cover edition.*
NOT ONE WORD HAS BEEN OMITTED.

THE ZIMMERMANN TELEGRAM
*A Bantam Book / published by arrangement with
The Macmillan Company*

PRINTING HISTORY
Viking Press edition published 1958
Macmillan edition published October 1966
4 printings through 1970
Book-of-the-Month Club edition published December 1966
Bantam edition published December 1971

*Bantam Books are published by Bantam Books, Inc., a National
General company. Its trade-mark, consisting of the words "Bantam
Books" and the portrayal of a bantam, is registered in the United
States Patent Office and in other countries. Marca Registrada.
Bantam Books, Inc., 666 Fifth Avenue, New York, N.Y. 10019.*

PRINTED IN THE UNITED STATES OF AMERICA

Contents

Author's Note

Nothing in this book has been invented. All persons mentioned are real persons; everything they said or did, as reported in the following pages, is based on documentary (or, in one of two instances, on verbal) evidence, which will be found in the Notes at the end of the book.

To the many who have given me willing help I am deeply grateful. Particularly I wish to express my debt and thanks to Mrs. Julia B. Carroll of the Diplomatic Records Branch, National Archives and Records Service, in Washington, for her indispensable assistance in guiding me through the archival maze and for her warmhearted cooperation in digging up evidence in answer to many puzzled queries; to Admiral Sir William James of Churt, Surrey, for his great personal kindness in aiding my Room 40 researches, as well as for his book, *The Eyes of the Navy,* to which I owe so much; to Commander P. K. Kemp, Admiralty Archivist, Whitehall, for supplying the facts on the cable-cutting voyage of the *Telconia;* to Mrs. Ruth Hotblack of London, Admiral Hall's secretary, for her personal reminiscences; to the late Wildon Lloyd of Washington, D.C., for making available to me his researches in the Szek case; to Mr. David C. Mearns, Chief, Manuscripts Division, Library of Congress, and to Mr. Howard B. Gotlieb, Librarian of Historical Manuscripts, Yale University Library, for help in locating information from the Wilson and Lansing, and the House papers respectively; to Mr. Boyd C. Shafer of the American Historical Association and Mrs. Agnes F. Peterson of the Hoover Institute and Library, Stanford University, for valuable suggestions as to sources; to the Honorable

Amos J. Peaslee for information from his records; to Dr. Paul Sweet, Chief, German Documents Division, Department of State; to Miss Anne Orde, Foreign Office Archives, London; to Mr. Walter Fried of New York for clarification of certain obscurities; to Mr. Alfred Romney and Mr. Henry Sachs of New York for supplementing my inadequate German.

For permission to quote from several manuscript collections, I wish to thank Mrs. Chandler P. Anderson for the Chandler P. Anderson Diary; Miss Mabel Choate for Ambassador Choate's letter; the Honorable Joseph C. Grew for his own papers; Mr. Arthur W. Page for the papers and diary of Ambassador Walter Hines Page; the Honorable William C. Phillips for his own papers; Houghton Library, Harvard University, custodian of the Grew, Page, and Phillips papers; and Yale University Library, custodian of the House and Polk papers.

I would like to thank the New York Society Library for books, open stacks, and newspaper microfilms, and especially for that greatest of boons, an undisturbed place to write.

To the anonymous reviewer of George F. Kennan's book, *Russia Leaves the War,* who wrote in the *Times Literary Supplement* (London), January 4, 1957, this sentence, "We still do not know at any level that really matters, why Wilson took the fateful decision to bring the United States into the First World War," I would like to say hello.

March, 1958

Preface to New Edition

Since this book was first published, new information has become available affecting the cryptographic problem of the telegram, though not to its historical and political circumstances, which stand as described.

A hitherto classified Signal Corps bulletin, "The Zimmermann Telegram of January 16, 1917 and Its Cryptographic Background" by William F. Friedman and Charles J. Mendelsohn (War Department, Office of the Chief Signal Officer, Washington, GPO, 1938) was declassified in 1965. Its primary author as Chief Cryptanalyst for the War Department, 1921–47, was the man responsible for breaking the Japanese code in 1941 and is America's leading figure in cryptography. At the time of writing I knew of the existence of the bulletin, but despite application to Mr. Friedman, who remained kind but close-mouthed, I was unable to examine it or learn its gist. It now appears to modify my account by disclosing that a second German code, No. 0075, was involved in the telegram, with implications as regards decoding which are analyzed in a forthcoming book, *The Codebreakers,* by David Kahn, former president of the New York Cipher Society. The chief conclusion drawn from the new evidence is that decryptment of the message was accomplished to a greater degree by "solving" than by the help of a German code book or copy of the code in Room 40's possession.

While venturing no dispute, I have retained in the following pages the stories suggesting a code copied by Szek or captured from Wassmuss because some measure of truth may yet lie buried in them and because the second story in particular was based on Admiral Hall's own affidavit, as follows: "The German cipher book covering this system of ciphering is in our possession, it having been captured by the British authorities in the luggage of a German consul named Wasmuss [sic] who was stationed at Shiraz while Wasmuss was engaged in an endeavor to cut a British oil pipe line." Friedman and Mendelsohn, reasonably enough, doubt that a diplomatic code book would have been entrusted to an agent like Wassmuss on his hazardous mission. Other new evidence, however, while supporting that doubt, now appears to confirm the story of a captured code book from the Persian Gulf.

Mr. C. J. Edmonds, who was Acting British Vice-Consul at Bushire on the Persian Gulf in 1915, was moved by the first appearance of this book to publish his own firsthand account of what took place there ("The Persian Gulf Prelude to The Zimmermann Telegram," *Journal of the Royal Central Asian Society,* January, 1960). He relates that Wassmuss' escape inspired the British staff at Bushire, including himself, to stage a thoroughly illegal arrest of the German Consul, Dr. Helmuth Listemann, and that among his effects, "wrapped up in several pairs of long woolen underpants," were found "two 'dictionary' cyphers." Mr. Edmonds writes that the interception of Wassmuss and raid on Listemann were "a single operation in two parts," adding that, while the first was given publicity, the second "for obvious reasons" was not. Herein may lie the explanation of Admiral Hall's affidavit. Since the arrest of Listemann was illegal he may have preferred to pass over it in silence and ascribe the finding of the cipher book, or books, to Wassmuss' luggage instead. As we now know from the many recent accounts of World War II espionage, the truth often does not get into the record while the cover story does.

Progress in filming and classifying the German Foreign Office Archives captured after World War II has made possible a number of scholarly studies, since this book was written, on the German-Japanese peace negotiations of 1915–16 and the declaration of unrestricted submarine warfare of January, 1917. Among these are Gerhard Ritter's *Die Tragödie der Staatskunst: Bethmann Hollweg als Kriegskanzler 1914–17* (Munich, 1964); a French study of the captured documents by Andre Scherer and Jacques Grunewald, *L'Allemagne et les problemes de la paix;* Vol. I, *Des Origines à la declaration de la guerre sous-marine à outrance, Août 1914–31—Janvier 1917* (Paris, 1962); and an article by Professor Frank W. Iklè, "Japanese-German Peace Negotiations During World War I," *American Historical Review,* October, 1965. These add to, but do not essentially alter, what was known at the time I wrote.

The role of a minor official in the German Foreign Office, Legation Counselor von Kemnitz (first name unknown), as originator of the idea for the telegram has recently been confirmed by a German investigator, Dr. Friedrich Katz, in his *Deutschland, Diaz und die mexikanische Revolution; die Deutsche Politik in Mexiko, 1870–1920* (Berlin, 1964). His researches have been made available to American readers by Professor Arthur S. Link in the fifth volume of his life of Wilson published in 1965. Although unmentioned by Dr. Katz, von Kemnitz' role was first disclosed by Professor Moritz J. Bonn as reported in the German press in October, 1918, and subsequently referred to by von Kemnitz himself when he was candidate of the German People's Party for election to the Reichstag in 1920. I did not include this rather shadowy figure in my account since the responsibility was in any case Zimmermann's and since there was too little information on von Kemnitz to bring him into focus, and what there was was uncertain. He was variously described as a Far Eastern and a Latin American specialist in the Foreign Office, a confusion which apparently persists because Dr. Katz calls him the one and Professor Link the other.

Dr. Katz makes the further point worth mentioning, that Zimmermann's proposal was warmly endorsed by the ultimate authority in Germany at the time, as shown by the fact that the renewed offer of alliance, after the fiasco of the telegram, was brought to Mexico and presented to Carranza by a representative of the Supreme Command.

BARBARA W. TUCHMAN
May, 1966

1

A Telegram Waylaid

The first message of the morning watch plopped out of the pneumatic tube into the wire basket with no more premonitory rattle than usual. The duty officer at British Naval Intelligence twisted open the cartridge and examined the German wireless intercept it contained without noting anything of unusual significance. When a glance showed him that the message was in non-naval code, he sent it in to the Political Section in the inner room and thought no more about it. The date was January 17, 1917, past the halfway mark of a war that had already ground through thirty months of reckless carnage and no gain.

On duty that morning in the inner room, the most secret in Whitehall, were two civilians diverted to cryptographic work masked under the guileless name of Room 40. One was the Reverend William Montgomery, a tall gray-haired scholar of forty-six, and the other Nigel de Grey, a young publisher of thirty-one borrowed from the firm of William Heinemann. Neither knew they were about to midwife a historic event. De Grey spread open the intercept, revealing rows of numerals arranged in four- and five- and a sprinkling of three-figure groups. Mute and passive on the paper, they gave forth no hint that a key to the war's deadlock lay concealed in their irregular jumble. De Grey noticed only that the message was of unusual length; more than a thousand groups, he estimated.

The gray morning was cold as Britain's fortunes, dingy as her hopes in this third winter of the war. The ghastly losses on the Somme—sixty thousand British casualties in a single mad day, over a million Allied and enemy losses in the five-month battle—had been for nothing. The

Hindenburg Line was still unbreached. The whole war had been like that, regiments of lives spent like water, half a million at Verdun alone, without either side's winning a strategic advantage, but only being riveted together like two fighting elks who have locked horns. Now the French were drained, the Russians dying, Rumania, a late entry on the Allied side, already ruined and overrun.

The enemy was no better off. Germans were living on a diet of potatoes, conscripting fifteen-year-olds for the army, gumming up the cracks that were beginning to appear in the authority of Kaiserdom with ever harsher measures. The German offer a few weeks before to negotiate a peace had been a mere pretense, designed to be rejected so that the General Staff could wring from the home front and faltering Austria yet more endurance and more sacrifice. Room 40 suspected it must have an ulterior purpose, for there was no evidence so far that the German leaders were any less obstinately fixed on total victory than the Allies.

England had fortitude left, but no money and, what was worse, no ideas. New commanders stumbled forward in the old rut, not questioning whether to assault the Western Front again, but merely where along its wall to bang their heads. No prospect of any end was visible.

Montgomery and de Grey examined the close-packed groups of numerals they were supposed to transform into verbal intelligence, expecting no more than another piece in the prolix correspondence they had been intercepting lately between Berlin and Washington about a negotiated peace. This was President Wilson's cherished goal. Bent on stopping the war, he quested after a compromise peace between mental blinkers, blind to both combatants' utter unwillingness to compromise at all. Berlin kept him talking in order to keep him neutral. The talk exasperated the Allies. It was not mediation they wanted from America but her great, fresh, untapped strength. Nothing else could break the war's deadlock. Arms, money, ships, men—everything the exhausted Allies needed was waiting in America, but Wilson would not budge. He remained unmoved behind his eyeglasses, lecturing both sides how to behave. It seemed there was nothing that would bring in the Americans before Europe exhausted itself beyond recovery.

De Grey's eye caught the top group of numerals in the message, 13042, and recognized it as a variant of 13040, title number of the German diplomatic code. He pointed it out to Montgomery, who unlocked the safe and took from it a book which he handled as he might have a bottle labeled POISON! If there was no visible skull and crossbones on the book's cover, there was more than one in its history, for the sea-bottom had been scraped and blood and life and honor spilled to assemble it. It was a reconstruction of the German code book for Code No. 13040. With it Montgomery took out another book that contained all that Room 40 had collected on the variants of the code. Through painstaking filing and collation of hundreds of intercepts, they had progressed toward a solution of the variants and so had built up a partially reconstructed key to use in cases like the present one.

The decoders tried first for the signature, which might give them a lead as to the nature of the message. A group in the 90000 range, 97556, appeared as the last group but two in the last row. High numbers such as this were usually reserved by the encoders for names or special words of infrequent use which were added as a supplement after the body of the code was made up. Working from earlier reconstructions in the code book, Montgomery and de Grey concentrated upon 97556. Obediently, as if tapped by a wand, it transformed itself into a name they knew well, "Zimmermann," the German Foreign Secretary.

Going back to the beginning, they searched for the addressee, but instead of a name the first words to emerge were "Most secret," and then they made out, "For Your Excellency's personal information." As the message was directed to Washington, the Excellency in question must be the German Ambassador there, Count von Bernstorff.

Routine so far, they were just about to decide, when an unexpected word appeared—"Mexico." Wondering what the Germans could be saying about Mexico, they worked on with added interest, decoding the word "alliance" and farther on, to their astonishment, "Japan," which was repeated in a phrase that came out as "us and Japan." The decoders looked at each other with a wild surmise. Was it possible that Japan, one of the Allied powers, was changing sides? Urgently now they renewed the attack, their muttering dying away into concentrated silence as their scribbling speeded up. The code book pages flipped back and forth with an agitated rustle while sheets of paper filled up with words tested and discarded, with more words fitted together until, after two hours and in spite of many gaps in the sequence, an intelligible version had come clear.

It fell into two parts, for the intercept contained two separate telegrams. The first and longer one, addressed to Bernstorff, informed him of Germany's intention to resume "unrestricted" submarine warfare on February 1, a decision expected and dreaded by the Allies for many months. "Unrestricted" meant that the U-boats were to be permitted to sink without warning all neutral as well as enemy merchant shipping found in the war zones. Bernstorff was instructed not to deliver the notice to the United States government until February 1, the very day the torpedoes would be let loose. Preparing for the belligerency that they believed would be America's answer to the U-boat, the Germans had added another telegram. It consisted of 155 code groups and was headed, "Berlin to Washington. W 158. 16 January, 1917. Most Secret. For Your Excellency's personal information and to be handed on to the Imperial Minister in Mexico by a safe route."

The message for the Imperial German Minister in Mexico, von Eckhardt, was headed "No. 1" and, in the incomplete version so far decoded, read:

WE PROPOSE TO BEGIN ON FEBRUARY 1 UNRESTRICTED SUBMARINE WARFARE. IN DOING THIS HOWEVER WE SHALL ENDEAVOR TO KEEP AMERICA NEUTRAL . . . (?) IF WE SHOULD NOT (? SUCCEED IN DOING SO) WE PROPOSE (? MEXICO) AN ALLIANCE UPON THE FOLLOWING BASIS: (JOINT) CONDUCT OF WAR, (JOINT)

CONCLUSION OF PEACE . . . YOUR EXCELLENCY SHOULD FOR THE PRESENT INFORM THE PRESIDENT* SECRETLY (? THAT WE EXPECT) WAR WITH THE U.S.A. (POSSIBLY) . . . (JAPAN) AND AT THE SAME TIME NEGOTIATE BE-TWEEN US AND JAPAN . . . PLEASE TELL THE PRESIDENT THAT . . . OUR SUBMARINES . . . WILL COMPEL ENGLAND TO PEACE WITHIN A FEW MONTHS. ACKNOWLEDGE RECEIPT. ZIMMERMANN.

The significance of the message the decoders could hardly let themselves believe. Zimmermann had given Room 40 the lever with which to move the United States. Mexico was both America's chief foreign investment area and chief trouble spot, where twice in the last three years American troops had gone in shooting and where, at that moment, twelve thousand men under General Pershing were deeply engaged. The United States was also exceedingly jumpy about Japan. In the circumstances, Zimmermann's spectacular proposal, picked out of the endless whispering in the air, must surely dynamite the Americans out of their neutrality.

In the telegram there was a blank passage of thirty groups from which the decoders had been unable to pry any meaning whatever. They could not guess that it contained the most explosive material of all. Only after weeks of patient, unrelenting effort were they able to reconstruct this portion of the code and discover that the missing passage contained Germany's promise to assist Mexico "to regain by conquest her lost territory in Texas, Arizona, and New Mexico."

Enough was at hand to require immediate action. This was a matter for the DNI, otherwise Admiral Hall, Director of Naval Intelligence. Montgomery hurried out of the room to fetch him. He returned, preceded through the door by a small ruddy man with authority in his step and an admiral's gold stripes on his sleeve. The physical presence of Admiral Sir William Reginald Hall frequently nerved in men an impulse to do something heroic. For

---

*Of Mexico.

once de Grey, as he stood up and silently handed the scribbled sheets to the admiral, felt equal to the moment.

"Zimmermann, eh?" said Admiral Hall while his eyes darted over the pages. As he read, the intermittent eyelid twitch for which he was nicknamed "Blinker Hall" quickened, the compact little figure seemed, if possible, to stiffen, the brilliant blue eyes to blaze almost literally, and the tufts of white hair to bristle around the bald pink head until he looked like a demonic Mr. Punch in uniform.

Hall knew instantly that he held in his hands notice of what was at once a deadly peril and a possible miracle. Only the miracle of America's entrance into the war could outweigh the peril of the unrestricted submarine, which, once let loose, might well accomplish what the Germans hoped—cut the Allies off from their source of supplies before the Americans had time to mobilize, train, and transport an army to help them. That was the stake the Germans were playing for.

Hall had known for months it would have to come to this, for the submarine was never designed for the gentlemanly role President Wilson seemed to think proper. To demand that it rise to the surface to warn before sinking, making itself a sitting duck in case its prey should shoot first, made nonsense of its function. He knew the Germans had accepted Wilsonian restrictions not because of the moral force of the President's notes tapped out on his private typewriter, but only because they had not enough U-boats on hand to force the issue. Since then, he knew too, Kiel's machine shops had been burning day and night, forging U-boats as fast as they could toward the goal of the two hundred Germany needed before letting loose a massive naval Verdun she hoped would bring Britain to her knees. Today's telegram was the signal that the two hundred must be nearly ready.

"Two weeks," Hall said aloud. In two weeks it would be February 1, the date staring up at him from Zimmermann's dispatch, when Britain's war effort, already hanging by its thumbs from Persia to the Channel on a lifeline of sea-borne supplies, would meet its greatest test. "Compel England to peace within a few months," Zimmermann's closing words had boasted. Hall knew it was no idle boast.

His mind racing ahead, Hall tried to think like a German. They had taken a desperate gamble, knowing unrestricted warfare might flush the reluctant dragon in the White House out of his cave. Obviously they must have made up their minds that the U-boats could sink ships faster than the Americans could mobilize, and it was even possible the Americans might not mobilize at all, in which case the gamble would pay off. But here in Hall's hands was a persuader, thoughtfully provided by Herr Zimmermann himself, that should help to make up the American mind.

Hall understood well enough why Zimmermann had sent the telegram. In case America should answer the U-boat threat by declaring war on Germany, he wanted to arrange enough trouble for her to keep her busy on her own side of the Atlantic. It was the shrewd, the clever thing to do—and he had done it, aiming straight for Mexico and Japan, the two whose long hostility to the United States gave most promise of readiness to jump to the attack. How right and proper! How correct!

Ah, yes, the Germans were clever, thought Hall with an inner smile, but just that fatal inch short of being clever enough to suspect that their enemy might be clever too. Sublimely confident that their code was as nearly perfect as human minds could devise—was it not scientific? was it not German?—they had used it unchanged since the first day of the war, assuming its inviolability. In war, never assume anything, Hall reflected, in the happy knowledge that every German wireless message was being grasped out of the ether and read in Room 40.

As Hall headed back to his own room he was reminded of a duty. He would have to inform the Foreign Office, and the thought dimmed his satisfaction. He hated sharing news of Room 40's coups with anybody, lest even a whisper get abroad to warn the Germans. Now he was seized by the agonizing problem that always haunts the cryptographer: how to make use of his information without revealing that he knows the code.

Faced with such a problem, armies have been known to

avoid warning their own men of enemy movements when such a warning would show knowledge that could have been gained only by possession of the enemy code. How, Hall asked himself, could the Zimmermann telegram be revealed to the Americans without revealing how it had been obtained? They would never believe it on the mere say-so of the Foreign Office. They would ask inconvenient questions. If the Germans discovered Room 40 had solved their code they would never use it again, and a whole delicate listening apparatus, carefully constructed, wire by wire, over two and a half years, would go dead. A new code might take years to break, as it had taken years, the genius of a few men, the lives of others, the long, patient months of plugging, to break this one. Hall could not risk disclosure.

Room 40 had sprung from an act done in the first hours of the war. England had declared war at midnight on August 4, and before the sun rose the next morning a ship moved slowly through the mist over the North Sea until she reached a point some miles off Emden, where the Dutch coast joins the German. In the half-darkness she began to fish in a manner that was strangely clumsy yet purposeful. Heavy grappling irons were plunged into the water, dragged along the bottom, and hauled up, bringing with them an eel-shaped catch, dripping mud and slime, that clanged against the ship's side with a metallic sound. Several times the maneuver was repeated, and each time the eel-like shapes were cut and cast back into the sea.

They were the German transatlantic cables. Five of them ran through the English Channel, one to Brest in France, one to Vigo in Spain, one to Tenerife in North Africa, and two to New York via the Azores. The English cable ship *Telconia* cut them all. She had no need to move on to the Mediterranean, for the cables there were English-owned, but a few days later she returned to the North Sea and, to exclude any possibility of repair, wound up the severed cable ends on her drums and carried them back home. It was England's first offensive action of the war and was to have results more lethal than were dreamed of when the Committee of Imperial Defense planned the action back in 1912. For two years an order authorizing the cable-cutting had lain dormant in Admiralty files, until the morning of August 4, 1914, when the German Army, glistening in spiked helmets and polished boots, marched into Belgium. Someone, on that day that ended a world, remembered the order, dug it out of the files, and dispatched it to the General Post Office. By midnight, when England's ultimatum on Belgian neutrality officially expired, the *Telconia* was already on her way.

After the *Telconia*'s work was done, only one cable remained open to Germany; this was one that ran between West Africa and Brazil and was largely American-owned. For a short time Germany was able to wireless messages to Africa and have them sent on from there in safety to South America and thence to the United States. When the British government, unwilling to risk American displeasure, refused to touch this cable, Hall's predecessor, Admiral H. F. Oliver, took his problem directly to Eastern Telegraph, the company that owned the Mediterranean cables. The company quietly pulled cousinly wires and was delighted to inform Admiral Oliver a few weeks later that the matter was satisfactorily arranged: they had thirty miles of the Liberia-Brazil cable in their tanks.

From that moment on, for the duration of the war, Germany was sealed off from direct cable communication with the overseas world, and the burden of communication fell on Nauen, the powerful German wireless station a few miles outside Berlin. Nothing can stop an enemy from picking wireless messages out of the free air—and nothing did. In England, Room 40 was born.

When intercepts in code began pouring over the desk of the Director of Naval Intelligence, at that time Admiral Oliver, the painful discovery was made that no one had been trained to deal with them. For two years the rumble of approaching war had been heard, but the Senior Service, never doubting its mastery of the seas, had prepared for it in the spirit that often governs play rehearsals: "It will be all right on the night." Harassed and sleepless in the frantic first hours of the war, Admiral Oliver thought of a

soft-spoken Scot named Alfred Ewing, a former professor
of Mechanical Engineering who was Director of Naval
Education. Ewing, he remembered, had made a hobby
of constructing ciphers. Oliver sent for him and handed
him a bundle of intercepts. Under shaggy eyebrows the
blue eyes of the little Scot brightened with interest as he
agreed to see what he could make of them. Relieved,
Admiral Oliver gave orders that henceforth all intercepts
were to be delivered to Mr. Ewing, and turned his attention to other matters.

Ewing found himself surrounded by ciphers and codes
and was soon blissfully absorbed in an occupation he had
followed ever since as a small boy he had won a newspaper prize for solving an acrostic puzzle. As the intercepts
piled up around him, Ewing was obliged to call for help
from one or two discreet friends who were amateur cryptographers like himself or had a knowledge of German.
This was how Montgomery was recruited from the Presby-
terian ministry, for, besides being an authority on St.
Augustine, he was a gifted translator of theological works
from the German. No work, it was said, had ever been
so idiomatically and yet so faithfully rendered as Montgomery's translation of Schweitzer's *Quest of the Historical
Jesus,* published in 1914. He and Ewing's other recruits
studied code books at the British Museum, collected commercial codes from Lloyds and the G.P.O., plunged themselves into the intricacies of Playfair and Vigenère squares,
alphabet frequencies, single and double substitutions,
grilles, and word wheels.

All the while German submarines and other fleet units
were constantly chattering with one another and with
Berlin, while the wireless station at Nauen, conducting
policy over the air, issued streams of instructions around
the world. To catch this verbal outpouring, four new listening stations were set up along the English coast with
direct wires to the Admiralty basement; amateur wireless
operators who were picking up unintelligible signals on
their sets increased the flow of intercepts. Soon they were
coming in at the rate of two hundred a day, overwhelming
the staff Ewing had increased to five. He recruited more

assistants—university dons, barristers, linguists, accountants with a flair for mathematical pattern, all men who went into battle against the ciphers with a zest for the intellectual challenge.

Cipher differs from code in that it is constructed upon a systematic method in which one letter or group of letters (or number or group of numbers) represents another letter or group according to some prearranged pattern. Code, on the other hand, is based on arbitrary substitution in which the substitutions are listed in a code book made up by the encoder. Sometimes a word is substituted for another word or idea—as, for example, in its simplest form, "Overlord" in 1944 was the code word for "Invasion of Normandy." Or, as in the case of the Zimmermann telegram, a code can be based on the substitution of an arbitrary group of numerals for a word as, for example, in the telegram 67893 represented "Mexico." Generally, although not always, when the Germans used code they wrapped it inside an extra covering of cipher; that is, they enciphered the code. The key to the encipherment they changed frequently—as time went on, every twenty-four hours. But, being orderly Germans, they changed it according to an orderly system which, once solved by the cryptanalysts of Room 40, could be solved again each time by progressing according to a constant pattern. For some reason still obscure, the Zimmermann telegram, when it was sent, was not put in enciphered code.

From the beginning, the Germans, heaping the air with their messages, ignored the possibility of their codes and ciphers being solved because they considered the enemy unequal to such intellectual exercise. The very number they sent out, often in duplicate and triplicate over two or three different routes, greatly facilitated Ewing's task by giving him several versions of the same message, and it was not long before his band of amateurs, with the aid of technical methods and machines they had improvised, were reading Berlin's messages more quickly and correctly than the German recipients. One wizard, working upon a series of numerals extracted out of the air over Macedonia, was able to transform the cipher into words which he himself could not read but which turned out to be the instructions of the Bulgar General Staff in Bulgarian.

To the ordinary mind it seems impossible that a code based on substitutions arbitrarily chosen by the encoder can be solved—or, as the cryptographers say, reconstructed—by a person not in possession of the code book Yet in time, with a sufficient number of messages to compare, with ingenuity, endless patience, and sparks of inspired guessing, it can be done. One has only to imagine the infinite difficulty of the process to realize the worth of the short-cut provided when a copy of the enemy code book is captured.

On October 13, 1914, came one such extraordinary windfall. In response to a call from the Russian Embassy, Admiral Oliver and Ewing hurried over and were conducted to a private room where they were introduced to a staff officer of the Russian Admiralty who handed them a small, rather heavy package. Opening it, Oliver and Ewing could hardly believe their luck; under their eyes was the German naval code book, lined in lead for quick jettison overboard in case of need.

"Magdeburg" was the one-word explanation offered by the Russian officer. Oliver remembered a German light cruiser of that name that had been lost in the Baltic in August. She had been escorting mine layers in the Gulf of Finland, the Russian offcer told them, when she ran aground in a fog off the island of Odensholm. Through a break in the fog her captain had seen two Russian cruisers bearing down upon him. Quickly he ordered his signalman to fetch the code book, row out to deep water, and throw it overboard. Just as the dinghy was being lowered, a shot from the Russian guns tore into it and, in his moment of death, the signalman's arms clutched the code book to his body. The Russian cruisers, closing in, destroyed the *Magdeburg* and proceeded methodically to the rescue of the German sailors floundering in the water. Someone spotted a floating body, which was hauled aboard with the living; it was the dead signalman, still clasping the code book in his arms.

The Russian Admiralty at St. Petersburg, exhibiting rare

good sense, had decided the code could best be used by the British Admiralty and, with even rarer generosity to an ally, had sent it by fast cruiser to London. Oliver and Ewing found in the *Magdeburg*'s salt-soaked relic not only the word columns on which the naval code was based but also a key to the cipher system according to which the code was varied from time to time. This gave them a clue to German cryptography which was the root and fundament of all that followed.

In November, upon the promotion of Admiral Oliver to Chief of Staff, a crackling breeze blew through Admiralty corridors with the advent of Captain William Reginald Hall, fresh from the bridge of a battle-cruiser, as the new DNI. The new Director was known as a precedent-breaker. In 1913, sniffing war in the air, Hall had put his ship, for greater alertness, on eight-hour watches instead of the traditional twelve, and ordered gunnery practice for the crew instead of leaving the gun mounts with their paint unmarred, as was customary. His innovations outraged the Mandarins, as the naval Colonel Blimps were called, but Hall, operating on the quaint theory that the Navy might be needed for battle and that whatever increased the ship's efficiency was a criterion for change, had continued trampling on the toes of orthodoxy.

His first act as DNI was made on the same principle. On finding the Intelligence staff overflowing its original space, he moved out of the main Admiralty building into a quiet backwater next door known as the Old Building. Here, set apart from bustle and visitors, was an isolated suite of rooms giving off Number 40. Although the staff later moved again to larger quarters, the name Room 40, O.B., so noncommittal that it stirred no curiosity, stuck to the operation throughout the war, as it has in the halls of cryptographic fame ever since. By the time the Zimmermann telegram was intercepted, Room 40 employed eight hundred wireless operators and seventy or eighty cryptographers and clerks.

Hall knew nothing about cryptography, but he instantly saw the absorbing opportunities for thwarting the Germans that were being opened by Ewing's cracksmen. The war had just become world-wide, spilling over the Middle East when the Turkish Empire joined the Central Powers a few days before Hall arrived in Whitehall. Hall soon jumped the original horizon of Naval Intelligence and arrogated to himself the task of counter-plotting against German intrigues anywhere in the world. He began at once to penetrate into every cranny of espionage, until no man's pie was free of his ambitious finger. Scotland Yard, tracking German spies, found Hall helping them; the censorship bumped up against him; so did the Blockade Bureau, the War Department, the Secret Service. Wherever intelligence was being gathered and turned against the enemy, there was Hall; wherever was a spot from which trouble might come, there he placed an agent or established contact with an Allied sympathizer. Like God in the British national anthem, Hall was ready to confound the politics and frustrate the knavish tricks of Britain's enemies. He was ruthless, sometimes cruel, always resourceful. His piercing eye, his unrelenting drive, his magnetism could get anything he wanted out of anybody. Wherever Germans were plotting, Hall was listening and, like dogs who can hear high-pitched sounds that never reach the human ear, Hall could hear intrigues hatching anywhere in the war. The more Room 40 decoded, the more came into his net: Indian revolutionaries and Irish rebellions, Sir Roger Casement and Mata Hari, German-fomented strikes and German sabotage. But all this activity was carefully masked by a bland pretense of ordinariness that implied that Naval Intelligence was no more than it was supposed to be, a lot of chaps busily tracking German fleet movements, locating U-boats by intercepted wireless signals, and charting mine fields. As this, in fact, was just what Room 40's outer group was doing, it provided the perfect cover for the activities of the inner group.

Leaving cryptography in Ewing's charge, Hall himself directed the efforts to acquire the German code books. Sooner or later any whisper or hint of a code picked up by Army, Navy, diplomatic, or other agents found its way to him. In December 1914 an iron-bound sea chest was delivered to Room 40 and identified as having come from one of a group of four German destroyers that had been sighted, chased, and sunk by the English on October 13. For two months the chest had lain on the bottom until by chance it was hauled up in the net of an English fishing trawler. Among the charts and confidential papers it contained, Room 40 found a code book whose use remained obscure for some time. After months of bafflement, comparison with certain intercepts proved it to be the code used by Berlin for communicating with German naval attachés abroad.

In the meantime, two strange dramas, a tragedy and a frontier adventure, were being enacted simultaneously, one in Brussels and one in Persia, each to have its denouement in Room 40.

When the Germans occupied Brussels on August 20, 1914, they found there a powerful wireless sending station that had gone out of order, and a twenty-year-old university student of wireless engineering who, it was said, could fix it. The young man, whose name was Alexander Szek, was of dual nationality by virtue of British birth and Austro-Hungarian parentage. He had grown up in England with his parents, but two years before the war he had moved with his father to Brussels, where he remained to study while the father went back to Vienna to live. Someone of Szek's family, either his mother or a sister, had remained in England. (The facts in this part of the Szek case are fuzzy, so we do not know exactly who it was.) The Germans naturally chose to consider young Szek an Austrian citizen and, as the alternative to sending him to Vienna for military service, commandeered his services for the Brussels station. Working there, he had access to the code.

Intercepts from the repaired Brussels station were soon streaming into Room 40 in a code no one could make out. Reasoning from this failure that Brussels was using the German consular or diplomatic code, Ewing requested extramural help. Allied Intelligence had contact via neutral Holland with a Belgian agent in Brussels, and, after careful reconnaissance in the Rue de la Loi, where the wireless station was located, the agent was able to report back the interesting fact that a trusted code clerk in the German employ could be claimed as a British subject, having been born in Croydon, just outside London. With this clue, Szek's sister—or mother—was located in England, acting as a governess. She was half Austrian, and her sympathies, like those of not a few full Austrians, were anti-German; she was without great difficulty persuaded to write a letter to her brother—or son—urging him to work for the country of his birth.

Even with this letter the Belgian agent was hard put to overcome Szek's fears and reluctance; but at last, early in 1915, he agreed to steal the code. His initial proposal, however, to escape outright with it to England was worse than useless, as the Germans would then have known that the code had been taken. More persuasion was required to convince the trembling clerk he must copy it bit by bit. Painfully, half a column or a column at a time, he began to do it, taking three months before it was completed. At the beginning he passed on the slips to the agent as they were completed, but, becoming increasingly nervous, he grew balky and at the last moment refused to hand over the rest of the code. With it on his person as his only assurance against being left behind, he insisted that he and the agent leave together.

It was then April 1915. What happened next no one knows for certain, but Szek was never seen alive after the war. The copied sheets of code, however, did reach an English Intelligence agent in Holland, who forwarded them to their proper haven in Room 40. As to Szek, some have claimed that the Germans captured and shot him, but Szek's father, after the war, accused the English of having done away with him in order to prevent the Germans from ever finding out that the code was taken. All we know is that his life was the cost of a code which the English got, which reached Room 40, and which the Germans went right on using.

Meanwhile, far away in Mesopotamia, in February 1915, a man very different from Szek embarked in a small boat to sail down the Tigris on a grandiose mission—no less than to bring Persia into the war on the German-

Turkish side. For years the Kaiser had hankered after his Berlin-to-Baghdad dream, and now his empire-builders saw themselves ending Anglo-Russian domination of Persia, swinging all Islam behind the Central Powers, bringing in Afghanistan after Persia, and ultimately marching triumphantly into India. More immediate strategy required the cutting of the Anglo-Persian pipeline.

The man in the boat who was to accomplish all this was Wilhelm Wassmuss, for many years German Vice-Consul at Bushire on the Persian Gulf. Like Lawrence over in Arabia, Wassmuss was part mystic, part fanatic, part charlatan, with a dash of hero. Like Lawrence, who was similarly trying to swing Turkey's Arab subjects over to the British, Wassmuss fancied himself as the destined liberator of desert tribes whose flowing robes both he and Lawrence liked to wear and be photographed in. At Constantinople he had been briefed on the proposed mission (or more likely proposed it himself), and he was on his way back to Persia now, armed with several bundles of propaganda leaflets and an intimate knowledge of the country and its people.

Wassmuss left the Tigris forty miles below Kut-al-Imara, and crossed secretly into Persia. His first objective was the Bakhtiari tribes through whose territory ran the Anglo-Persian pipeline. On February 5 the pipeline was cut, though it seems doubtful if it was at the instigation of Wassmuss, for he would hardly have arrived in the area by then. Shortly afterward he passed through the market towns of Dizful and Shushtar, conferring with tribal chieftains and distributing his pamphlets inciting them to a *jihad* or holy war against Britain as the enemy of Islam's Caliph, the Sultan of Turkey.

"Jihad! Jihad!" the whisper flashed through the bazaars, and from then on Wassmuss's progress was about as secret as that of a fox in a henyard. A pounce upon his party by local gendarmes at Shushtar was foiled when he was warned and fled in time, but a hundred miles farther south, where he next appeared, at Behbehan, the local Khan decided to make his fortune by presenting Wassmuss to the British. First he invited Wassmuss to his home as his

guest, then, with something less than traditional Moslem hospitality, locked him up under armed guard and sent off a messenger to the British at Bushire. The messenger, meeting a British detachment on the road, excitedly urged them forward to take his master's prisoner into custody. The mounted officers of the detachment galloped into Behbehan, spent precious minutes exchanging the politenesses of Eastern protocol with the beaming Khan and arranging his reward, turned to take their prisoner, and found him gone. Rushing to the roof, they saw only a flurry of dust in the distance marking the escape, but down in the courtyard they found assorted bundles and baggage left behind.

These were dejectedly carried back with them to Bushire, where, when the pamphlets were read, the British blew loudly for the hunt. Because of Persia's neutrality, a full-scale expedition was impossible, and Wassmuss again slipped through the hands of a small party that ran him to earth in a mud village. He made his way to Shiraz, the provincial capital, where he cut a wide swath of trouble, including a raid that resulted in the murder of the British Vice-Consul and the arrest and rather rude removal of the Consul and entire British colony to the coast.

In the course of these activities, one thing that marked Wassmuss' progress was a seemingly disproportionate irritation over the loss of his baggage. Witnesses reported his bursts of anger, how he "lashed the tribesmen into transports of rage over the seizure of his pamphlets," how he demanded to see the Governor at Shiraz, to whom he presented a formal protest and a claim for the return of his baggage. Since by now his purposes were known to all Persia as well as to the British, who had in the meantime raided the German consulate at Bushire and found in its files the full plans for his mission, his rage would appear to have been pointless unless the baggage contained something of extraordinary value known only to him. In any event, the baggage was beyond his reach, the British in Bushire having sent it on to London.

In London late that summer, Admiral Hall was listening to the account of a naval officer invalided home from the Persian Gulf. Naturally the tale of Wassmuss' hair-breadth escapes and depredations figured largely. A private buzzer sounded inside Hall's mind, and as soon as his visitor had left he sent aides scurrying through Whitehall, discreetly inquiring for the Wassmuss baggage. The day was ending when a call came through from one of the searchers, saying the baggage had been located in the cellar of the India Office, not three minutes' walk away. It had not been touched since it came from Persia. Hall had it brought over, and blinking like a semaphore, cut the rope holding it together. Carefully separating the papers, he found in their midst, as his sixth sense had told him he would, the German diplomatic code book, Code No. 13040.

Because Room 40's records have never, with a few exceptions, been made public, and because Admiral Hall was refused permission to publish the autobiography he began in 1932, some dates are necessarily imprecise. Sometime between June and September 1915 can be fixed as the time when both the Szek and the Wassmuss codes reached Room 40. Whether the code obtained through Szek was also the diplomatic code, or another, has never been made clear. But in any event, Ewing's staff now went to work on certain boxes of intercepts hitherto set aside as belonging to some category unknown but recognizably non-naval. No. 13040 was discovered to be one of the two codes used for communication between Berlin and Washington and, with Washington as the transferral point, between Berlin and all German missions in the Western Hemisphere.

With 13040 in his possession Admiral Hall could listen in on a remarkable correspondence—the uniquely informative reports from Washington of Ambassador Bernstorff to his government in Berlin. Since November 1916 these had centered on Wilson's efforts to bring the combatants to terms, revealing to Hall how obstinately set the American President was on preserving his country for the role of mediator, not belligerent. Without American belligerency, he well knew, the Allies could never win, would, in fact, despite all public protest to the contrary, soon be forced to negotiate.

Back at his desk, with the Zimmermann telegram in his hand, Hall believed he held the instrument that would puncture American neutrality—if it could be used. That "if" was his problem. He looked out across the open space of the Horse Guards Parade to the Renaissance bulk of the Foreign Office. His eyes picked out the second-story window that was the Secretary's room, where he could picture Arthur Balfour at that moment, slouched back in his chair, his long legs stretched out beneath the table in the deceptively sleepy pose caricaturists had made famous through three governments. No one had ever seen Balfour animated off the tennis court. During the past year, when Balfour had been First Lord of the Admiralty, Hall had learned that very little ever ruffled the tall, cool, skeptical man who had once been Prime Minister, who cheerfully accepted any post and cared for none, and who, when escorted to the front, nonchalantly admired the bursting shells through his pince-nez. But Hall knew how desperately Balfour needed what Room 40 had found. Behind that serene façade he must be despairing of the waiting game he was forced to play with the United States, trying always sauvely, imperceptibly, to nudge them over the edge of neutrality, yet without ever seeming to interfere.

At that moment Balfour's need was urgent. England was spending £5,500,000 a day on the war, and cash and credit were as low as they could go. Six weeks ago the American Federal Reserve had warned its member banks against making long-term loans to belligerent governments or even short-term loans that were liable for renewal. It was Wilson's way of trying to pressure the belligerents into a negotiated peace. Britain would never negotiate on any terms Germany could offer. But if the loan embargo was maintained, the collapse of the Allies would be a matter of months.

Admiral Hall was still staring fixedly at Balfour's window. To go over there now and give Balfour the telegram to use as he liked in Washington would be to stake all on the likelihood that it would indeed bring the Americans in. But suppose it did not; he would have gambled the code and gained nothing. Personally he could not see how the Mexican-Japanese threat could fail of its effect, but if that mulish fellow in the White House remained still "too proud to fight," he might sidestep it somehow. Hall had to be sure. He knew, as the Admiralty's former First Lord, Winston Churchill, was to say later, that United States action depended solely on the workings of this one man's mind. But who in England understood how that mind worked?

Hall wished desperately that he knew half as much about the White House as he did about the Wilhelmstrasse. To release the telegram meant risking the code; but to withhold the telegram meant throwing away the greatest triumph possession of the code could bring. He was in an agonizing dilemma. But he was determined to find a way out. Already half-formed schemes were tickling at the back of his mind, but they would take time, and time was running thin. He still had two weeks' grace, for when the German order to resume unrestricted submarine warfare on February 1 became known, the United States might come in of its own accord, sparing him the necessity of using the Zimmermann telegram. If not, the telegram would have to be published, but in the meantime he might be able to cover Room 40's tracks.

He hesitated, still held by the window opposite. Had he the right to keep this knowledge from his government? Years on the bridge had not only disciplined him to lonely decisions but given him a positive taste for them. He relished the responsibility of sole command. Turning his back on the window, he locked the dispatch—and with it two weeks of his country's life—inside his private safe.

Then Admiral Hall sat down to work out a plan and to wait.

In Berlin they were waiting too—for the answer of Mexico and Japan. The league of these two nations in alliance with Germany was no last-minute makeshift but a plan that had evolved over many years since the moment when one of the most meddlesome sovereigns in history sat down in his palace to paint a picture.

The Clever Kaiser and
the Yellow Peril

Late in the year 1895, Kaiser Wilhelm had a revelation. He decided to commit it to paper in the form of a drawing, and when he had finished he was delighted with his artistry; the ominous Oriental figure dominating the picture was truly admirable. Suddenly it inspired in his fertile mind a title in one succinct and striking phrase: *Die gelbe Gefahr!*—the Yellow Peril.

Europe had been shocked earlier in that year by the quick, cut-and-slash victory of Japan over the ancient colossus of China. He alone, the Kaiser believed, grasped the significance of that event. Germany, France, and Russia had joined to force Japan to disgorge the larger part of her territorial gains and, as their price for thus coming to China's aid, had taken most of these gains for themselves. Tsingtao and a naval base on Kiaochow Bay had fallen to the Kaiser's share, but Wilhelm, who dealt in world dynamics, had been brooding over the rise of a new power in Asia. Vividly he saw its yellow hordes overwhelming Europe. "Under the glitter of the Christmas-tree candles," as he described it to his cousin Nicky, the Czar of Russia, he drew his vision on paper and ordered the court painter, Knackfuss, to immortalize the sketch in a painting.

The picture showed a Buddha riding upon a dragon through a thunderous sky, leaving smoking cities in ruins beneath him as he advances upon Europe. Apprehensively watching this apparition are seven long-haired ladies in helmets and breastplates, representing the nations of Europe, of whom the foremost, Germania, with streaming blond locks beneath an eagle headdress, has drawn her sword and leans forward aggressively. Upon a height an archangel exhorts the ladies, "Peoples of Europe, guard your most precious possessions!"

Seized by the brilliance of his conception, the Kaiser caused copies to be engraved and presented to all the embassies in Berlin and to royal relatives of the various reigning houses and other distinguished persons. Wilhelm's forays into personal diplomacy often dismayed the European chanceries, in some of which he was known as William the Sudden. Because he swung wildly between feelings of persecution and a rosy optimism, no one ever knew what to expect of the German Emperor. Bismarck said of him that "he wanted it always to be Sunday." Wilhelm's Byzantine court assisted him in this illusion by providing him with his own morning paper, in a special imperial edition of one, made up of carefully excerpted items from the world press, printed in gold.

Wilhelm was interested in gold-plated news only and disliked above all else those tiresome visits from ministers with their reports of inconvenient facts that did not fit in with his schemes. To avoid listening to them, the Kaiser would walk up and down, do all the talking himself, and dismiss the minister in twenty minutes. It was his task, he believed, to preserve the balance of Europe. Indeed, who but he in Europe was equal to it? Government officials from the Chancellor down were nothing but a pack of clerks. Europe needed a master mind if it was not to fall apart under the fumbling of these petty bureaucrats. Dynastic rulers were the only persons fit to manage international affairs, but really it was not fair the whole burden should fall upon him. Immediately the Kaiser, a man of volatile moods, felt deeply sorry for himself. Alone he shouldered this terrible burden, and no one realized how it weighed upon him. But he must bravely carry on, misunderstood, unappreciated though his efforts were. His fat uncle, King Edward of England, hated him as Wilhelm's own mother, Edward's sister, had hated him. Emperor Franz Josef belonged to a past generation, an ancient recluse who understood nothing of modern times. France had no ruler worth talking to. Anyway they were all conspiring behind his back, trying to encircle him. Only Nicky, the Czar, was his friend, neither clever nor strong like himself, but at least malleable. He had to hold on tightly to Nicky, wheedle him, flatter him, frighten him judiciously from time to time, for the Czar too they were trying to draw into this terrible encirclement.

He formed the habit of writing Nicky confidential letters, gossiping, advising, warning, admonishing, and signing himself "Yours Affectionately, Willy." The letters, written in English (accounting for their occasional curiosities of spelling and grammar), were found in the Russian archives by the Bolsheviks after the war. The Czar's replies are not extant, but the Kaiser evidently derived considerable pleasure from the correspondence. It charmed his ego to mold the Czar of all the Russias to suit his schemes.

Proud of his new naval base on the Pacific, Wilhelm now embarked on a program to make Germany a first-class naval power. Bismarck, content for Germany to dominate the land mass of Europe, had warned against collision with England on the seas, but the Kaiser wanted empire and took the fatal path. It occurred to him that Germany ought to have a foothold in the Americas, and the direct method he favored, as did the Count of Monte Cristo, was to buy one. In 1901 his roving eye alighted on the Santa Margarita Islands off the coast of Venezuela, but when Secretary of State John Hay learned that German warships were surveying the islands, he dropped a *démarche* in Berlin, and the enterprise was heard of no more.

If Colonel Hay thought his protest had stopped the German Emperor, he was wrong. The Kaiser had thought of something better than Venezuela: why not a piece of Mexico? On the desolate coast of Lower California, the thousand-mile-long peninsula which hangs down from California along the Pacific coast of Mexico, there was another Santa Margarita island, enclosing the superb natural harbor of Magdalena Bay. In 1902 an American lawyer practicing in London called upon Ambassador Joseph H. Choate with a startling piece of news which the Ambassador promptly reported to Secretary Hay. The lawyer told him, Choate wrote, that he had been approached by a German gentleman doing business in the City, "to draw options giving him the right to purchase the principal part of the peninsula of Lower California." He did not disclose for whom he was acting, but after some weeks of transactions the American lawyer, who found he would be required to go to Mexico to obtain the concessions, insisted on knowing where the money was coming from for so extraordinary an adventure in real estate.

The real purchaser, he was told, was "the Emperor of Germany in his personal and individual capacity," and it was he who would furnish the money. Amazed, the American lawyer asked what the German Emperor could possibly want with such a property. His German client pointed to two harbors on the map, Magdalena Bay and Whale Bay farther north, remarking that they were excellent harbors "for naval purposes." At this stage of the business the American lawyer, disinclined to assist the German Emperor's proposed penetration of the American continent, withdrew his services.

"We have a decidedly exposed flank there," concluded Ambassador Choate's letter to Hay, "and it seems pretty clear the property is for sale and the Germans are after it." He added, perhaps unnecessarily, "We are concerned that it should not fall into the hands of any foreign power under any disguise whatever."

Whether the options lapsed after the American lawyer's withdrawal, or whether Hay took some action of which he left no record, is not known, but Magdalena Bay was not sold to the Kaiser. His happy thought of acquiring a naval base in the American hemisphere was balked again.

In the same year the Kaiser's pride suffered a more serious setback. The perfidious English, ignoring the warning of his picture, had gone behind his back and made an alliance with Japan—had actually joined hands with the Yellow Peril! And some months later, when he generously tried to help them out over the affair of the Venezuelan debts and sent his warships to blockade Venezuela, he stirred up a crisis. President Theodore Roosevelt shook the big stick at him and threatened to send Admiral

Dewey and the fleet in the name of the Monroe Doctrine. The Kaiser was disgusted. The Americans were always calling upon the Monroe Doctrine as if it were some sort of covenant established by God, giving them rights over the rest of the hemisphere. Wilhelm believed that if God were going play favorites He would choose Germany. (It is recorded that one Sunday when the Kaiser went to church the Court Circular reported, "This morning the All-Highest paid his respects to the Highest.")

Even his gold-tinted morning newspaper could not cheer from the Kaiser's mind the suspicion that everyone was against him. Once, when he suspected France of calling a European Congress without Germany, his anger, echoing across the Atlantic, prompted Roosevelt to remark, "The Kaiser has had another fit. What a jumpy creature he is anyhow!"

His feelings of persecution centered upon the English, whom he loudly hated and secretly admired. In the midst of a long tirade against England addressed to Roosevelt he suddenly blurted out, "I ADORE the English!" but he never could quite suppress the suspicion that his mother's countrymen thought him vulgar. Like Captain Hook in Peter Pan, he was haunted by doubt that he was not quite "good form." And like Captain Hook, who was feared by all, but himself quivered at the approach of the ticking crocodile, Wilhelm quivered at the approach of encirclement. The form of it he most dreaded was an alliance of Russia at his back with France and England at his front.

In an effort to turn Russia's energies eastward, away from Europe, he determined to urge Nicky into war with Japan. It is "the great task of the future for Russia to defend Europe from the inroads of the great Yellow Race," he wrote the Czar and assured him he would keep Europe quiet, guard his rear, and "help you as best I can." Unfortunately the Russo-Japanese War of 1904–1905 turned out disastrously for Nicky, but that, as Willy never tired of reminding him, was not Willy's fault. In fact, after the Japanese had won all the battles, the Kaiser could not make up his mind whether they were now more of a Yellow

Peril than ever or, on the other hand, the Prussians of the East who might very well be his natural allies.

At this juncture, in 1906, the United States acquired the ground for the Panama Canal. Across the Pacific, Japan was swelling out of her narrow islands like a jinni out of a bottle; all Europe considered a clash between her and the United States inevitable. The Kaiser waited hopefully. And one day in 1907 his gratification was immense when he personally uncovered a Japanese plot to seize the Panama Canal with a hidden army of ten thousand men already stationed in Mexico! A private informant just back from the coffee plantations of southern Mexico had reported to him having seen the ten thousand Japanese, "all in military jackets and brass buttons," secretly drilling after sundown under the command of sergeants and officers "disguised as simple laborers." The Kaiser wrote Nicky all about it. His informant had himself counted the ten thousand Japanese. "They are reservists who have hidden arms with them and intended as army corps to seize the Panama Canal and cut off communications with America." As a thousand miles of Central American jungle separates Mexico from Panama, it is hard to say just where the Kaiser thought the canal was, but a king with vast problems on his mind may be forgiven if his geography is slightly askew. "This is my *secret* information for YOU PERSONALLY" he continued. "It is sure information and good as you well know by now that I never gave you a wrong one."

He went on to instruct Nicky in the world implications of this startling news. "London" he pronounced, "is afraid of an encounter between Japan and America because they must take sides with one of them, as it will be a question of Race, not of Politiks, only *Yellow* vs. *White*." Now, he ended triumphantly, the English have "for the first time used the term 'Yellow Peril' from *my picture,* which is coming true!"

The Kaiser's mind leaped ahead to a vision of the Japanese pouncing upon the half-dug ditch of which President Roosevelt was so proud. The prospect of a war acted on Wilhelm as does the ringing of the bell on the laboratory dog. It made his saliva run. "Whenever war occurs in any part of the world," he once said to Arthur Balfour, "we in Germany sit down and we make a plan." Now the Kaiser had found in Mexico a new pressure point, and already he was forming a plan. The news set off in the mind of that "autocratic zigzag," as Roosevelt called him, a train of ideas that was to bewitch German policy through the next ten years and culminate in the Zimmermann telegram.

The Kaiser savored the effect his discovery of the Japanese in Mexico would have on the American President, who was even now flinging thousands of men and more money into the digging in Panama. Mr. Roosevelt would have to admit the reality of the Yellow Peril about which the Kaiser had so earnestly warned the Western World. Wilhelm's vigorous imagination envisaged the United States and Japan locked in conflict on a battlefield in Mexico. He saw the most fortunate results for Germany. The moment the United States invaded Mexico the smoldering anti-Yankeeism south of the border would burst into flames throughout Latin America. Yankee domination of the continent would end. Germany, ambitious to expand her commerce and influence, would at last have the free field she deserved and had long sought.

Properly exploited, the Japanese menace would surely provoke the Americans to invade Mexico. Another pleasing consequence occurred to the Kaiser. In a war between the United States and Japan, England would have to support America, and that would cost her her Japanese ally. The Kaiser's whirring mind, endlessly scheming, had now found a new candidate to defend the white race against the yellow—America! And Mexico would be the battleground. How simple, how natural! One had but to convince the heedless Americans of their mission.

The Kaiser felt sure America's virile president would appreciate the glory offered to him. Mr. Roosevelt, Chancellor Prince von Bülow had told him, "is a great admirer of Your Majesty and would like to rule the world hand in hand with Your Majesty, regarding himself as something in the nature of an American counterpart of Your Majesty." Clearly Mr. Roosevelt was just the man to fight the

Yellow Peril. In January 1908 the Kaiser summoned the American Ambassador, Charlemagne Tower, and told him about the ten thousand Japanese in brass buttons, whom he now described as distributing themselves "throughout" Mexico. Inform the President, he told Tower, that there is no doubt they are soldiers who will certainly move against the Panama Canal the moment there is war in Europe.

Mr. Roosevelt, informed of this threat to the canal by his Ambassador, was not disposed to take up the challenge offered him. The Kaiser, however, had convinced himself it was his clear duty as well as an act of friendship to awaken Mr. Roosevelt to his opportunity. He determined to prod him, as he had prodded Nicky into war with the Japanese, by promising him Germany's assistance. The extraordinary idea suggested itself of proposing an alliance among Germany, the United States, and China.

At this moment fate, like an obedient courtier, laid an opportunity at Wilhelm's feet. An American journalist named William Bayard Hale, representing *The New York Times,* arrived in Berlin especially to secure an interview with the Kaiser. This is the first appearance of a man who will reveal a curious affinity for turning up at crucial junctures in the coming entanglements. In August 1908, Hale, not yet a German agent, was granted an interview by the Kaiser of such startling indiscretion that the *Times* felt obliged to consult the President personally before publishing it.

What the Kaiser told Mr. Hale was that "within a year or two the Americans would certainly have to fight the Japanese" and therefore he was arranging an alliance among China, Germany, and the United States that would very shortly be announced. He inveighed bitterly against England as a traitor to the white race because of her alliance with Japan. Germany would soon have to go to war against England, and the time had nearly come. With one of his characteristic leaps over consistency, the Kaiser said he was arming the Mohammedans as a bulwark against the Yellow Peril. He said Russia had been fighting for the whole white race against Japan, but of course, if

Germany had been doing the fighting, Japan would have been beaten. He continued to harangue Mr. Hale along these lines for two hours.

The Germanophile Mr. Hale had an uncomfortable feeling that the Emperor might not be serving Germany's best interests by these remarks, and took the precaution of showing them to the German Foreign Office, which "had a spasm," and to the American Ambassador, who was horrified, before he cabled the interview to the *Times*. The *Times* took it to Roosevelt, who in his "strongest manner" advised against publication. Sacrificing a front-page sensation, the *Times* complied. "I really like, and in a way, admire him," Roosevelt wrote some months later, "but I wish he would not have brain storms."

The Kaiser was not to be foiled of his heroics by the mean tactic of silence. He gave another interview, similar in spirit although different in substance, to the London *Daily Telegraph*, which published it on October 28, 1908, causing an explosion that rocked Europe and almost rocked Wilhelm off his throne. Hurt, astonished, and bewildered, he escaped Berlin, where his sanity was even being questioned by the press, and fled to Pless, where a royal hunt was loyally got up to soothe the All-Highest spirit, though without much success. "Oh, I am most unhappy, I am always misunderstood," he told the beautiful English Daisy, Princess of Pless, at dinner and, as he spoke, "a tear fell on his cigar."

Meanwhile what of the Japanese? The fact is the Kaiser's information was not entirely groundless. Something was going on between Japan and Mexico, no one knew exactly what. In 1908, some months before the Kaiser's famous interview, the American Minister in Guatemala advised Washington of a rumor that Japan, by secret treaty, had acquired lease of a naval base at Magdalena Bay, the largest and most secure base on Mexico's Pacific coast, the same place the Kaiser had once coveted. Washington's worried queries were met by official denials, but the reports persisted over the next years, usually accompanied by the story of disguised Japanese soldiers (reminiscent of the Kaiser's ten thousand) ready to swarm across the Rio Grande or, alternatively, seize the Panama Canal.

There may have been a secret treaty; the archives do not say. But certainly Japan was making common cause with the Mexicans, who had not forgiven the loss of Texas. Japan had a fresher cause of resentment in the American restrictions on the entry of Japanese labor. They began to talk about the Mexicans as their racial brothers, descended from Japanese fishermen who had long ago been blown across the Pacific on a raft. Japanese training ships visited Mexican waters. In 1911 came Admiral Yashiro, Grand Admiral of the Japanese fleet, on a state visit. Entertained by the Mexican Minister of War at a splendid banquet at Chapultepec, the Admiral rose, rather unsteadily after seven courses and seven wines, to toast this "fraternal feast" of the Mexican and Japanese Army and Navy and to make a speech teeming with portents of common action against a certain common enemy. He stressed the similarities of the Mexican and Japanese people: "The same blood" flows in their veins (clamorous applause); both have terrible and untameable volcanoes which, though now quiescent, can erupt and make the world tremble in their fury (cries of approval); both are building up their Armies and Navies to resist insults to their national honor (*Viva Japon! Abaja los Gringos!*). No doubt was left of the identity of the common enemy.

If America did not or would not understand these portents, Berlin determined to bring them forcibly to her notice. In February 1911 a Germany spy named, almost too Teutonically, Horst von der Goltz, arrived in Paris under orders to steal the draft of a secret treaty which the Mexican Finance Minister, José Yves Limantour, was believed to be negotiating with Japanese agents in France. Limantour, regarded as the cleverest man in Mexico and the probable successor of President Porfirio Díaz, was in Paris raising a loan while waiting out the results of an insurrection that was threatening to oust old Díaz at last. Von der Goltz, according to an embellished confession he later made, attached himself to Limantour and, with the aid of a Rolls-Royce, several Apaches from the Paris underworld, a wild party, and a drugged bottle, succeeded in rendering the Mexican minister unconscious and extracting from him the vital document in the most approved cloak-and-dagger manner. Immediately two silent, black-coated couriers from Berlin appeared and relieved him of his loot, and in a few weeks a photographed copy of the secret treaty was laid under the startled eyes of the American Ambassador to Mexico, Henry Lane Wilson.

Ambassador Wilson was to deny this ever happened, and courtesy suggests more credence in the word of an American ambassador than in that of a German spy. Yet early in March, Ambassador Wilson did scurry up to Washington to consult President Taft, Roosevelt's successor, and the Cabinet in person. The morning after his arrival, March 6, the country was astounded by the news that the President had mobilized twenty thousand troops, two-thirds of the regular Army, on the Mexican border, and had sent the fleet steaming to the Gulf. Mr. Taft said it was maneuvers, but everyone else said it meant war with Japan. Correspondents converged upon El Paso, mobilization headquarters, to send home stories of bugles, campfires, baked beans, and martial confusion. Among the crowd in El Paso a stranger in uniform attracted particular notice. He was discovered to be Major Herwarth von Bittenfeld, German military attaché in Washington. What is this gentleman doing in Texas? Keep your eye on the major, for he has not come down just to watch the maneuvers.

Texas and the border states were in a ferment. At Fort Sam Houston men assured each other that the Japanese fleet had appeared off the Pacific Coast; at San Antonio people were saying the Army would be in Mexico City by Easter. Every Japanese ship arriving at Seattle and San Francisco was said to be disembarking colonists who were being speedily transshipped to Mexico. Alert patriots spotted suspicious Orientals on the Mexican side of the border who wore civilian clothes but walked with a "military carriage" and did not seek employment. A cache of fifty thousand rifles was reported located at strategic spots along Mexico's Pacific coast.

Foreign capitals buzzed with "authoritative" stories (of remarkable unanimity) about the secret treaty. Japan was credited with having obtained not only a fleet-coaling base at Magdalena Bay but also rights to the trans-Mexican Tehuantepec Railway linking the Pacific and Atlantic coasts. Despite anguished denials by Japanese ambassadors in all the capitals, and by Mexican officials, the report persisted, reverberating with most relish and embellishments from Germany. The German press, in an access of wishful thinking, firmly predicted that the Americans would cross the border within three days, overthrow Díaz, and annex Mexico to protect the Panama Canal.

So fast flew the rumors that President Taft felt obliged to deny publicly that the mobilization was concerned in any way with Japan. He was telling the truth, but nobody believed him, the less so because Germany took a certain step to make sure nobody would. On April 9 a sensational story headlined SECRET TREATY PHOTOGRAPH! appeared on the front page of the respectable New York *Evening Sun*. It told much the same story von der Goltz was later to tell in his published confessions, though without mentioning his share. The secret treaty with Japan indeed existed, the *Sun* informed the world, and had been ratified by the Díaz government. Ambassador Wilson had obtained the original, had kept it only long enough to have it photographed, after which it was returned to the innermost archives of the Mexican Foreign Office. The Ambassador, the *Sun* continued, immediately entrained for Washington, wiring ahead that he was coming, and upon arrival laid the incriminating document before a startled President and Cabinet. Chief of Staff General Leonard Wood, lunching at his club, received a White House summons and, throwing down his napkin, hurried there for consultation. Mobilization orders were issued the same day. Ambassador Wilson went on to New York to meet Limantour, who was arriving that very moment from Paris, and told him, declared the *Sun,* that he must take an oral message to President Díaz demanding abrogation of the secret treaty within six days or the United States would take positive action.

This inside story, circumstantial, dramatic, and supported by the *Sun's* prestige, convinced the public that Mexico was to be Japan's invasion base. The Yellow Peril became as popular as the turkey trot, creating in the American mind a special sensitivity to alarums from over the border that was to last for some years.

What did Ambassador Wilson, the only man who could have scotched the story, have to say? Publicly, nothing. Privately he told the State Department that no secret treaty had ever been placed in his hands. He told them something else. Mr. Ritchie, the *Sun's* special correspondent, had admitted to him having written the famous article entirely from information supplied by (as the clever reader will instantly have guessed) Major Herwarth von Bittenfeld.

It was, of course, a German invention. The fact is that President Taft mobilized the American Army to foil not a Japanese threat to American territory but an internal Mexican threat to American business from the increasingly menacing insurrection. Ambassador Wilson's hurried trip north and Taft's response were made in the hope of overawing the rebels and of bolstering the Díaz regime, not overthrowing it. They had no intention of invading Mexico and, though it was unfeeling of them to disappoint the Kaiser, did not cross the border.

Whether there ever was a secret Japanese treaty with Mexico, or von der Goltz ever stole it, is unresolved but irrelevant. For the purposes of history, what actually happened is less determining of later events than what people think happened. Germany had succeeded not only in making Americans believe in the possibility of joint Japanese-Mexican action against the United States but in making herself believe in it. So the pit was dug for Zimmermann.

Meanwhile the Kaiser still itched for Latin American adventure and was soon to try again. The insurrection in Mexico, already lapping at Díaz's boots, gave him his next opportunity.

"Seize the Customs House at Once!"

When Francisco Madero, leader of the revolution that broke the iron grip of Porfirio Díaz in 1911, rode in to the capital on a white horse, the peons hailed him as Mexico's apostle and redeemer, but the old regime, priming its guns, crouched for a counterattack. It came in less than two years, all the time that Madero was given to try to graft democracy on the trunk of feudalism. After ten days of terror and bombardment ten thousand were dead and Mexico had a new iron man who, behind the blood and cannon smoke, had made his spring to power. He was General Victoriano Huerta, a pure-blooded Indian with a flat nose, a bullet head, a sphinx's eyes behind incongruous spectacles, and a brandy bottle never far from hand. Wily, patient, laconic, and rarely sober, he had risen carefully through the Army, step by step, to its command, serving under both Díaz and Madero, whom he now betrayed and arrested. Gratefully the ruling class and foreign investors welcomed him as *their* redeemer.

Two weeks after Huerta's coup, during the night of February 22, 1913, Madero and his Vice-President, Pino Suárez, while being moved under guard from house arrest in the National Palace to the National Prison, were assassinated—murdered, the world believed, on Huerta's orders, though no evidence was ever found to prove his direct complicity.

History chose this precise moment to inaugurate Woodrow Wilson as the new President of the United States. In his way he too was an apostle, not a messiah like Madero, but rather a Luther, intent upon a reformation, schooled, incorruptible, and sure of his purpose, mandated by himself as by the electorate to sweep out the old iniquities and the new greeds and redeem the level of American politics. Reform was what the time demanded, and reform was the device on Wilson's banner. With him he brought into office other devotees of the New Freedom, among them William Jennings Bryan, the most improbable Secretary of State America ever had, and Josephus Daniels, a pacifist, as Secretary of the Navy. To them, as to Wilson, General Huerta was everything that was abhorrent. Yet Wilson, in the long duel with Huerta that was to follow, could not suppress a "sneaking admiration" for his opponent's nerve. Fulminating publicly, privately he confessed to finding Huerta "a diverting brute . . . so false, so sly, so full of bravado, yet so courageous . . . seldom sober and always impossible yet what an indomitable fighter for his own country." To Huerta, a man of few words, Wilson was simply the "Puritan of the North."

The murder of Madero, a reform president like himself, occurring only a few days before his own inaugural, brushed Wilson almost too closely and shocked him inexpressibly. It need not have, since hardly a ruler of Mexico in a hundred years had failed to die a violent death, but Wilson felt Madero's death like a brother's. Perhaps a sense that it might have been his own added to his indignation. From the day he took office on March 4, 1913, he was obsessed by the idea that it was his "clear duty" as a knight of the New Freedom and foe of the "Interests" to tear General Huerta, the "usurper," off the backs of the Mexican people. He determined that Mexico should be ruled by the consent of the governed and that it somehow devolved upon him to accomplish this goal.

Just at this time Japan was aroused to fury when California passed a law forbidding Japanese nationals to own or lease land in that state. Unable to believe that the federal government was powerless to abrogate a state law, and convinced that the action was a deliberate insult, Japan protested hotly to Washington. The air over the Pacific became electric with tension; the long-predicted war seemed about to break.

Wilson, bursting with plans for domestic reforms, for busting the trusts, breaking the "interlocking directorates," driving the dollar diplomats from the temple, had hardly got inside the White House door before he was confronted by possible war with Japan and a major crisis in Mexico. "It would be the irony of fate," he said wistfully, "if my administration had to deal chiefly with foreign affairs"— a remark which fate, in a malicious mood, promptly proved the understatement of the era.

At such a moment, when fresh rumors were circulating that Japan was even then offering a secret alliance to Mexico, a less high-principled man than Wilson would not have risked throwing Mexico into Japanese arms by simultaneously weakening and alienating the Mexican government. But Wilson's peculiar strength, as well as his ultimate weakness, was that, conscious of the purity of his motives, he unwaveringly pursued what he believed was right, regardless of expediency. He spurred against "that scoundrel Huerta," determined to unseat him with the weapon of non-recognition. Withholding recognition from Huerta naturally encouraged the rise of a rival in the person of General Carranza, who had already got an insurrection going in the north, near the American border. His forces now spread southward, swelling daily, set up a rival government, and made of Mexico a Latin American Balkans inviting foreign intrigue. With both parties seeking guns, money, and other forms of support from abroad, Mexico was opened to any enterprising trouble shooter with an eye for a crack in the Monroe Doctrine.

More than one was watching for the right moment. Japan, in that summer of 1913, gladly sold Huerta a fat pack of arms and, to annoy Wilson the more, requested a special mission, which arrived in the person of Señor de la Barra, Mexico's Foreign Minister, who was personally received by the Emperor and made the object of cheering demonstrations. Germany's expectations of trouble warmed up at once. It looked as if the long-bruited alliance of Japan and Mexico was really taking shape. Mexico had two thousand miles of undefended coastline on the Pacific. Her northern border with the United States stretched for twelve hundred miles from Texas to California, touching all along its length against territory that had once been her own. Mexicans remembered the Alamo too. Mexico was, in short, the soft underbelly of the United States.

President Wilson, however, was not concerned with strategy but with reform. Seduced by the magic of the word "Constitutionalists," which Carranza chose for his party, or perhaps by the nobility of Carranza's long white beard, which made him look like a combination of John Brown and the prophet Isaiah, Wilson believed he saw in him a new leader of the oppressed. This was the man for Mexico, he decided, on behalf of the Mexicans. The Mexican people must be given democracy, ready or not. "My passion is for the submerged 85 per cent who are struggling to be free," he said. Unfortunately the submerged 85 per cent, unable to distinguish a difference between Huerta and Carranza, were cowering in their huts or had taken to the hills, hoping to save one burro or a bag of corn from the battle of the rival tyrants.

In vain Ambassador Henry Lane Wilson drew a fearful prospect of the turmoil and anarchy that would again beset Mexico unless General Huerta was quickly confirmed in power. The President, who scorned the other Wilson as the most egregious of the dollar diplomats left over from Taft (and believed him half responsible for Madero's murder for having denied the Mexican President asylum), refused to communicate with his Ambassador.

President Wilson's policy made the European nations equally uneasy. Having shuddered for their investments during Madero's regime, they had been delighted by Huerta's coup and his promised re-establishment of the old order. They were pained and distressed by Wilson's refusal to recognize him. They all urged upon Wilson the necessity of supporting a safe and stable government in Mexico. "The best thing that can happen is to get as soon as possible a dictator who will keep order and give a chance for material and educational progress," advised Lord Bryce, who could not be shrugged aside as a tool of the Interests, though he was British Ambassador in Washington. The Kaiser put it more succinctly. "Morality," he said, "is all right, but what about dividends?"

But Wilson was not to be swerved from his self-appointed mission to unseat "that person who calls himself the President of Mexico." Although some sixteen nations had recognized Huerta's right to call himself President, Huerta remained to Wilson a symbol of political sin, a golden calf around whom backsliding Mexicans and dollar diplomats were bowed in worship, an idol whom he, bidden by a voice from some inner Sinai, must smash.

Oil was the factor that quickened the coming of a climax. The world's navies were just then completing the conversion from coal to oil, and Mexican oil supplied one-quarter of the world's needs. Mexico supplied also, from the holdings of one man, Lord Cowdray, practically all the oil used by the British Navy. In this eleventh hour, as the sands of peace were running out, the rivalry of the British and German Navies was paramount. The British Navy depended upon Mexican oil; Britain depended upon its Navy. Lord Cowdray was becoming distinctly restless. His friend Sir Lionel Carden, the British Ambassador to Mexico, was squirming with frustration at not yet being allowed to hang the guerdon of recognition around Huerta's neck as he believed Britain's interests required. He bedeviled London for recognition. London bedeviled Washington. Wilson only dug his heels into the ground more firmly. He regarded the British Ambassador, as he did his own, with cold distaste, while over Sir Lionel's shoulder the figure of Lord Cowdray loomed before his eyes like some dark monster dripping oil-stained footprints wherever he walked.

England, however, had come to feel that Lord Cowdray's contract with the Royal Navy spoke more cogently than President Wilson's passion for the submerged peons. On May 3 England recognized General Huerta. Wilson's annoyance at this act was hardly soothed when on top of it came Japan's angry protest against the California alien-exclusion act. The President remained calm, but the Joint Army and Navy Board did not. Upon its own authority it ordered five cruisers from the China station to Manila and recommended that the Pacific fleet be sent at once to Hawaii and two warships to Panama. This drastic move, carefully leaked to the press, left the country gasping and so infuriated the President that he dissolved the Joint Board, with the result that it remained out of existence throughout 1914 and most of 1915.

The Yellow Peril was the talk of the hour. Secretary Daniels complained that his admirals "sat up nights thinking how Japan was planning to make war on America and steal a march on us by taking the Philippine Islands and going on to Hawaii." As this was a blueprint of Pearl Harbor twenty-eight years in advance, these admirals of an earlier generation at least were wide awake. But Daniels was, as he put it, disgusted with their "obsession," and the President regarded it as "bad taste" at a time when he was trying to soothe Japanese feelings and keep the peace.

And he was getting nowhere in Mexico. Alarmed by the growing anti-Americanism Wilson's policy was fostering, the leading American investors sent him a memorandum urging recognition of Huerta on condition that Huerta and Carranza each guarantee a free election, for, they said, "If Mexico is helped out of her trouble by Britain and Germany, American prestige will be destroyed in that country."

For once Mr. Wilson paused, listened, and almost took advice. He went so far as to draw up a message to Huerta along the lines suggested by the businessmen, but when it came to actually giving recognition to "that desperate brute" he kept turning it round and round in his hand like a glass of nasty medicine. Had he gulped it down then, the American record would never have been stained by the blood of Veracruz.

But advice more to his liking now reached him. William Bayard Hale, to whom the Kaiser had confided that indiscreet interview, once more crosses the path of this history. Having journalistically embraced the New Freedom, Hale had been chosen to write Wilson's campaign biography in 1912. Impressed by his talents, the President had sent him on a confidential fact-finding mission to

Mexico. His qualifications for the mission consisted in knowing nothing whatever about Mexico but a good deal about Wilson. A quick glance around was all he needed to report back what he knew Wilson wanted to hear: that Huerta was indeed the archfiend, that his regime could not last, that Ambassador Wilson had actually invited the archfiend to dinner! Well! Wilson flung away the cup of recognition and sent another confidential emissary with a letter to Huerta informing him that he must remove himself as a candidate in the coming election. America, Wilson wrote, was "seeking to counsel Mexico for her own good."

Like Cromwell against the Cavaliers, Wilson was right and Huerta reactionary. But, in his genuine desire to put an end to the exploitation of the Mexican people, Wilson took toward a neighboring chief of state a hectoring tone that was not well designed for persuasion. Huerta, however wicked, had sovereignty; as an Aztec, he had pride. His answer to Wilson's advice was neat and unmistakable. He swooped down upon the Mexican Congress, arrested 110 of its members, and dissolved the rump. When the scheduled election duly took place a few weeks later, no one was less surprised than General Huerta to find himself confirmed as President of Mexico.

Wilson, who persisted in expecting Mexico to behave like a modern democracy although its political development was about on a level with pre-Bastille France, was terribly shocked by the arrest of the deputies. He took it as a personal insult and "impossible to regard as otherwise than an act of bad faith toward the United States." Nor was he comforted when his Ambassador in London, Walter Hines Page, reported that there was no appreciation in England of his "moral" position on the Mexican problem. Exasperated, Wilson now publicly announced that he considered it his "clear duty" to force out the usurper by "such means as may be necessary to secure this result."

Anger had led Wilson out on a limb; now Britain was to ease him off. Sir Edward Grey, the Liberal Foreign Secretary, unhappy over Wilson's course in Mexico, sent to Washington an emissary, Sir William Tyrrell, who, overcoming Wilson's suspicions of him, charmed the President into a frank talk. Among the impressions he brought home was the report that Wilson, on being asked what his Mexican policy was, replied, "I am going to teach the Latin American republics to elect good men!"

Within a few weeks of Tyrrell's return, Wilson's gratification was immense to learn that his *bête noire,* Sir Lionel Carden, had been transferred to another post; further, that Lord Cowdray, as reported by Page, had lost his aplomb and "they are taking to their tents." This pleasing change was not due to England's having a sudden rush of morality to the head but to Sir Edward Grey's having set his heart upon an object for which he needed Wilson's active support: repeal of the Panama Canal tolls. Grey did not believe that morally there was much to choose between Huerta and Carranza. He decided that British support for Huerta in preference to some replica of Huerta by another name was not worth making an issue of at the risk of gaining Wilson's hostility. Hence the handsome gesture recalling Sir Lionel, to which Wilson responded with a handsome plea to Congress for repeal of the Panama Canal tolls. A gentlemen's understanding, all on the highest principles.

General Huerta, inscrutable behind his incongruous spectacles, did not need to be told what it meant when the English began to pull out. When, in February 1914, Wilson, now happy in England's new appreciation of his moral position, lifted the arms embargo upon Carranza, Huerta knew himself to be in an extremity. In that extremity help was reached out to him. Germany saw an opening. To Huerta came the German ambassador, Admiral von Hintze, with an offer of military aid against the rebels, provided he would cut off oil to the British Navy in case of war. Within a few days derricks on the decks of Hamburg were swinging huge crates of rifles and other munitions aboard the ships *Ypiranga, Bavaria,* and *Kronprinzessen Cecilie;* their destination, Veracruz.

Another ship now enters the picture, the U.S.S. *Dolphin,* flagship of Admiral Mayo, anchored in Mexican waters off

Tampico. On April 6 a gunboat from the *Dolphin,* carrying seven sailors and a paymaster, went ashore to load supplies. Tampico was then under martial law. A minor Huertista officer, carrying out orders not to permit any ship to dock, arrested the Americans and marched them off to his superior. This officer, confronted by a live *casus belli* walking into his guardroom, instantly ordered the men returned to the *Dolphin,* whither they were shortly followed by a Mexican officer bringing an explanation and the polite regrets of the Tampico commander.

Admiral Mayo, however, believing that American honor required a twenty-one-gun salute in token of official Mexican apology, as well as punishment of the arresting officer, issued an ultimatum answerable within twenty-four hours. Afterward he informed Washington of what he had done. Hardly knowing how it had happened, the government found itself plunged into a crisis from which neither Wilson, Bryan, nor Daniels could think of any quick egress in case Huerta refused to apologize. The hour appointed by the ultimatum came and went, but no guns saluted the American flag. Overnight the Tampico affair swelled into a national insult. Diplomatic hell broke loose, telegrams flashed, warships scurried to the Gulf, further ultimata clattered down on Huerta's head like hailstones. He would not yield. Why, he asked with a wry logic, should the United States demand a salute from a government it did not recognize? Nearly beaten, facing ruin, pressed by a power ten times his size, he fended off the final moment by one argument after another until Wilson, horrified and helpless, found himself maneuvered onto a pedestal of national honor from which there was no climbing down except by way of war.

Yet, caught on the horns of his own ambivalence, Wilson in fact welcomed the opportunity to oust the dictator Huerta and, as he saw it, free Mexico for democracy. He shrank from the use of force, but his hand reached out for the gun. He issued a last personal ultimatum to Huerta, which was due to expire at six o'clock on the evening of April 19. Military sanctions, in the event of Huerta's refusal, were to take the form of blockade and occupation of Mexico's largest port city, Veracruz, and the armed forces had been ordered to prepare for this action. Six o'clock passed without an answer from Huerta, but Wilson did nothing that night.

All next day, April 20, Washington was in turmoil; rumors buzzed, headlines blazed. Wilson called the Cabinet at 10:30 A.M. and told them he was going to ask Congress that afternoon to pass a resolution authorizing the use of arms to seize Veracruz. Although, needless to say, he cared little about a salute to the flag for its own sake, he narrowed the issue entirely to that question and left everyone feeling distinctly uncomfortable. The President himself, recalled one Cabinet member, was "profoundly disturbed" and closed the meeting with a plea that if any of them believed in prayer he should use it now before a decision that "might take the nation into war." The next moment, in one of those twists which often make Wilson difficult to follow, he told reporters waiting outside the Cabinet room that "in no conceivable circumstances would we fight the people of Mexico."

Shortly after the Cabinet meeting, he was informed by a telegram from the American consul at Veracruz of the approach of the *Ypiranga,* believed to be bringing a cargo of arms for Huerta. At 2 P.M. he met with four House and Senate leaders and read them the resolution which he wished Congress to pass justifying the use of force to secure amends for "affronts and indignities" to the United States. He also told the Congressional leaders that he wished to intercept the German ship, but when he went up to the Capitol an hour later to ask for the resolution in person, he did not mention the *Ypiranga.* Congress was left to debate the use of force solely on the issue of an outworn ritual of apology due to the national honor of the United States, and there were many who blushed for the cause. Uneasily the debate began; it turned sour; Wilson anxiously returned for a cloakroom conference at 6 P.M.; by nightfall nothing had been settled. Washington went to bed on a lighted fuse.

By now the ultimatum had lain unimplemented for over twenty-four hours. Legally Wilson did not need Congressional authorization but, still tortured by indecision, he did not act. He longed to pull the trigger against Huerta, but the flimsiness of his case, which even dollar diplomats, hardened to mainpulating Latin American affairs for their own ends, might have hesitated to use, held him back. It was the German arms ship that precipitated what happened next.

In the still hours before dawn of April 21 the shrill ring of the telephone pierced the sleep of the President. Struggling to come awake in the dark, he picked up the receiver and heard the voice of Secretary Bryan, who was calling in pajamas from his home in Calumet Place. Another voice joined in, that of Secretary of the Navy Daniels, who, previously roused from bed, was plugged in on a three-way hookup. Downstairs in the White House, the President's secretary, Joseph Tumulty, also in pajamas, listened in on an extension.

"Mr. President," said Bryan, tuning the famous larynx to a solemnity suitable for midnight crisis, "I am sorry to inform you that I have just received a telegram from Veracruz reporting that the *Ypiranga* is due to dock at ten this morning."

"What? Oh, yes, yes. Go ahead, Mr. Bryan."

"The telegram is from our consul at Veracruz, William Canada. He wires, 'Steamer *Ypiranga,* owned by Hamburg-Amerika line, will arrive tomorrow from Germany with 200 machine guns and 15,000,000 cartridges; will go to Pier 4 and start discharging at 10:30.' Consul Canada also says that three trains, each coaled up and ready, are waiting on the pier to load the munitions and will leave as soon as loaded and that the Veracruz commander, General Maas, has stated 'he will not fight but will leave with all soldiers and rolling stock tomorrow tearing up the track behind him.' "

"Do you realize what this means, Mr. Bryan?" Distress and hesitation wrinkled the President's voice. "Daniels, are you there, Daniels? What do you think?"

"The munitions should not be permitted to reach Huerta," Daniels answered. "I can wire Admiral Fletcher to prevent it and take the Customs House. I think that should be done."

A pause fell upon the listeners as each in his separate room, gripping the telephone that linked him with the others, felt the heaviness of the decision the President must make. Then the pause was broken. "Daniels," came the President's voice, "send this order to Admiral Fletcher: Take Veracruz at once!" This pre-dawn parley, since known to history as the Pajama Conference, launched the United States upon the invasion of a neighboring state.

Over in the Navy Department a light went on, and minutes later the Secretary of the Navy's message went tapping through the night air to Admiral Fletcher at Veracruz: SEIZE THE CUSTOMS HOUSE. DO NOT PERMIT WAR SUPPLIES TO BE DELIVERED TO HUERTA GOVERNMENT OR TO ANY OTHER PARTY.

Next day Wilson, pacing the floor, waited for news along with Bryan, white-faced and fidgety, and Daniels, drained of all his bounce and cheer. Secretary of War Garrison and Robert Lansing, Counselor of the State Department, waited with them while up on Capitol Hill a bewildered Congress now found itself debating in anger and incredulity a resolution approving the President's midnight action in virtually putting the United States at war over what appeared to the public to be "some medieval points of punctilio" in a petty quarrel about a salute.

Already at 8:30 that morning Admiral Fletcher's flagship, with ominous signals wigwagging from its deck, had blocked the path of the *Ypiranga* and sent its engines clanging into reverse. Three hours later American marines and bluejackets poured ashore at Veracruz and took possession of the Customs House, the railroad yards and rolling stock, the cable, telegraph, and post offices.

Then occurred a regrettable mischance: the Mexicans resisted. How were they to know the running bluejackets with fixed bayonets had really come down to Mexico, in Wilson's words, "to serve mankind"? Mexican cadets barricaded a stone fort and opened fire upon the invaders. Encouraged by this sign of defense, angry citizens rushed to shoot from upstairs windows. In reply the guns of the

U.S.S. *Prairie* shelled the city. Blood spattered the walls, dead bodies fell in the streets.

FOUR OF OUR MEN KILLED, 20 WOUNDED. FIRING ALL AROUND THE CONSULATE, wired Consul Canada at 4 P.M. to the men waiting in the White House. When all the casualties had been counted after the occupation of Veracruz was completed, 19 Americans and 126 Mexicans had been killed, 71 Americans and 95 Mexicans wounded.

These irretrievable deaths stared Wilson in the face and left him shaken. Facing the press next day, he looked, one of the newsmen remembered, "preternaturally pale, almost parchmenty—the death of American sailors and marines owing to an order of his seemed to affect him like an ailment." On top of tragedy came humiliation. Even before the echo of the firing reached Washington, Germany lodged a protest at the State Department.

His Excellency Count von Bernstorff, correct in his Homburg, with pearl-gray cutaway and gray pearl stickpin, called in person upon the Secretary of State to protest the halting of the *Ypiranga* without prior declaration of blockade or state of war. Bowing him out, Mr. Bryan worriedly consulted his legal experts. Precedents hastily examined revealed the painful truth: the German Ambassador was right. Secretary Bryan, seeming almost to relish the opportunity for a public display of Christian humility, proceeded at once to the German Embassy to apologize in person. While exposing his country's embarrassment he managed to spare his own by blaming the whole thing on Admiral Fletcher, who, he said, "through a misunderstanding exceeded his instructions." Full tilt upon public confession—for Mr. Bryan tended to conduct diplomacy like a penitent at a revival meeting—he let it be known that "by direction of the President" he had offered an explanation and apology to the German Ambassador and that Admiral Fletcher had been instructed to call personally upon the captain of the *Ypiranga* and do likewise. With somewhat less relish, Secretary Daniels was forced to inform the bewildered admiral of this duty.

Publicly the Germans announced that the munitions would be returned to Hamburg, but while American attention was focused on Veracruz they privately ordered the *Ypiranga* to slip down the coast to Puerta Mexico, where, after she was joined by the *Bavaria* carrying 1,800,000 rounds of ammunition and 8327 rolls of barbed wire, both ships quietly completed delivery of their cargoes to the Huerta forces. Whether it was to compel a salute from General Huerta or to prevent delivery of German arms to him that nineteen Americans had died, it was now difficult to avoid the conclusion that they had died in vain.

Germany was entranced by the results of her experiment in Latin American meddling. "Mexico is a god-send to us," privately wrote Count Bernstorff. The United States would soon annex Mexico, explained *Der Tag,* and thus arouse all Latin America to unite to throw off the Yankee yoke. Germany could then move in. *Der Tag* foresaw the United States sucked into a war in Mexico's mountains and jungles, lasting five years at least. "The intervention of Japan is more than a possibility," it affirmed and drew a happy picture of Japanese forces landing on the coast of Mexico and marching on California.

Veracruz did, in fact, provoke the resentment Germany was hoping for. American travelers returning from South America reported the people seething with antagonism toward the United States. Unhappily Germany was prevented from taking advantage of it, owing to the consequences of the midsummer murder of an Austrian archduke at Sarajevo.

The dauntless Kaiser, optimistic as ever, was not to be diverted by the unfortunate affairs at Sarajevo from seizing the golden opportunity for German expansion opening at last in Latin America. Playing his usual personal hand, he dispatched an emissary to London to invite England to collaborate with Germany to block the evident design of the United States for the conquest of Mexico. "I am ready to give you the highest official assurance" the emissary told an astonished Foreign Office, "that your country and my country would have no difficulty in arranging our respective spheres of influence in Mexico." Considering that the hour was July 1914, the Kaiser's proposal was an odd one and evoked only a British stare of hauteur.

President Wilson knew nothing of this at the time, but he was unhappy enough already. Rather helplessly he told the country at the funeral of the Veracruz casualties, "We have gone down to Mexico to serve mankind, if we can find out a way. We do not want to fight the Mexicans. We want to serve the Mexicans if we can." But in a personal letter to a friend he acknowledged, "I am longing for an exit."

Again he was given one, this time by the ABC powers, Argentina, Brazil, and Chile, who offered to mediate. With equal relief Wilson and Huerta accepted, but for Huerta it came too late. Veracruz was a blow from which his regime never recovered, and before long Carranza had marched upon the capital and ousted him. Luckier than Madero, he got away to exile, and, as Díaz had done before him, he sailed to exile on a German ship. On July 17, Captain Kohler and the entire officer complement of the cruiser *Dresden* in dress uniform stood at attention on the station platform of Puerta Mexico to greet the departing dictator and escort him to their ship. Díaz died in exile, but, unlike Díaz, General Huerta would return—with Germany, still lured by Mexico, behind him.

In the meantime Huerta went to Spain, arriving there on August 1, three days before the world exploded.

The Third Partner—Japan

One day in September 1914, when the war was but a month old, an American in New York unexpectedly met on the street a man whom he had last seen, resplendent in medals, at a diplomatic dinner in Mexico City. The American was about to greet him when the man put his finger on his lips and with a silencing glance "disappeared around the corner of Wall and Nassau Streets." Such stealth seemed bizarre on the part of a distinguished diplomat, for the American knew the man to be Germany's Minister to Mexico, Admiral Paul von Hintze. His appearance on Wall Street was the beginning of a remarkable adventure upon which rested Germany's hopes of detaching the imperial power of Japan from the Allies. Six months later von Hintze was Minister in China, having outwitted the secret services of three countries to reach there. He had been personally selected for the post by the Kaiser, and his mission was to persuade Japan to change sides.

The Germans' time table for quick victory in the European war had gone wrong when the defense of the Marne barred them a bare taxi ride from Paris; it was a dead letter by November, when the desperate defense of Ypres barred their way to the French Channel ports. After that all hope of the "decisive battle" preached by Clausewitz was lost, and the German war plan—to smash France fast before Russia could effectively open a second front—lay derelict in the death-saturated mud of Flanders. From then on the war on the Western Front became transfixed along a line of trenches from the Alps to the Channel, where first one side and then the other threw away fresh assemblies of men and guns in monstrous, useless assaults to break the deadlock.

It was then, from imperative necessity to weaken the Allies, that America and Japan and Mexico became important in the German scheme. Germany had two goals in mind. One was to cut off America's supply of war materials to the Allies by embroiling the United States in an all-absorbing war with Mexico or Japan, or preferably both. The other was to frighten Russia out of the war by inducing her recent enemy, Japan, to leave the Allies and join the German camp.

Japan, having declared war on Germany on August 9, had won more for herself out of the war in a shorter belligerent time than any of the Allies. By November 7, 1914, she had snapped up Germany's naval base and leased territory at Tsingtao and the German Pacific islands —Yap, Truk, and the other Marshalls and Carolines whose names were to become famous one war later. At that point her active belligerency stopped.

Germany could not help thinking that Japan, whose rapacity she considered only natural, had chosen the wrong side. She seemed to belong with Germany in spirit. The Kaiser was still not sure whether he should combat Japan as the Yellow Peril or associate with her as the Prussia of the East, but in times like these expediency must decide. Expediency unhesitatingly said that, as an ally, Japan would not only contain Russia but deter the United States. Mexico would provide the occasion and the place, but how much more effective as a deterrent Mexico would be if she were joined by the organized power of America's other natural enemy, Japan!

It was no coincidence that these theories took shape in the mind of a diplomat familiar with Mexico, an astute and resolute envoy who was also an intimate of the Kaiser, a friend of Ludendorff, a former adjutant of the Czar, a high-ranking officer, and a future Foreign Minister whose fate was to be to arrange the conditions of the Kaiser's abdication in the final months of collapse. In Mexico City the blue-eyed, clean-shaven von Hintze was considered one of the more agreeable members of the diplomatic corps.

Though an ardent pan-German and Junker into whose mind never entered any question of the divine right of German militarism, he tempered his normal arrogance with amiability, and he even, later, reasonably suggested that his countrymen might have locked up Miss Edith Cavell instead of shooting her. He was intelligent, cultivated, sociable, spoke English without an accent, and, evidently sharing every Prussian's secret ambition to be taken for an English gentleman, dressed in impeccable English clothes except for the anomaly, noticed by an American diplomat's wife, that he wore a large amethyst ring.

Von Hintze's earlier experience had included a brush with Americans on a famous occasion. In 1918, as a "capable, tactful young officer" attached to Admiral von Diederichs' Pacific Squadron, he had been sent during a tense moment at Manila Bay to deliver a provocative message from his commander to Admiral Dewey. He was said to have reported back with such verisimilitude Dewey's red-faced roar, "If your Admiral wants a fight he can have it now!" that Diederichs advised the Kaiser that perhaps the Philippines was not worth a war after all.

Afterward von Hintze went as naval attaché to St. Petersburg, where he stayed seven years, part of the time as the Kaiser's personally appointed adjutant to his imperial cousin Nicky. In 1911 he returned to become aide-de-camp to the Kaiser and in the following year was named Minister to Mexico. It was he who, after the Veracruz attack, proffered Germany's help to Huerta if Huerta would in return agree to cut off Britain's oil in case of war. During that crisis the natural association of Germany, Mexico, and Japan was taking visible shape. Huerta asked Japan to represent him at Washington and, though Japan declined, the press, both American and European, was full of talk that Japan would interfere on behalf of Mexico and the United States.

Von Hintze carried these ideas with him when he went to China to establish contact with Japan. But first he had to get there. It was not with the intention of going to the Far East that he had left Mexico when the war broke out, but of resuming active service in the Navy. Having publicly stated his intention, however, he could not obtain safe conduct as a diplomat and had to make his way home secretly. This accounts for his mysterious behavior on Wall Street. Disguised as a steward, he got across the ocean on a Norwegian steamer without allowing the dirty dishes and smells that disturbed his fastidious tastes to give him away. Enjoying his own bravado, he took a day's stroll through London and, undetected, continued on to Berlin via Rotterdam. His Majesty, on hearing von Hintze's account of his adventures, said, "If you can do it once, you can do it again. I shall send you to China."

Peking, then neutral, was a place where enemy envoys, if need be, could discreetly meet. Who better fitted to be sent there than von Hintze?—a man of experience and finesse with first-hand knowledge of both Russia and Mexico, in both of which countries Japan was deeply interested. Besides, as a naval officer he might be expected to appeal to the Japanese. But how was he to reach Peking? He could not, of course, cross Russia, and if he went via the United States and the Pacific he would have to run the gantlet of the Japanese, who dominated the sea approaches to China.

Admiral von Hintze felt himself equal to the challenge. On his behalf Berlin asked the American government to request a safe conduct from Japan, but von Hintze did not bother to wait for the answer. He had already crossed the United States and reached San Francisco, where he booked passage on an American steamer, when word came from the Japanese Ambassador that the Imperial Japanese Government regretted its inability to entertain the request for a safe conduct for Admiral von Hintze. For some reason Secretary Bryan let a week go by before passing on this information, but von Hintze picked up the hint in San Francisco. He cancelled his passage on the American steamer, which was due to call at three Japanese ports on her way to Shanghai, and then he dropped out of sight.

Meanwhile the German bugle was loudly sounding the Yellow Peril, hoping its shrill note would scare the

Americans into keeping their arms at home. Daily in Berlin, all during the winter of 1914, highly placed German visitors called upon United States Ambassador Gerard to whisper the great danger that threatened America from Japan and relay confidential reports that Mexico was full of Japanese colonels and America full of Japanese spies. In Washington the German press attaché, Baron von Schoen, transferred from Tokyo when Japan joined the Allies, publicly proclaimed upon his arrival in September that Japan's intense hatred for the United States, coupled with her strong pro-Mexican feeling, made war "unavoidable." His remarks prompted the President to suggest that it was "not only desirable but imperative" that this gentleman should not remain here. He was shortly followed by a more discreet colleague, Dr. Fuehr, who also came from Tokyo, where he had been Germany's commercial attaché. He gave no interviews but was deputized, according to an American Military Intelligence report, "to foment trouble between the United States and Mexico with Japan as a side line." A few weeks later the West Coast became excited by a wave of rumors that Japanese troops had landed in Mexico. Long afterward, when the diary of a German commander came into the hands of United States Naval Intelligence, these rumors were traced to the German cruiser *Geier,* which had taken refuge from the British Navy in Pearl Harbor and sent the rumors out over its wireless while its band played afternoon concerts to cover the sound.

Next was heard, through the courtesy of the Hearst press, which made a specialty of the Yellow Peril, Professor Ludwig Stein, billed as a great German expert on the Orient, who warned America, "Today, because of the Panama Canal, your geographical and moral position as the forepost of the White Race against the Yellow Race imposes upon you a great duty: to hold back the East." It might have been Willy advising Nicky.

But among the synthetic phobias and the rumors were some hard facts. In December 1914, while von Hintze was on his way to the Far East, the commander of a

Japanese warship visited Mexico City, which at that time was occupied by General Pancho Villa, who had momentarily displaced Carranza. Villa was then at the height of his power and was having himself photographed sprawling in the golden chair of state with a smirk on his face as if to say, "Look who's sitting here now!" This was at a time when, Wilson having become disillusioned in Carranza and veering toward Villa, it looked as if that enterprising bandit might soon control the whole country. What would be Mexico's attitude, the Japanese envoy asked General Villa, in the event of war between Japan and the United States? He went on to say, as Villa recounted it to his *amigo* General Hugh Scott, American commander at the border and later Chief of Staff, that Japan was greatly grieved against the United States and that she had been preparing for war with us for three years and would be ready in two years more. Having said this, he put out his feeler as to possible joint action. Villa, basking then in an American friendship he did not know was soon to be withdrawn, told the Japanese inquirer that his forces would always be at the disposal of the United States in any foreign war she might get into.

This Japanese overture was one fact. Mexico's geography was another. The American General Staff's plans assumed that if ever Japan undertook to invade the United States it would be by way of Mexico into the Mississippi Valley, with the object of splitting the country in two. Mexico's network of railways, which met the American border at regular intervals and had terminals on both the Pacific Ocean and the Gulf, provided a perfect transportation system for moving up troops and supplies in any invasion of the United States. "Every European and Asiatic General Staff which had studied a possible war with this country," said one of General Pershing's staff, "recognizes the great advantage of an alliance with Mexico."

While the Japanese were taking this advice to heart and calling upon General Villa, a small Norwegian tramp steamer, the *Christian Bors,* departing from San Francisco, was chugging slowly eastward across the immense expanse of the Pacific. She reached Shanghai on January 9, 1915, and disembarked a passenger who registered at the Astor House under the modest signature of "Mr. V. Heintze." In Shanghai's waterfront bars word quickly got around that the captain of the *Christian Bors* had been paid one thousand dollars in gold by this modest gentleman to proceed to Shanghai without touching at any Japanese port. By the time inquiries had been made, the modest gentleman had vanished. In Peking a week later Admiral Paul von Hintze, with the cherished *von* duly restored in place of the inglorious *V*, presented his credentials as Germany's Minister.

He felt sanguine about the feelers to Japan he had been instructed to initiate, for he quite agreed with the Kaiser and the other thinkers of Berlin that Japan's alliance with the Allies was a brittle affair—as, in fact, it was. Lacking any real community of interest, the alliance was an artificial arrangement which the Japanese had entered into for the sake of the gains on the Asiatic mainland which they hoped to exploit from it. Their war role was outlined with gloomy foreknowledge by President Yüan Shih-k'ai of China at the outset: "Japan is going to take advantage of this war to gain control of China." Within a few months, while her allies and enemies were too busy battling to interfere, Japan had got her foot well inside the door of Chinese sovereignty when she wrung from China acceptance of the Twenty-one Demands. The rest she intended to get by assuring herself a front place at the winners' peace table and, until that happy day, by every now and then notching up her price for staying loyal.

Since her loyalty was doubtful and her contribution small, her only value to the Allies was the negative one of her not being allied to Germany. But this was vital. Because of the effect a Japanese switch of sides would have had on Russia, it was essential to keep Japan out of the German embrace. Japan, aware of the nature of her value, was not at all reluctant to let it be known that Germany was wooing her. Whenever Germany whispered tempting offers it was quite remarkable how quickly judicious hints of them reached Allied ears.

That, for all his finesse, was to be the fate of Hintze's overtures. He had begun sounding out the Japanese immediately upon his arrival in Peking. He assured the Japanese Ambassador there that he was voicing the personal views of the Kaiser in suggesting an alliance, and he repeated the proposal in a private talk with the correspondent of a leading Tokyo newspaper, the *Asahi Shimbun*. He said Germany would let Japan keep Tsingtao and the Pacific islands after the peace and would assure her a freer hand in China than would ever be allowed her by the Allies. He suggested the possibility of German financial support for Japan's expansion in China. In Stockholm too—another neutral capital where the envoys of opposite sides could meet—the Japanese Ambassador found himself suddenly popular. In March and April 1915 he was visited variously by the German, Austrian, and Turkish envoys, each bearing on behalf of the Central Powers a proposal echoing von Hintze's. The Japanese listened attentively to the overtures and leaked them discreetly to Russia. No one knows to this day whether they seriously considered accepting them, but the Russian Ambassador in Peking was worried enough to believe they might.

Just at this moment, in April 1915, Americans were swept up in a first-class, genuine Japanese war scare by the news that a Japanese battle cruiser, the *Asama,* was mysteriously maneuvering in Turtle Bay on the coast of Mexican Lower California. The Hearst press screamed, admirals and generals scurried in and out of the State Department, military intelligence reported Turtle Bay had been used for months by Japanese warships, Japanese radio signals were picked up, and Admiral Howard of the Pacific Fleet asked for reinforcements.

Had the *Asama* really run aground, or was she pretending? What was she doing in Turtle Bay anyway? Reports said she had been there since December, that she was caught fast on a rock, or, alternatively, that she was only stuck in the mud and could easily be pulled off in a week. In that case, why were three other cruisers and several supply ships hovering around? Government agents rushed down from Los Angeles, and the cruiser *New Orleans* was sent out to investigate. The press frenziedly recalled all the Japan-in-Mexico alarms of recent years: the secret treaty of 1911; Japan's alleged attempt to buy Magdalena Bay in 1912; the rumors that Japan had been giving Huerta credit for arms, then Carranza credit for arms, that Japanese officers were in Huerta's army, in Carranza's army, even in Villa's army. New reports proliferated that Japan was planting coaling stations at Santiago Bay and fishing colonies at Manzanilla Bay, and peopling Mexico with fishermen who spoke two or three languages and, instead of rods and nets, carried surveyors' apparatus.

Japan's spokesmen abjured all evil intentions and said the Turtle Bay story was fabricated by German agents. The German press retorted that Japan was certainly establishing a naval base in Mexico and wistfully suggested that, if this should lead to war with the United States, Germany would not find it hard to reconcile herself to America's misfortune.

Japan was not displeased by the universal suspicion of her intentions. The greater the doubts of her loyalty, the higher the price the Allies would pay to keep her loyal. She did not mind letting it be known to the Allies that she had been approached by the enemy. Admiral Hall heard about it in London. The State Department heard about it in Washington. In June 1915, Sir Cecil Spring-Rice, the neurasthenic British Ambassador, hurried over in his most harassed manner to say that relations with Japan were exceedingly bad at present, in fact could hardly be worse, and he was confident that Japan would join forces with Germany after the war. Although Sir Cecil was a perennial worrier, on this occasion his forebodings were taken seriously and set official pens to scratching gloomily in diplomatic diaries. Chandler P. Anderson, Counselor of the State Department, to whom Sir Cecil had voiced his belief that Japan would join Germany, noted in his diary, "I had already independently formed the same conclusion." Colonel House wrote in *his* diary that if Germany and Japan linked fortunes "it would be a serious day for the United States." The new Secretary of State, Robert Lansing, who had just replaced Bryan, was even more explicit. "I think," he wrote in one of his careful memoranda, "that if German militarism and autocratic government survive the war, they will renew the attack on democracy and the two powers they will approach will be Russia and Japan, equally autocratic and expansionist."

Disparaged Lansing, though "meticulous, metallic and mousy," as Secretary Daniels called him, had a way of sizing up matters correctly. In this instance he was wrong in only one respect: the Germans were not waiting until after the war; they were approaching Japan and Russia already, in pursuit of that great natural triple alliance of the three autocracies that was their dream and the Allies' nightmare. Together, von Hintze openly told a Japanese correspondent, Germany and Japan and Russia would form an invincible combination that would "dominate the two hemispheres and ensure world peace." He had sympathetic listeners among Japan's military leaders, who always believed Germany would prevail in the war and said so loudly and often. The Japanese government made no attempt to silence these sentiments. It found them useful in leading on both Germany and the Allies to expect that Japan might succumb to the German temptation. Throughout the war the German hope and the Allied fear that Japan might one day apostasize were never absent.

Of course Japan obligingly adhered to the London Pact pledging each of the signatories not to make a separate peace, but this did not seem to set anyone's mind at rest. Washington nerves were not soothed when Ambassador Gerard wired from Berlin late in 1915, "I suspect the Germans and Japanese of getting together," and a week later picked up new evidence that von Hintze was still trying to come to an understanding with both Japan and Russia. In April 1916 Germany sent her giant of industry, Hugo Stinnes, to Stockholm, as if on some labor of Hercules, to wrestle for a separate peace. He had many interviews with the Japanese Ambassador but, mortal after all, came home empty-handed.

Although the Allies were dutifully informed by Japan of the bids she was receiving, they could never altogether quell an uneasiness that one day she might turn around and accept them. The uneasiness was fully shared in Washington, where officials knew that, with Europe's attention absorbed, the moment was as opportune as might come again in a long time for a Japanese adventure against the United States via Mexico. Here the facts are difficult to separate from the imaginings of people who looked through yellow glasses and saw the Peril wherever they looked. Whether Japan was actually planning an attack at this time it is impossible to say because few, if any, Westerners have had free access to Japanese archives. But it can be said without question that most people, including responsible people, in Germany, in the rest of Europe, as well as in America, believed that Japan was planning and might undertake at any time some action in Mexico aimed at the United States.

German propagandists in the United States as well as the Hearst press and similiarly minded interests were forever alerting the public to the danger of a Japanese attack by way of Mexico. Hearst's film company produced a serial movie starring Irene Castle, in whose idolized person American womanhood was made to suffer the cinematic perils of a Japanese-Mexican attempt to conquer the United States. In ten weekly episodes she struggled and escaped and battled for her virtue against Japanese who, led by a villainous samurai at the head of the Emperor's secret service, invaded California, committing appropriate atrocities as they went.

Japan's real intentions in Mexico at this time were probably opportunist; she was ready to take advantage of favorable circumstances but not ready for open aggression. Whatever the purpose of the *Asama*'s mission to Mexico, it is unlikely that she ran aground in Turtle Bay by accident or through careless seamanship, and the possibility of a Japanese reappearance in Mexico remained wide open. In the same month—April 1915—that the *Asama* lay stuck in the mud, surrounded by Japanese fleet units so unaccountably awkward in their attempts to pull her off, two other visitors arrived on the opposite coast of the American continent. They too had a secret mission in Mexico.

5

"Von Rintelen Came Here, Backed by Millions . . ."

Since 1914 General Huerta had been waiting in Barcelona, like Napoleon at Elba, for the moment of return. Germany had brought him out of Mexico, and Germany now proposed to put him back. To him came an envoy in February 1915, Captain Franz von Rintelen, a German naval officer in mufti who offered to back a military coup that would restore Huerta to power in Mexico, win him sweet revenge on Wilson—and incidentally, it was hoped, provoke a war with the United States that would conveniently absorb American munitions now going to the Allies.

A comeback for Huerta staged by Germany could be counted on to make Wilson lower his head and charge blindly into another misadventure in Mexico more disastrous than Veracruz. He was now tangled in a worse mess than ever amid the wrangles of the revolution below the Rio Grande. Begun by Madero, interrupted by Huerta's brief reign, renewed by "First Chief" Carranza and his furiously battling rivals, the revolution had in the past year reduced Mexico to a bleeding ruin roamed by the pistol-happy private armies of Generals Villa, Zapata, Obregón, and other competing chieftans, while General Felix Díaz and Orozco, adherents of Huerta, marshaled their forces for the counter-revolution. In this murderous tangle Wilson was hopelessly lost. Each Mexican faction had its own set of American supporters and detractors trying to pressure Washington this way or that. American property-owners and bandit-harassed border residents were screaming for intervention; the liberals were screaming against it. No wonder the German High Command hoped, by reintroducing Huerta into the turmoil, to explode a situation that would keep United States energies fully occupied on her own side of the Atlantic.

Rintelen, the man whom the High Command selected to carry out the mission, was the possessor of intelligence, daring, and that streak of megalomania, characteristic of Wassmuss too, that may be the secret agent's most important qualification. With a self-confidence no less sublime than that of his counterpart in Persia, Rintelen determined to open an American front in Mexico. As a side effort he planned to buy out Du Pont's munitions works and tie up the remaining arms output by strikes and sabotage. He was thirty-eight at this time, a tall, prepossessing, well-born, well-tailored man who spoke excellent English and knew the United States, Mexico, and South America at first hand. After early service with the Navy and some years with the Deutsche Bank, he had first come to America in 1906 as representative of Germany's second biggest bank, the Disconto Gesellschaft. Three years' residence in New York had given him wide acquaintance in business and banking circles, not to mention the New York Yacht Club, on whose exclusive roster he had acquired membership. He had lived at the Yacht Club, had his office with the solid banking firm of Ladenburg, Thalmann & Co., had made himself a delightful bachelor guest at dinner tables from Southampton to Newport, and left sorrowing friends when he departed for Mexico in 1909. There and in South America he spent a year extending banking connections, returned to Germany in 1910, married a lady of wealth, fathered a daughter, and upon the outbreak of war rejoined the Navy, serving out of uniform as financial adviser to the Admiralty General Staff.

He took his mission seriously, for, unlike the Berlin officials, he justly estimated, from his personal knowledge, the weight the United States might eventually throw in the balance, and he believed the war would be won not on the battlefields of Europe but in America. According to boasts overheard in the course of his exploits here, he hoped to add to his official mission the pleasure of personally "telling Wilson what's what" about his heinous munitions traffic. In this trade, the Germans, who had sold arms in the Spanish-American war, the Boer war, and the Russo-Japanese war, found something particularly criminal and had worked themselves up to a foam of rage against Americans that far exceeded at this time the local and sporadic indignation against Germans in America.

Rintelen arrived in New York on April 3, 1915, to be followed ten days later by General Huerta, who arrived on April 13. Their chances of success were by no means unlikely. "Poor Mexico," Porfirio Díaz once lamented, "so far from God and so near the United States." That indeed was her tragedy. It was not only Germans who smelled profit in a counter-revolution in Mexico. Mexico's anarchy was then America's number-one foreign problem, and the sound of shooting from over the border made more noise in American ears than the shooting in Europe. American oil interests led by Doheny and Senator Fall (the future Teapot Dome twins), Guggenheim copper and other mining and railroad interests were heavily invested there. That was the day of the tycoon in Mexico, and almost to a man the tycoons would have been happy to see Huerta restored. Within Mexico, conditions were begging for a strong man's coup. The country, as Wilson had to admit, was "starving and without a government." Carranza's rule was in chaos; the First Chief himself, chased out of the capital, was operating from Veracruz while the raffish Pancho Villa and fiery-eyed Zapata looted Mexico City and clowned in the throne room of the National Palace. Along the roads rotting bodies swung from the trees, crops and cattle were stolen by galloping bandits draped in cartridge belts, black smallpox and typhus prowled the cities, fields lay unsown, railroads and bridges were wrecked, firing squads outnumbered food lines, death was as common as dirt, and the peon, the "submerged 85 per cent" in whose name the revolution had been launched, huddled in the dust of deserted villages.

Any one of the warring factions, regardless of ideology, might be induced to sell out to Huerta, and there were of course generals, landowners, *cientificos,* and other powers of the old regime ready to rally to him at the first signal. Most of the more prominent ones were already in New York, busily engaged in intriguing for the exile's return with American groups and Mexican factions.

Rintelen therefore had plenty to work with. And he had ready-made channels of German influence in Mexico through the German Minister, German consuls, German commercial agents, a German community of some four thousand, German-subsidized newspapers, German wireless operators whom Huerta before his fall had installed in Mexico's receiving station, a German officer, General Maximilian Kloss, who was director general of Mexico's munitions and ordnance manufacture, and some fifty naturalized Germans who held commissions in the Mexican Army.

Unfortunately, the one thing Rintelen and Huerta did not find in New York was a decent privacy for the maturing of their plot. From the moment of their arrival several varieties of secret-service agents began to converge upon them, tripping over one another as they sniffed in and out of New York hotels on the scent of the conspirators. The scent was the stronger because of the stew of jealousy and intrigue stirred up among German embassy personnel by Rintelen's advent. Particularly he was resented by a future Chancellor of the Reich, Major Franz von Papen, then a dapper military attaché who, being accredited to Mexico as well as to Washington, regarded Rintelen as an intruder upon his private province. Papen's affinity for diplomatic espionage was to continue over a career of thirty years until his last post as Hitler's Ambassador to Turkey in World War II, but at this time he was just embarked upon those more informal duties of a diplomat that were to get him expelled before the year was over. When Rintelen moved in on him with his I'll-take-over air and his tactless announcement that the General Staff had sent him to "do something positive" about the munitions traffic, he made an enemy inside his own camp who immediately began scheming for his removal. And the odds were on Papen, who was far more wily and subtle than Rintelen and would, as his future was to show, manage always to fall on his feet on the side of the ins, never the outs—whether it was the monarchy, the Weimar Republic, or the Third Reich. Today he is living comfortably in Germany, the only one of all the actors in this story still alive.

Papen's colleague, Captain Boy-Ed, the naval attaché, a strong, silent half-Turk with the eyes of a fanatic, equally resented Rintelen as presuming to take precedence over him upon the higher orders of the Admiralty. There were at this time numbers of German ships interned in Atlantic ports, which together with their idle crews provided ready-made headquarters and personnel for carrying out sabotage. Rintelen's claim that these ships and crews were now under his orders annoyed Papen and Boy-Ed, who were doing their best as hard-working diplomats in a neutral country to arrange for the blowing up of piers, canals, railroad bridges, and other objectives. Whether they were responsible for any of the troubles that soon began to enmesh their new colleague is not proved, but Rintelen always believed they were and carried on a lively feud with them for years after the war.

Another colleague was the commercial attaché, Heinrich Albert, whom Wilson described as "the directing and most dangerous mind in all these unhappy intrigues." As paymaster of all German undercover activities in the United States, Dr. Albert was not pleased by Rintelen's command of independent funds.

Albert's chief, the suave Count von Bernstorff, found all these matters very distressing. Elegant, aristocratic, intelligent, Ambassador and son of an Ambassador, Count Johann Heinrich Andreas Hermann Albrecht von Bernstorff was a cosmopolitan, born in England, whose six years as envoy to the United States had been adorned by social éclat and honorary degrees from five universities, including Wilson's Princeton. Knowing America, he understood better than anyone at home that Germany, despite all her initial victories, would not be able to withstand the addition of the United States as an active enemy. He channeled all his efforts toward one goal only: to keep America from joining the Allies. Although bound to comply with Berlin's orders, he deplored the use of tactics that could give America cause for irritation against his country and upset the nervous balance of neutrality. No ambassador ever had a more tact-demanding task or was more fitted to perform it. His charm, his candor, his easy adaptability, the sweetness of his manners, the hint of deference in his tone so different from the usual Prussian bluster, opened all avenues to him. He won ladies with his waltzing and warm blue eyes, men with his golf and poker, and newspapermen by giving orders to embassy guards to admit any gentlemen of the press who called. He spoke and wrote flawless English and French and, though on occasion a brilliant talker, he could sit for hours through dinners and over cigars with the men, letting others do the talking while he listened with an understanding smile kept in constant play over what was otherwise an oddly baffling countenance. The secret of his success, it was said, was his willingness to be bored.

As the ranking German diplomat in the Western Hemisphere, Bernstorff was responsible for carrying out German schemes in that area; all instructions to and reports from envoys went through him, and on him lodged the blame when extra-legal acts were uncovered. The bellows and blunders emanating from Berlin did not help his efforts to keep America neutral. He was in the position of a cultivated young man whose wooing of a Puritan maiden of the most sensitive morals is hampered by the social solecisms of his coarser relatives.

Rintelen's arrival did not ease Bernstorff's task; but Rintelen had come under the highest auspices, and after avoiding him for some weeks the Ambassador summoned him to a conference at his New York headquarters in the Ritz-Carlton, and shortly afterward communicated with the General Staff concerning Rintelen's mission. Besides the suite the Ambassador kept at the Ritz, each of the German embassy personnel maintained separate offices in New York, Papen at 60 Broadway, Boy-Ed in the German Consulate at 11 Broadway facing the Customs House on Bowling Green, and Dr. Albert in the Hamburg-American building at 45 Broadway. All used the German-American Club at 112 Central Park South as a meeting place and held frequent conferences in the Manhattan Hotel at 42nd Street and Madison Avenue.

Into this hotel one afternoon strolled Rintelen. As he waited, nonchalantly poking at the potted palms with his cane, a black limousine drew up at the entrance and discharged into the lobby the shrewd, tight-lipped Indian in pince-nez, General Huerta, attended by an escort of émigré Mexican plutocrats in velvet-collared overcoats. The group, joined by Rintelen, disappeared upstairs. None of them was aware that the rooms flanking their suite had been engaged by several gentlemen who kept watch there around the clock. To be introduced to them we must take a long jump back to London in the early weeks of the war.

Wickham Steed, foreign editor of the *Times,* on leaving his house one morning, met on the doorstep a thick-set Slavic individual of medium height, unshaven, grimy, and close to exhaustion, who said simply, "I'm Voska. The Professor sent me." The Professor, Steed knew from long acquaintance with Balkan politics, was Thomas Masaryk, one day to be Czechoslovakia's first president, but he had no idea who Voska was until the tired man explained that he was head of the Bohemian Alliance in America. He had just come with his daughter from five days' travel across Europe, bringing secret documents prepared by Masaryk on the Austro-Hungarian war potential. Some of them he had sewn inside the soles of his shoes before leaving Prague; the rest were rolled up and inserted in place of the bones of his daughter's corset. Neither shoes nor corset had been removed during the journey, father and daughter having slept in their clothes for five days. This seems to have been the first piece of espionage performed by a man who, as a volunteer, was to become the most valuable secret agent of the Allies in the United States.

Expelled as a youth from his native Bohemia by the Austro-Hungarian government on charges of socialist activity, Voska had emigrated to the United States, where he had prospered, acquired a Kansas marble quarry, and was now devoting the wealth gained from it to organizing the Czech colony in the United States for the nationalist cause. He had gone to Prague early in 1914 and after Sarajevo had been chosen by Masaryk to arrange a courier service and liaison between the Czech nationalists—whose hopes depended, of course upon the collapse of Austria-Hungary—and the Allies.

Voska, having completed his arrangements with the British, returned to the United States with a letter from Steed to the *Times* man in Washington. His first coup was to secure from a Czech patriot serving as mail clerk in the Austrian consulate a list of German and Austrian reservists who, with neutral passports bought from unemployed seamen, were planning to sail within the next few days, disguised as Dutch or Swiss or Swedes, to rejoin their regiments. Through the *Times* the list was made available to the British embassy. Voska, uncertain whether the man who had given him the list was really a Czech patriot or an *agent provocateur,* waited nervously for results. Within a week Madam Gruich, wife of a Serbian diplomat, invited him to tea and told him "a man" wanted to meet him secretly. He was to go to an address on the upper West Side, where he would find an apartment house, take the elevator to the fourth floor, open the first door on the right, which would be unlocked, enter, and wait until somebody came.

Voska followed instructions, pushed the door open, found a furnished apartment with no one in it, and sat down to wait in the silent room, wondering nervously who would appear. Fifteen minutes went by. Suddenly the door opened to admit a slender, smartly dressed young man who bounced cheerfully in, locked the door quickly behind him, introduced himself as Captain Guy Gaunt, British naval attaché in charge of Naval Intelligence. He complimented Voska on the list of pretended neutrals, all of whom had been duly caught and interned. "Splendid work, my dear chap, splendid!"

Like his opposite number, Captain Boy-Ed, though rather more discreetly, Captain Gaunt was doubling in secret service and reporting directly to Admiral Hall of Naval Intelligence. He now proposed to Voska that the members of the Bohemian Alliance be utilized as the

Allies' counter-espionage wedge in the United States. Speaking the German they had been forced to learn at school as their second language, they had held many sensitive posts under Austria-Hungary, which never realized the strength of the passion for freedom in its Czech and Slovak subjects. Britain, Gaunt said, had only two or three agents in the United States, France and Belgium had none, and the Russians, who always traveled in a cloud of secret agents, could not be trusted because too many of them were Baltics of German blood and sympathy.

The two men worked out their plans. By the time Rintelen arrived in America, Voska had recruited a band of compatriots who had infiltrated most of the missions and offices of the Central Powers. One of his agents was Countess von Bernstorff's personal maid; one was assistant chief clerk in the Austrian embassy; four were in the Austrian consulate; two were in the Hamburg-American Office; one was chauffeur at the German embassy; one was an operator at the Sayville wireless station on Long Island, which was used by the Germans for communication overseas. Others, eventually to the number of eighty, were clerks or waiters or messengers or scrubwomen in German clubs, commercial firms, consulates, and German-American newspapers throughout the country. Voska's home on East 86th Street in the Yorkville district was headquarters of the organization, a hive of hurried visits and oral reports, of telephones, papers, conferences, and photostat machines going day and night copying documents brought in on stolen time. Every day the faithful mail clerk who had started it all came at his lunch hour and sat munching a sandwich while letters he brought were photostated; they were then returned by him to be delivered as newly arrived mail.

The material gathered by Voska, passed on by Captain Gaunt to the American government, gave the government its first authentic evidence of German intrigues and violations of neutral soil. Nor was Captain Gaunt reluctant to have the revelations reach the American public. In the Australian-born and English-educated editor of the *Provi-*

dence Journal, John R. Rathom, he found a willing collaborator whose paper soon exhibited a startling and intimate acquaintance with German secrets. By prearrangement, Rathom's exposés appeared simultaneously in *The New York Times,* whose opening line, "The *Providence Journal* will say this morning . . ." soon became famous.

It was Voska's men, of course, who were listening in the room next to the German suite in the Manhattan Hotel. One of them, employed in the German embassy, had, in fact, arranged the meeting place. He had come up the day before, accompanied by a man carrying a black bag. The man was a master electrician and a passionate Czech who had performed many remarkable services for Voska. He prowled through the suite, studied a large round table in the sitting room; decided this was where the talk would take place; pushed the table a little nearer to the window, which was hung with heavy drapes, inner curtains, and shades; concealed his dictaphone behind the hangings; and ran the wire through the window frame to the room next door, where he connected it with a pair of headphones. Voska himself lunched in the hotel for two days and sat afterward in the lobby, ostensibly reading a newspaper. There he saw the tall German and the party of Mexicans meet and disappear together upstairs.

Huerta's arrival in the United States had naturally alarmed both Carranza and Villa, who immediately howled for the arrest of this "ruffian," this "monster shame of humanity," or for his deportation or, hopefully, for his extradition to Mexico on the old charge of Madero's murder. Carranzista agents shadowed Huerta and everyone he talked with. That made two sets of agents keeping watch on the plot, and when they were joined later on by a third there were enough spies in the Manhattan Hotel to start a convention. The third set was American. Department of Justice Agents had picked up Rintelen's trail through his sabotage activities. Unlike Huerta, Rintelen had entered the country pseudonymously on a forged Swiss passport under the alias Emil V. Gasche. The name was borrowed from his sister Emily, who had married a

Swiss named Gasche. In New York he transformed himself into the E. V. Gibbons Co., listed as an importing and exporting firm and representative of the Mexican Northwest Railway, with offices at 55 Liberty Street. From here he was to pour out half a million dollars to organize a group called Labor's National Peace Council, designed to cause strikes and slowdowns among longshoremen and munitions workers. His agent in this business, which was to come under Senate investigation, was a character known as the "Wolf of Wall Street," otherwise David Lamar, who fed Rintelen extravagant reports of the Peace Council's progress while pocketing the large share of Rintelen's money.

When Rintelen was not being Gibbons, he was being Frederick Hansen, in whose name he took another set of offices around the corner at 57 William Street, in the same building as the Transatlantic Trust Company, where his funds were deposited. As Hansen he carried on his designs against the munitions traffic, using as his headquarters the engine room of the *Friedrich der Grosse,* one of the interned German ships. Here, under his direction, a chemist named Dr. Scheele fabricated time bombs to be placed in the holds of ships carrying arms to the Allies. Several of these, successfully exploding in mid-ocean, were to provide the charge on which Rintelen was eventually tried and convicted.

Between being Gibbons and Hansen the inexhaustible Rintelen found time, in his own person, to rediscover old friends in the yacht basins of Long Island Sound and to attend to his main purpose—arranging for a war with Mexico through the restoration of General Huerta.

The American government, uneasy host to President Wilson's least favorite character, had been watching Huerta from the moment of his arrival but did not know at first of German complicity in his plans. In May, Wilson took a step that was to enter yet another group of agents in the secret-service sweepstakes going on in New York. For some time Colonel House had been relaying information received from Captain Gaunt about German violations of neutral territory. The President had avoided pressing the issue because he wished to keep relations with the Germans reasonably smooth for the sake of the overriding goal on which his heart and mind were set: ending the war by American mediation. Then on May 7 the *Lusitania* was sunk and the country enjoyed a frenzy of horror over the crime of the Hohenzollerns. Some of the national anger rubbed off on the President. On May 14 he instructed Secretary of the Treasury McAdoo, whose department controlled the Secret Service, to put a watch on German and Austrian embassy personnel to uncover any conduct unbecoming to diplomats.

"We rented an apartment," testified Secret Service Chief William J. Flynn some years later, "and the telephone man led the wires in and hooked them up so that we had a telephone matching every telephone in the two embassies. When a receiver was taken down in the embassy a light flashed in the Secret Service apartment. When a phone bell rang in the embassy one rang in our apartment. Four stenographers worked in relays, all expert linguists."

Each night Flynn received a stenographic report of all conversations of the previous twenty-four hours, copies of which were given to the State Department in a procedure known to the President. Among the interesting data furnished by these calls were Count von Bernstorff's lively conversations with Washington ladies. No, he modestly protested to one caller, he really should not be compared to the title character of a current play called *The Great Lover,* because, unlike the play's hero, he had "stopped." "Perhaps you have taken a rest, but not stopped," a female voice replied, adding in a sharper tone, "You *needed* a rest."

In New York the even busier German wires were tapped with the cooperation of Police Commissioner Arthur Woods. Two of Flynn's men were sent to trail the busy visits of German diplomats in New York, and the Bomb Squad of the Department of Justice, whose job was to track saboteurs, joined the proliferation of watchers. In the course of these duties both sets of American agents eventually picked up Rintelen's trail, although they did not as yet connect him with General Huerta. Department of

Justice agents, following saboteurs, spotted him as Frederick Hansen and reported that he had unlimited funds and was having some negotiations with a Mexican whom they mistakenly believed to be Villa's representative. In July a State Department official learned from a lady informant that she recognized Hansen as her old friend, Captain Franz von Rintelen.

Meanwhile Rintelen had been conferring with Huerta again, both at the Manhattan Hotel and at an unnamed Fifth Avenue hotel, probably the Holland House, another favorite German meeting place, at Fifth Avenue and 30th Street. Upon one of these occasions he noticed two detectives who had frequently shadowed him and who now followed Huerta as he left the hotel. "Our interview," Rintelen recalls dramatically in his memoirs, "had been observed!" Nevertheless, using the German naval code, he reported the substance of the meeting to Berlin. Huerta, he said, wanted funds for the purchase of arms in the United States, moral support, and U-boats to land weapons along the Mexican coast for his adherents who would rise when he crossed the border. On his part he would, after regaining power, take up arms against the United States. That Huerta, a hard-headed realist, intended seriously to make war on the United States is unlikely, but plotters who want something from each other are frequently generous with promises. It is also possible that Rintelen, carried away by the heroic role in which he saw himself personally engineering a war that would cut off American munitions, exaggerated the prospects to Berlin.

Whether Room 40 intercepted this message is not recorded. Communication between Berlin and Bernstorff's embassy was coded variously in the diplomatic code, No. 13040, in another code, designated 5950, and in the naval cipher, VB 718, two of which—and possibly all three—Room 40 could read at this time. Two months later Admiral Hall was able to use one of the three codes to lure Rintelen himself into a trap.

Absorbed by his multifarious conspiracies, Rintelen now left further negotiations on the Mexican matter to Papen and Boy-Ed, and delegated practical preparations for the rising—purchase of arms, arrangements at the border, deals with the factions in Mexico—to Dr. Albert's chief assistant, Carl Heynen, formerly Hamburg-American agent at Tampico, and to Frederico Stallforth, a prominent German banker in Mexico who had come up to New York to assist Huerta's return. Stallforth and his brother Alberto, who handled the Mexican end, were focal points on Mexican intrigue whose many contacts opened as many possibilities of betrayal, and they were naturally closely watched by the Carranzistas. At some point during these weeks, eight million rounds of ammunition were purchased in St. Louis, orders placed for a further three million in New York, and a preliminary sum of $800,000 deposited to Huerta's account in the Deutsche Bank in Havana as well as $95,000 in a Mexican account. Arrangements were made with General Felix Díaz, nephew of the old dictator, to lead a rising in the south when Huerta should cross the border in the north. Papen, who knew the ground from earlier trips to Mexico in 1914, was now sent down to the border to study the terrain from the military point of view, to arrange for a sort of underground railway by which German reservists in the United States could enter Mexico, and to distribute funds for Huerta's use in Brownsville, El Paso, and San Antonio.

Back in New York, Boy-Ed carried on the negotiations with Huerta. Driven by the embassy chauffer, who was one of Voska's men, he went to see Huerta at his hotel, the Ansonia, at Broadway and 72nd Street. A cautious answer had come through from Berlin, promising that further funds would be forthcoming and that U-boats and auxiliary cruisers would lend support when Mexico should enter upon hostilities with the United States. At further meetings with Boy-Ed, with Voska's men listening in, Huerta was promised ten thousand rifles and a first credit of ten thousand dollars. By now deeply committed, Huerta, whose family had come from Spain to join him, moved forward to his destiny.

He could not have chosen a more frenzied moment. Americans had hardly recovered from the Japanese war scare over the presence of the *Asama* at Turtle Bay in April, when they were flung into a furor over the sinking of the *Lusitania* in May. Wilson issued condemnatory notes, Germany rejected his principles, Secretary Bryan resigned when Wilson's further notes became too strong for his peace-loving soul, America and Germany moved to the verge of war, and the whole country was on edge.

In the midst of his furor, on Friday, June 25, General Huerta, after attending a baseball game, telling a census taker that he was *not* retired, and buying tickets to a policeman's ball, boarded a westbound train, saying he was going to visit the Exposition at San Francisco. On Saturday afternoon Secretary Lansing, a man of precise and invariable habits, made his usual neat notation on his desk calendar, "half holiday," and went home at one o'clock. At eight that evening the Department called him with news that Huerta had changed trains at Kansas City and was expected at El Paso next morning at six-thirty. Cobb, the State Department agent at El Paso, was waiting for instructions. The moment for the return from Elba had come.

It was a moment touchy in the extreme. If Huerta crossed the border, Washington would be on the brink of another Veracruz. If there was anything Wilson did not want at that moment, when he was close to a crisis with Germany over the submarine question, it was another Veracruz. But Wilson had himself just left Washington the day before for a vacation in New Hampshire. Meantime Huerta's train was speeding southward, and something had to be done. Lansing wired Cobb to cooperate with Department of Justice agents in the area and advise immediately. The eager Mr. Cobb took this to be authorization enough to act on his own responsibility, as he had already found out that the Justice men were without instructions. He had also found out that Huerta planned to leave the train at Newman, New Mexico, twenty miles from the border, where he was to be met by General Orozco, who would drive him to Mexico by car. After rounding up an Army colonel, twenty-five soldiers, and two deputy marshals, Cobb sped through the night to

Newman, arriving on Sunday at dawn, just before the train.

At sunrise, as the train slowed to a stop at Newman, General Orozco drove up in his car, General Huerta descended from his Pullman, and Mr. Cobb, followed by his escort, stepped from behind a baggage crate, made his arrest, and took both generals in custody to El Paso. There Huerta was released on a fifteen-thousand-dollar bond when his embarrassed captors found that news of his arrest by Americans had excited the Mexican populace of whatever faction in his favor. Washington sent Cobb a telegram of congratulations, but he worriedly reported back that business sentiment was strong for Huerta, the Mayor of El Paso had agreed to be his attorney, partisans were giving him ovations, the town was full of former Huerta officers and henchmen, the border restless. Huerta could buy out the garrison of Ciudad Juárez across the river any time he wanted, ten thousand mercenaries assembled by Orozco were waiting to rally to him, if he got a foothold Villa would collapse, the way to the capital would be open. The American Army had agreed to arrest him the moment he crossed the border but in the meantime had invited him to dinner at Fort Bliss. As long as he remained in El Paso, poised on the edge of Mexico, agitation would grow. Cobb begged Washington to get Huerta away from the border quickly.

But in Washington the anxious question was, how? Remembering the horrid consequences of the affair of the salute only a year ago, no one in Wilson's administration cared to risk another too precipitate brush with the foxy Aztec that might provoke another incident. Wilson's attention was momentarily engaged in New Hampshire by a growing acquaintance with his daughters' new friend, the delightful Mrs. Galt. While Lansing held one conference after another with the Secretary of War, the Chilean Ambassador, the Attorney-General, and other colleagues, Cobb harried him daily with telegrams pleading for action to get Huerta away "before the night passes." Then, on July 2, Orozco escaped to Mexico, and Washington, unable to delay longer, ordered Huerta rearrested and lodged in the county jail. But he was hot property, and every means was tried of persuading him to vanish painlessly away. He was threatened with deportation as an alien, he was wheedled with offers of liberty if he would only leave the border and consent to live in the northern part of the United States. But Huerta, stubborn as in the old days when he had refused to fire the salute, now refused to disembarrass Washington, refused to go away, refused to post higher bail, refused to accept any conditions in exchange for his freedom. "I will leave this jail only if I leave it unconditionally," he said. "I will agree to no compromise. I will stay in my cell rather than accept terms for my liberty." He took to studying English from a child's primer and complained only that the ice water his jailer brought him was "a little thin." Sadly he told reporters, "I have not had a drink these one-two-three-four days"—but even for brandy he would not make terms.

Cobb's telegrams now waxed frantic: "Orozco gathering forces in the mountains," he reported, "movement very thorough and strong." In Washington the benefits Germany expected to reap from an explosion in Mexico were being made all too clear by reports coming in from the agents in New York. Holding Huerta in the county jail was like holding on to a stick of dynamite with the fuse lit. On July 9 the War Department ordered Huerta transferred to military prison at Fort Bliss. Gasping with relief, Cobb wired, "This solves the problem."

He was wrong, for Huerta did not cease to be a problem until he was dead, and that was not yet.

A footnote was Bernstorff's characteristic washing his hands of the affair. While still under civil arrest, Huerta had wired him asking for the protection of the German government for his wife and children because the American officers "do not let them sleep or eat and search my house at will." Bernstorff blandly forwarded the message to Lansing with a covering note saying he had neither answered the note nor taken any notice of it. Shown to the President, Bernstorff's note elicited Wilson's one-line comment, "This is truly extraordinary."

Rintelen too was now about to come to the end of his usefulness. On July 6, two days after Huerta's arrest, he had received a telegram in the German Admiralty code, recalling him on the ground that his activities were becoming known and he was in danger of arrest. Once again traveling as Emil Gasche, he sailed on the neutral Holland-American liner *Noordam* on August 3, just four months after arriving in New York. When the *Noordam* touched at England she was boarded by an armed search party which took an unusual interest in the Swiss citizen Mr. Gasche. Declaring themselves dissatisfied with his identity, the search party took him off the ship and, despite his indignant protests, escorted him to London for further examination. Carefully rehearsed in the details of the real Gasche's life, Rintelen was so convincing in his first interview at Scotland Yard that his interrogators' confidence in a certain tip they had received was shaken. They agreed to his demand to be taken before the Swiss Minister, who, equally convinced by his story, vouched for him. As a last precaution before apologetically releasing the Swiss gentleman, the Yard decided on one more interview, to which the man who had given the original tip was invited.

When Rintelen, still indignantly Swiss, entered the room, he at once felt fixed upon him the gaze of a newcomer in naval uniform, a short, pink-cheeked admiral. While an aide questioned him in German, the admiral, from beneath intermittently blinking eyelids, watched him unwaveringly, like a cat. Why not, suggested the admiral, speaking for the first time, ask the English legation in Bern to ascertain whether it was possible for Emile Gasche to be in London? The presumed Swiss knew he would not be Swiss much longer. Preferring to be held as a prisoner of war in England, rather than as a criminal in America, he admitted his identity as Captain von Rintelen of the Imperial German Navy. Admiral Hall nodded, having known Rintelen's identity from the beginning. Either, as some have suggested, he himself sent the telegram recalling Rintelen from America, or he intercepted a genuine telegram of recall.

For the next twenty-one months Rintelen remained in a prisoner-of-war camp in England.*

His departure from America had not finished the story. On August 4, the day after he sailed from New York, Gaunt's mouthpiece, the *Providence Journal,* using evidence obtained from Voska, published an exposé of the German plot to restore Huerta and provoke war with Mexico. It did not mention Rintelen but ascribed the conspiracy to Bernstorff and Boy-Ed, whom it was more to England's interest to discredit. Bernstorff, whose invariable rule was to deny knowledge of anything nefarious any of his subordinates might be accused of, repudiated the newspaper story; but even as he spoke, another exposé—the famous affair of the Purloined Briefcase—was in preparation.

---

*After America entered the war, Rintelen was sent back to the United States, where he was tried for conspiracy with the National Peace Council to foment labor agitation. He was convicted and sentenced to a fine of two thousand dollars and a year's imprisonment. A German offer to exchange him for twenty-one Allied officers of equal rank was not accepted. Two more trials and two more convictions followed in 1918 on charges of passport fraud and conspiracy to plant bombs on British ships. Altogether he was sentenced to a total of four years and two months. The Mexican conspiracy was never one of the charges. On November 19, 1920, he was released and his sentence commuted by the Attorney-General to the astonishment, indignation, and avid speculation of the public, or at least of the press. The rest is anti-climax. Embittered by the German Republic's disavowal of his mission after the war, he published his version of the truth in two volumes of memoirs notable for a Munchausen-like quality of stretching the possible into the preposterous. Befriended by Admiral Hall, he took up residence in England and on the outbreak of World War II, predicting that Hitler would soon disappear and be replaced by Pastor Niemöller, he offered his services to the British Navy. They were not accepted. He survived the war in an English detention camp for aliens, from which he emerged, grandiose to the last, with an offer to go to Nuremberg to defend the ten leading Nazis in the war crimes trials, describing himself for the occasion as a "specialist in international law," a designation that raised eyebrows on people with long memories. He died in London in 1949, aged seventy-two.

At three o'clock on the afternoon of July 24, Dr. Albert and George Sylvester Viereck, the American propagandist who worked for the Germans, had left Albert's office at 45 Broadway, followed by an American Secret Service agent, Frank Burke. Of the two, Burke recognized only Viereck, but he noticed that Viereck treated his companion with deference and that this man fitted a description of Albert as a man of fifty, six feet tall, with a face marked by dueling scars, and further that he carried a heavily stuffed briefcase. The two men took the Sixth Avenue El at Rector Street, and when Viereck got off alone at 23rd Street, Burke stuck with his companion. Albert fell asleep but woke just as the El doors were opening for the 50th Street station. He jumped up and hurried out, forgetting his briefcase, which Burke promptly laid hold of and, seeing Albert rushing back, got off at the far end of the car. While Albert looked frantically around for the person who could have taken his briefcase, Burke flattened himself against the wall of the platform, pretending to light a cigar. Albert dashed down to the street; Burke took the other stairway and jumped on a moving trolley just as Albert spotted him. Burke told the conductor that the wild-eyed man running alongside was a "nut" who had just created a disturbance on the El. The conductor told the motorman; the motorman obligingly passed up the next stop. At 53rd Street, Burke changed to a downtown trolley and rode it all the way to the carbarn, where he immediately telephoned his chief, Flynn. Flynn came up, examined the contents of the briefcase, sent off a wire to Secretary McAdoo, who was vacationing in Maine, and took the portfolio up to him the same evening.

The Albert papers, though not supplying evidence of illegality sufficient for prosecution, were a revelation of the various kinds of German undercover activity. The government, deciding they could best be handled by public exposure, gave the papers to the New York *World,* which accorded them half the front page on August 15. It was a midsummer sensation and the *World* kept it going with serial publication of all the incriminating documents. Bernstorff, adept at avoiding the scandals his subordinates got themselves into, retired to the Adirondacks, where, the State Department was informed, "he has been buried for the last ten days with his inamorata," while the unfortunate Albert became famous as the "Minister without Portfolio." Rintelen's name still did not appear, but the public, made aware by the Albert portfolio that German plots were no respecters of American soil, was more disposed to accept further revelations.

These were not long in coming. Voska's invaluable agents discovered an American citizen acting as one of the couriers on whom the Central Powers, lacking cables, were forced to rely to eke out their crippled communications. Every neutral ship that sailed carried a courier protected by a neutral passport, and the *Rotterdam*, sailing from New York in the last week of August, carried one John J. Archibald. Alerted by the Voska-to-Gaunt-to-Hall signal, the British neatly picked him off when the ship touched their shores. A haul of 110 documents as full of plums as a fruitcake was taken from Archibald, including a report from Count Dumba, the Austrian Ambassador, to his government, describing strikes promoted among Hungarian munitions worked and other indiscreet efforts; seventeen reports from the German embassy to the German Foreign Office; cancelled checks and payments to saboteurs and propagandists; sabotage progress reports by Papen and Boy-Ed; as well as a private letter from Papen to his wife, expressing his opinion of "these idiotic Yankees." Boy-Ed's dealings with Huerta figured in the correspondence, as did Papen's visits to Mexico the year before for the purpose of organizing the German community there for "self-defense," for which he was recommended for a medal.

When Admiral Hall, sorting over the papers, discovered what he had netted, he took considerable pleasure in presenting the evidence, with Britain's compliments, to Page, the American Ambassador. Page, passionately pro-Ally and sick with frustration over the blind side Wilson turned to him, was only too delighted to forward it to Washington. As a precaution the British, not quite trusting Wilson to become appropriately indignant, published the most incriminating of the documents in a Parliamentary White Paper in September.

Rising reluctantly to the occasion, the President declared the Austrian Ambassador *non grata* and demanded his recall but took no action, as yet, against the German attachés. The real effect of the Archibald papers, coming on top of the Albert portfolio and the Rintelen-Huerta conspiracy, was more profound, if less public. At that moment the official temper was so irritated with Germany over the long-drawn-out *Lusitania* issue that final rupture seemed to be at hand. The revelations of sabotage and plots woke the State Department with a shock of surprise to the fact that the Germans were dangerous. "A break may come before you get this letter," wrote Colonel House in mid-September. Everybody took another look at America's trouble spot, the Mexican border. Wilson's Mexican policy came to a screeching halt, backed up, and reversed itself.

Viva Villa!—Made in Germany

From the day Carranza had replaced Huerta he had been a disenchantment to Wilson, who complained, "I have never known a man more impossible to deal with." His once admired "constitutionalism" took the form of decrees against foreign property, he proved no more amenable to American pressure than Huerta, and, really, it seemed that he differed from Huerta only in that he had not murdered his predecessor. (He made up for it by murdering General Zapata some years later.) Sorely tried, Wilson for a while considered that General Obregón might be "the man of the hour" but subsequently, abetted by Secretary Bryan, he had come to the remarkable conclusion that Pancho Villa, the illiterate marauder with the fat mustache and whirling eyes who controlled all northern Mexico and was Carranza's chief opponent, was perhaps "the safest man to tie to."

Bryan, the grape-juice teetotaler, had decided that Villa was an "idealist" because he did not smoke or drink. In Bryan's mind the Idealist apparently remained uncontaminated by his command of a rabble that got drunk twice a day on tequila and smoked marijuana in between. But Bryan's strong point was not logic. His and Wilson's new candidate was a swaggering rooster who would far more readily shoot a man in the belly than shake hands with him. On one occasion, when annoyed by the yells of a drunken soldier while he was being interviewed by an American journalist, Villa casually pulled his pistol and killed the man from the window, without interrupting the conversation.

Villa was delighted to consider the American President his *amigo*. On the American side, as late as August 9,

1915, Secretary Lansing, Bryan's successor, was recommending support for Villa in order that the "appearance, at least," of opposition to the vain and obstreperous Carranza would make Carranza more amenable.

But then came the Albert and Archibald shocks, the full revelation of German designs behind Huerta, and the deepening crisis over the U-boats. It was in expectation of an imminent break with Germany that the Mexican reversal took place. In October 1915 the United States, with a jerk that startled the world, suddenly recognized Carranza as President of Mexico. Villa, ditched by his *amigo*, was maddened; everybody else was mystified, but the reasoning was clear. Lansing wrote it down in his diary:

Germany desires to keep up the turmoil in Mexico until the United States is forced to intervene; *therefore, we must not intervene.*

Germany does not wish to have any one faction dominant in Mexico; *therefore, we must recognize one faction as dominant in Mexico. . . .*

It comes down to this: Our possible relations with Germany must be our first consideration; and all our intercourse with Mexico must be regulated accordingly.

Immediately the new policy went into action. The Americans made a deal whereby Carranza's northern commander, who was expecting attack by Villa's forces at Agua Prieta, was enabled to bring in reinforcements, bypassing the mountains, on American railroads across American territory. When early in November the unsuspecting Villa charged down from the hills, his force was decimated. The battle of Agua Prieta broke his power and forced him into a winter retreat over the snowbound sierras that left him with nothing but a barefoot, frostbitten, half-starved remnant and a maniacal rage for revenge upon the gringos who had betrayed him. That was to be unfortunate.

On November 7 the torpedoing of another merchantman, the *Ancona*, exacerbated relations with Germany.

Wilson wished to take some action sterner than notes, which would make America's displeasure unmistakable. Could we not send home "the obnoxious underlings"? suggested Colonel House. We could. The evidence of the Archibald papers against Papen and Boy-Ed was dug out and their recall stiffly demanded. It made a sensation. All the papers began printing everything they could get hold of on German plots, while the government, for added emphasis, carefully leaked much of the information collected by the four sets of secret agents during the previous summer. Now for the first time the public learned the full details of the German conspiracy to restore Huerta and of Rintelen's directing role in it. The *Times* trumpeted the scandal on December 8: UNCOVER GERMAN PLOT TO EMBROIL U.S. WITH MEXICO. VON RINTELEN CAME HERE, BACKED BY MILLIONS, FOR THAT PURPOSE, GOVERNMENT LEARNS. ESPOUSED HUERTA'S CAUSE. NEW REVOLUTION WOULD DIVERT FROM ALLIES THE FLOW OF MUNITIONS.

Thirty million dollars had been appropriated by the Germans to finance Huerta's counter-revolution, said the *Times*. Twelve million had already been spent for arms and preparations. Department of Justice agents had traced the funds and located enough stores of rifles and ammunition "to equip a formidable expedition." Papen and Boy-Ed had journeyed to the border to prepare the ground. Felix Díaz was ready to march on the capital from the south. Rintelen was revealed as the master mind, and columns were devoted to his dealings with Huerta and the Wolf of Wall Street.

In fact the Department of Justice had built up a card file of every man Rintelen had seen, every hotel he had visited, every phone call made, every telegram sent or received, and nearly every dollar spent of the five hundred thousand he had personally deposited in the Transatlantic Trust Company. He had gone through it all in four months, with little more to show for the expenditure than a few bombs placed in cargo vessels, which any mechanic could have made for ten dollars apiece.

In the furor the only person to remain unruffled was Bernstorff. Privately he wired home, "Convinced Rintelen was principal reason for recall of attachés. His immediate disavowal absolutely necessary." But when called in to see Lansing, Bernstorff seemed "very much surprised and said he knew nothing about it." Lansing told him he had very good proofs and certainly was convinced that Captain Boy-Ed had seen Huerta several times at both the Manhattan Hotel and the Hotel Ansonia. Coolly the Ambassador denied any knowledge of the affair, insisted that the Secretary of State should repudiate the accusations, and himself announced publicly that he had been instructed to disavow Rintelen.

Papen tried to brave it out by taking the same tone. It was all "utterly false," he said in a formal protest to the Secretary of War, and neither he nor Boy-Ed "had directly or indirectly approached any Mexican government, faction, individual, or sets of individuals for any such purpose." His aplomb was thin, however, and, along with Boy-Ed, he had to go. Treading lightly around every trap, Bernstorff alone remained, not because the government had not got plenty to incriminate him but because he was indispensable to Wilson's hope of negotiating a peace.

The last and central figure of the whole affair was soon to go. At the Mexican border General Huerta was dying. In Fort Bliss he had sickened mysteriously; yellow jaundice was the diagnosis, but rumors that he was being poisoned got about. It would not look well if General Huerta were to die in American custody, and so in November he was released in the care of his family, who had followed him to El Paso. But the indomitable Indian refused once more to do the convenient thing; instead of dying he got well, whereupon he was promptly pulled back into Fort Bliss. Again his malady returned, and again the Americans, hastening to unburden themselves of a prisoner *in extremis,* released him, just after Christmas. Up in Hot Springs, Virginia, the President was enjoying a two week's honeymoon over the holidays with the new Mrs. Wilson. Did he know that his old opponent was dying at last? There is no record of whether he knew, or cared. But even dying, Huerta was not allowed to do without American intervention. Day and night American soldiers were stationed at his bedside and removed only when he fell into a coma. On January 14, 1916, on alien soil within sight of his unrecovered country, he died.

Neither his death nor Rintelen's removal halted Germany's unrelenting effort to provoke war between the United States and Mexico. Where Huerta had been, now there was Villa, a new enemy raised up by the United States herself. To Germany, Villa now appeared to offer a better prospect than ever of embroiling the United States with Mexico. And the appearance was soon borne out. On January 10, at Santa Ysabel in the province of Chihuahua, a band of Villistas waylaid a train carrying seventeen American mining engineers, lined them up, stripped them, and shot them down one after another. One man, Thomas H. Holmes, lay on the ground, still breathing. After the bandits rode off, he crawled through the night and stumbled, gasping and bleeding into Chihuahua City at seven next morning with the news of the deaths of all his companions.

The Massacre of Santa Ysabel, as it was immediately labeled, threw the country into an uproar and evoked a thunderous demand for intervention. Angry protest meetings and citizens' petitions shrieked for action to avenge "this foul and brutal murder." El Paso, whose citizens went out looking for Mexicans with guns, had to be put under martial law. A volunteer posse of a thousand mining and cattle men threatened to rush the border, hunt down the bandits, and take vengeance into their own hands unless the army was called out. Congressmen, especially Texans, perorated about murder, rapine, and pillage, about American women outraged, fates worse than death, American lives and sacred honor. Senators from the border states fumed that the only murder that had ever mattered to Wilson was the murder of Madero. Business interventionists declared it no longer safe for any American to enter Mexico while Wilson was president. Ex-president Roosevelt, receiving a petition from the border, called for the regular Army to march into Mexico at once.

Wilson, home from his honeymoon barely a week, was not to be moved. Deep within him was shame as an

American over the first Mexican War, overlaid by the stain of his own foray upon Veracruz. Never, he declared to a friend through shut teeth, would he be forced into a war with Mexico that could possibly be avoided. He closed his ears to epithets of cowardice that the nation flung at him and held on tight to the lines of Lansing's memorandum: Germany wants us to go to war with Mexico, therefore we must *not* go to war with Mexico; what we do in Mexico must be governed by the state of our relations with Germany. He knew well what a voice from an unexpected source—the Governor of Texas—pointed out, that it would be the wildest folly to act precipitately when the United States was totally unprepared for war with anybody, even ravaged Mexico.

Villa, spoiling for a fight, with Germany whispering encouragement in his ear, danced up and down the border like an enraged rooster trying to provoke the rush of a large dog. He saw himself, since Venustiano Carranza had received the American nod, facing oblivion, his power withering, his followers slipping away, and he believed his only hope lay in forcing an American invasion that would rally the peons in an anti-American rising behind his banner. Then he, not Carranza, would be the national hero. "Viva Villa!" would resound again from Sonora to Yucatán in one great battle cry that would sweep vain old "Don Venus" into the dust pile and leave nothing but his long white whiskers to make a hatband for valiant Pancho. This suited Germany perfectly. She did not believe Carranza likely to be ousted, but Villa, chasing that dream, could be helped to suck Americans into armed conflict in Mexico, German strategy would be freed of a great weight.

Germany's campaign opened with Theodore Roosevelt's bugle call to arms, which, unknown to him, was a German plant. An alert agent discovered that two German businessmen of El Paso, Edgar Held and Louis Hess, had circulated the petition addressed to Roosevelt and had been loudest in their denunciations of Wilson's failure to act. As a leading Hun-hater, T.R. would not have relished being a German tool, but he was fortunately spared that embarrassment when his summons thudded dully against the stone wall of Wilson's resistance.

But even that wall cracked under the impact of Villa's next blow. For Pancho came back. On the night of March 9, 1916, the little town of Columbus, New Mexico, was shattered out of its sleep by four hundred Mexican horsemen who galloped through the streets, shrieking and shooting, killed a score of residents, burned houses, sacked stores, and disappeared back over the border at dawn. This time, no matter what the counsels of caution and policy, America had to hit back. Bitterly, against every better judgment, Wilson for the second time in his administration found himself forced to order attack in Mexico, the one act he had wished above all things to avoid. Moving as circumspectly as he could, he first obtained Carranza's edgy consent to the entry of American troops, "for the sole purpose of capturing the bandit Villa." After searching vainly for some saving alternative that never came, when he could no longer help it, Wilson gave the command for a punitive expedition under General Pershing to cross the frontier.

It was a prolonged and famous fumble. Within a month Pershing, with 6600 men, was 300 miles inside Mexico, getting closer to a clash with Carranza and no nearer to Villa every day. In Washington the General Staff, preparing for the worst, drew up plans for a full-scale invasion. Ten, twenty, unnumbered times Villa was reported dead, captured, run to earth, beheaded, hung by his own men, caught by Carranzistas, until it seemed as if his face grinned at the scorched Americans out of every cactus only to vanish like the Cheshire cat.

Berlin's press was ecstatic and, harking back to an old theme, suggested the Japanese were secretly backing Villa. Our ambassador, James Gerard, telegraphed, "Am sure Villa's attacks are made in Germany." Everyone wondered where they were made, for the bravado of the Columbus raid, with its lack of apparent goal, was puzzling. Even in Mexico they called it Pancho's *delirio de grandeza*. Many Americans, including the President, believed it to have been inspired by the oil and metal greed of American business, while others, such as the *Collier's* correspondent, deduced a "certain European nation now at war whose interest is to keep the United States very busy."

Evidence of Germany's complicity, though in fact filtering in constantly, was kept very hush-hush in Washington, because the government, plunged at this moment into a new crisis over the torpedoing of the *Sussex,* did not want to provide the public with additional reasons for getting into war with Germany. But every few days through May and June, Lansing's desk diary bristled with notes of Secret Service reports: "reputed German officer at Tampico," "German plots in N. Mexico," "Justice reports of Germans on Mexican border." Enterprising as ever, Agent Cobb, who had once gone after Huerta with such avidity, now wired Lansing asking for permission to employ extra operatives to help him investigate "all the Germans who are mixing into our Mexican troubles." Although the Department had to blush when several of Cobb's suspicious characters turned out to be War Department agents following the same trails, enough other evidence was coming in to cause anxiety. Voska's men discovered that the arms Rintelen had bought for Huerta were now going to Villa, transported over the border in cheap coffins or shipped in sealed casks in chartered oil tankers whose tanks were then filled with oil, which was drained on reaching Mexican ports so the munitions could be lifted out intact.

Other German connections were evident. Why was it that Max Weber, the German Consul in Juárez, always smiled knowingly when people brought in new rumors of Villa's capture and, from some private source, was able to refute them? Why was it that only the German firms, with names sounding like the drill commands of a Prussian sergeant—Krakauer, Zork & Moye, Ketelson & Degetau—were passed by when the Villistas ransacked every other store and warehouse in Chihuahua City and again in Parral?

Germany was not satisfied with the footling, self-limited Pershing expedition, and every night, reported Gerard, "fifty million Germans cry themselves to sleep because all Mexico has not risen against us." To exacerbate matters, Germany, while nudging Villa with one hand, with the other offered one of the Díaz generals exiled in Cuba several million marks to start a counter-revolution. At the same time she redoubled her efforts to encourage the Carranza regime into a shooting war with the United States. Our consul in Veracruz, where Carranza had his headquarters, reported that a German agent in personal conference with Carranza had offered to lend the Mexican Army thirty-two officers in return for a grant of the San Antonio Lizardo peninsula, thirty miles south of Veracruz, which had an excellent natural harbor. This, with its implication of a possible submarine base, sent a chill through Washington and evoked from the presidential typewriter an order for immediate investigation.

General Funston, in command of the Mexican border, was troubled by information from Monterey that the German and Austrian Consuls there were financing a group of conspirators who were preparing an attack on Texas. All at once a number of sinister rumors began seeping in from Monterey, referring to a mysterious "Plan of San Diego" and the interest therein of the German Consul, a prominent merchant named Pablo Burchard. He had surreptitiously visited a Carranzista officer, Colonel Guerrero, said to be leader of the Plan, after midnight. He had held frequent conferences with another of the leaders, Colonel Maurilio Rodríguez. He had presented a very handsome diamond ring to a third Mexican conspirator, Luis de la Rosa, who was sporting it around town. What was it all about? When the American Vice-Consul in Monterey obtained the full details of the Plan of San Diego they left him gasping. Its aim was a revolution that was to be started by arms and manifestos in Texas, was to spread over New Mexico, Arizona, California, Nevada, Colorado, and Oklahoma and establish in this former Mexican territory an independent republic of Mexicans, Negroes, and Indians. Eventually it was to affiliate with Mexico and ultimately to assist the Negroes of six more American Southern states to revolt and set up a Negro state. Paranoid as it was, it dripped with the authentic hundred-year-old hate for the white-faced gringo. Possibly some report of the Plan of San Diego from Herr Burchard to his chief, Zimmermann, may have first planted in the Foreign Minister's mind the idea of offering Mexico recovery of her lost states.

Lansing, reading reports like these, was uneasy lest the passions engendered by the presence of American troops inside Mexico, especially with Germany stirring the brew, boil over in some incident committing America more deeply than ever. Mexico concerned him less than the need to keep clear to meet Germany. He and the new Secretary of War, Newton Baker, advised Wilson to withdraw Pershing now, with or without Villa, before something happened to make withdrawal impossible. While withdrawal was being considered, Consul Canada wired on June 18 that the German Minister, von Eckardt, was doing everything possible to urge Carranza to make war on the United States and he feared that Carranza's "impetuous generals may lead him into war." Next day it was learned that German reserve and noncommissioned officers in the United States had been ordered to register at Mexican consulates, failing which they would be considered as deserters.

The signs were ominous. Too long Carranza's generals had listened to the German siren song. Two days later, on June 21, an American scouting party, ignoring a Mexican warning that Americans moving in any direction except north would be fired upon, was attacked by Carranza troops at Carrizal and suffered twelve killed and twenty-three captured. Too late had come the government's thoughts of withdrawal; the country would not stand for it now. Interventionists bellowed more blood and thunder. The President, whose every effort to be the friend of Mexico had turned sour, now had to order out the National Guard to protect the border and send warships to both Mexican coasts.

To Germany it seemed that America was satisfactorily embroiled at last. At last the years of plots and pressure and slush funds had paid off. Germany could not resist gloating. When the New York *Times* warned that Germany was behind Carranza's turning against us, a Berlin paper replied, "We consider it not worth denying that Germany is egging Mexico into war in order to prevent the export of arms to the Allies. The fact that America's profitable arms traffic with France and England will suffer through a war with Mexico is, to be sure, a consequence that will cause us no tears."

Indeed the Germans, impatiently waiting for the Americans to extend their operations into a war of annexation, could not understand why they were so slow about it. Neither could the itchy-fingered American business interests who thought a war with Mexico much more useful than mixing into Europe's troubles. "Fate offers us a golden apple in Mexico and only bitter fruit in Flanders," said the *Chicago Tribune*. "If we win a war with Mexico we know what we get out of it—a secure continent. And it is practically impossible for us to lose." The Germans could not have agreed more. Their propaganda had pounded into Latin American heads the belief that America would try to annex all the territory between Texas and the Panama Canal, and as this, to the German mind, was the only logical thing to do, they became quite exasperated at America's failure to grasp her opportunity.

"It is perfectly silly of you Americans," remarked Major Herwarth von Bittenfeld, an old expert in the business of provoking a United States–Mexican war, "to expect to control the canal without the territory in between." Speaking to an American lady in Berlin, he became quite heated. "The canal is of no use to you strategically. You don't own the land leading up to it. Imagine our holding the Kiel Canal without Schleswig-Holstein!"

Yet Major Herwarth and Berlin's other Latin American manipulators could congratulate themselves on Germany's growing influence with the Carranza regime. Don Venus, behind his majestic appearance, was truculent but vain, ambitious but susceptible, and of slender intellectual equipment. The German net was slowly being drawn around him; he surely could be gathered in. With the right inducement he might even be persuaded to abandon neutrality and become an open ally. The prospect was luscious. Tampico's oil would be cut off from Britain, U-boats could shelter in the Gulf of Mexico, America would be pinned down on the far side of the Atlantic, too busy to meddle, much less to fight, in Europe.

A New Mexican Minister, Señor Zubaran, arriving in Berlin that summer, was invited to long conferences with Zimmermann and, ignoring diplomatic protocol, pointedly failed to call on the American Ambassador. In Mexico the Union of German Citizens was happy to report it now had twenty-nine local propaganda committees spreading the spirit of German *Kultur* with such zeal that "a great number of Mexicans have been convinced that we are in the right in our methods of conducting warfare and are now disposed to accept our communiqués." With no less zeal the Iron Cross Society reported seventy-five branches with members engaged in every kind of enterprise in the country, some as clerks and bureau chiefs in the government, ten as officers in the Army, two at divisonal level, and two with Villa. German money subsidized the press and published a special picture paper of war news for illiterate peasants. German agents fomented strikes among Tampico stevedores and anti-Americanism among Mexican laborers in Arizona and California. German banks extended their grip on the finances of Carranza's government. German mining interests bribed the government to invent decrees enabling them to buy up the mines vacated during the enforced absence of Americans, which they did so efficiently that soon the incredible happened. A German firm, the Compañía Metallurgica de Torreón, actually exceeded the holdings of the Guggenheims' American Smelting and Refining Company. Genuine horror speaks between the lines of the American agent reporting this awful development.

Worse was Carranza's flourishing intimacy with von Eckhardt, the German Minister, who conferred with him frequently in person, without a go-between. Eckhardt, driving his automobile to the National Palace to meet with the President in his own office, became a familiar sight. Carranza's resentment of the United States fed his favorite dream of a Pan-Hispanic union of Latin American nations strong and tall enough to look the Yankees in the eye. It was a fertile field for explorations with von Eckhardt, and together they schemed counter-revolutions to set up Mexican- (or German-) oriented regimes in various Central American states.

Eckhardt, when he first reached Mexico to replace von Hintze, had found himself handicapped by the lack of telegraphic communication with Berlin. No transmitter existed in Mexico powerful enough to send messages across the Atlantic. Although German wireless messages could be received in Mexico, there was no assurance they would reach Eckhardt, because of a Mexican law forbidding the use of code by foreigners. When Eckhardt complained of this to Carranza, the Mexican Minister of Telegraphs, Señor Mario Mendez, was conveniently allowed to be bribed, at the rate of $600 a month paid by the German Citizens Union, to look the other way. This arrangement eased Eckhardt's inter-American communication with other German envoys and secret agents but did not help in the matter of overseas telegrams.

Germany, however, worked out a way to leap over the wireless gap. Her overseas messages to and from the Americas, most of which were channeled through Bernstorff, were getting through in some manner which, until now, Room 40 had been unable to trace. A puzzling dead spot in the air between Washington and Berlin had blocked the efforts to listen in. The interceptors could not discover what route the messages took.

Originally these messages had been sent over what was known as the "main line" between Nauen, the German wireless station a few miles outside of Berlin, and Sayville, the station on Long Island. In the summer of 1915 the United States had put Sayville under naval censorship on the ground that the Germans were using it to inform their submarines of ship locations, thus making neutral territory a base for naval warfare. Thenceforward the Germans were supposed to use Sayville for cipher messages only if the cipher was filed with the American government. In fact the censorship was ineffective because the Germans simply circumvented it by sending messages ostensibly signed by German steamship and other commercial firms, which were really Bernstorff's in code.

American restrictions, however, hampered them enough to evoke their repeated and bitter complaints about their supposed inability to communicate directly with Berlin. Unfair, unfair, Bernstorff was constantly telling the State Department, while in Berlin, Chancellor Bethmann-Hollweg and Zimmermann periodically called in Ambassador Gerard to listen to their wounded feelings on the same theme. These complaints were part of a deliberate campaign to acquire telegraph routes with neutral connivance. It succeeded.

Admiral Hall was baffled. "We have traced nearly every route," he wrote to Captain Gaunt, "and I am really reduced to the following: he sends them down to Buenos Aires and thence across to Valparaiso." So far Hall was right, but after Argentina and Chile the track vanished. "From there I cannot make out where they are sent," he told Gaunt, "whether via China or Russia through the connivance of a neutral legation or not." Now, in the last quarter of 1916, a clue picked up in Mexico supplied the solution.

One of the most noisily pro-German members of the diplomatic corps in Mexico City was the Swedish chargé d'affaires, Herr Folke Cronholm. Lately, it had been noticed by a certain inquisitive Englishman, Herr Cronholm had been frequenting the telegraph office more often than the routine and limited relations of Sweden with Mexico would seem to warrant. The Englishman was inquisitive with a purpose, for he was acting as an agent of Admiral Hall. Designated only as H., his identity remains secreted in Room 40's files.

Had Cronholm been more discreetly neutral his visits might have gone unremarked, but his admiration for the German cause being notorious, his traffic in telegrams became provocative. Mr. H. took note of it, wondered, and reported his observations to Admiral Hall with a promise to investigate further.

Some time later Admiral Hall found himself reading

an intercept from Eckhardt to Berlin asking for a reply to an earlier request for a decoration for his Swedish colleague, Herr Cronholm. Although the German passion for collecting and bestowing decorations was an understood thing in the Europe of that day, Hall's sensitive antenna twitched on reading Eckhardt's request. Why should a Swedish chargé in Mexico City want or deserve a German decoration? Admiral Hall did not like unanswered questions. He looked up H.'s reports and reread the mention of Cronholm's unusual frequenting of the telegraph office. Subsequently H., having with some ingenuity discovered that Cronholm's telegraph bills far exceeded his government's allowance for that purpose, had suggested a disquieting explanation. Was it possible that Sweden—granted that she was admittedly pro-German—could have so far violated her official neutrality as to be secretly sending German's messages for her?

So far this was only a suspicion, but now circumstantial evidence turned up to confirm it. A letter from Eckhardt to Chancellor Bethmann-Hollweg containing Eckardt's first request for a decoration for Cronholm came into Room 40's possession. It told why Cronholm deserved German gratitude. "He arranges the conditions," Eckhardt wrote, "for the official telegraphic traffic with Your Excellency." On each occasion "he goes personally, often late at night, to the telegraph office to hand in the dispatches." Herr Cronholm did not have a Swedish order but only a Chilean one. (How naked his Swedish chest must have felt when compared, for example, with that of General Maximilian Kloss, highest German officer in the Mexican Army, who wrote proudly home to his parents, "I now have nine decorations and three high orders to pin on my tunic and the Cross of Honor to wear around my neck.") Could not Germany show her appreciation, Eckhardt asked, by conferring upon Cronholm the *Kronenorden,* Second Class, privately of course, with no official announcement until after the war so as not to arouse the enemy's suspicions?

Here at last was the answer to the problem that had

baffled Room 40 for so long. Germany's overseas messages were being transmitted by Sweden! Proof was easily secured, for Swedish cablegrams touched at England in passing over the Atlantic cable. Hall had only to call for copies of the Swedish government code telegrams, and a brief examination showed the truth. After a few Swedish code groups, the characteristic German code appeared, and the rest of the friendly arrangement was not hard to reconstruct. German envoys abroad gave their messages in German code to their Swedish colleagues, as Eckhardt was giving them to Cronholm, and the Swedes transmitted them by cable, along with their own, to the Foreign Office in Stockholm. The Foreign Office gave them to the German Minister in Stockholm, who sent them on to Berlin. Outgoing telegrams took the reverse route. They went from Berlin via Stockholm to Swedish envoys in foreign capitals, who delivered them to their German colleagues. Most of the correspondence with Washington and Mexico went via Buenos Aires.

This, as it became known in Room 40, was the Swedish Roundabout. Once in possession of it, Hall could listen in not only on Eckhardt but on Bernstorff, whose intelligence service gave more insight into Wilson's intentions, policies, and peace maneuvers than anything else coming out of Washington, including the cloudy communiqués of the peregrinating Colonel House. Bernstorff used the Sayville-Nauen route, which, being operated under American naval censorship, was risky, and the Swedish Roundabout, which was slow. When he continued to complain— to Colonel House—about the difficulty of communicating with his government, he was granted a concession, one of such simple granduer that for us to accept it requires what the poets call a willing suspension of disbelief. Colonel House's arrangement will appear in due time.

It was now November 1916. Deadlock and discouragement hung in the air as thick as a coal-smoke fog. Half humanity was starving or sickening or dying in the trenches. When American relief was urged for Poles and Belgians and typhus-stricken Serbs, Bethmann-Hollweg looked helpless and shrugged. "What do these compare with the hecatomb of lives lost on the Somme?"

Relentlessly, every few minutes, the intercepts still dropped into the wire baskets at Room 40. They warned Hall that a dreaded danger, the letting loose of the U-boats, was looming closer. Von Eckhardt's wooing had prospered to the point where, in October, he had reported, "Carranza, who is now openly friendly to Germany, is willing, if it becomes necessary, to support German submarines in Mexican waters to the best of his ability." After intercepting this message, Hall had quickly passed it on to the United States. Lansing had sternly warned Carranza that such a violation of Mexican neutrality, if true, could only have "the most disastrous results" and compel "drastic action" by Great Britain. Carranza had hesitated. Berlin began to push. On November 12, Eckhardt was informed in Headquarters' most momentous tones that the imperial government was about to resume unrestricted use of the U-boat as "the most efficacious means of annihilating its principal enemy." This would include operations in American waters, and "it would be very valuable to have bases to assist the work of the submarines both in South American and Mexico." In a first feeler toward an alliance with Mexico, von Eckhardt was instructed to ask what "suitable advantages" Germany could grant in return for permission to use Mexican territory for submarine bases.

What would Carranza do? The longer American troops remained inside his borders, galling Mexican pride, the greater was the chance of his succumbing to Germany. U-boats operating from Mexican bases could cut off supplies from America. Worse, all Tampico's oil was at stake. Above all, what would Wilson do?

In America four-fifths of the regular Army was tied up inside or along the borders of Mexico. Pershing's twelve thousand troops were still vainly chasing Villa through the hills of Chihuahua. The possibility of Japan's taking advantage of Mexican resentment to woo her into an accord disturbed Washington. Officials were harassed by more than the usual number of reports from government agents and from agitated citizens about Japanese colonists and Japanese fishing fleets and Japanese wireless and Japanese deals with Villa, and had to investigate each one. The specter of the secret Japanese treaty walked again, not threadbare from repeated appearance but healthier than ever.

By November, when the prospect of involvement in Europe was getting blacker, the growing intimacy between Carranza and Japan was becoming plainer. The Japanese envoy in Mexico was lavishly entertaining government officials and being lavishly dined in return at the National Palace in an "ostentatious display of cordiality." Also in November a Mexican Army officer, Major Carpio, sailed for Tokyo aboard the *Empress of Asia* on a mission to buy arms. His activities on arrival, reported daily by watching Americans, included conferences with many high naval officials and escorted visits to Japanese naval bases at Kure, Sasebo, and Yokosuka. Despite Japan's agreement not to export arms to any except Allied nations, Major Carpio was able to purchase machine guns and rifles as well as all the equipment for an ammunition factory to be set up in Mexico. Nor did he find any obstacles put in the way of his engaging the services of several score Japanese ordnance experts to run the factory and a Japanese ship to deliver it. His activities set off so many wild rumors of Japanese infiltration that it really seemed as if the Yellow Peril had arrived in the flesh at last.

Berlin fervently hoped so. At that very moment the militarists were forcing the decision to risk American belligerency for the sake of an all-out submarine campaign. German admirals and generals with confident arrogance were promising their government that America could be discounted in advance because her flank would be turned by Japan, which would certainly seize the chance to attack Lower California or the Panama Canal. The German government was anxious to be persuaded. But who, as 1916 drew to its somber close, knew what Japan might do? Wilson at the same time was ardently, desperately trying to wring from the belligerents some sign of willingness to

negotiate a settlement before Germany should let loose
the U-boats and force belligerency upon America herself.
It was a grim race between Wilson and the Wilhelmstrasse.
No one was cheering.

"Our Friend Zimmermann"

In November 1916, when Europe was war-numb and longing for peace, America thought it saw a sign of hope in the appointment of "a very jolly large sort of German" (so described by Ambassador Gerard) as the new Foreign Minister. Disgusted with the war, increasingly nervous lest they be dragged in, Americans were ready to seize on anything that seemed to offer a prospect of breaking apart the belligerents, who were reeling back and forth in their hopelessly deadlocked wrestle. They believed they saw in the promotion of Under-Secretary Arthur Zimmermann the signal of an upsurge of liberal forces that would free Germany from the grip of military autocracy, open the way to peace and the salvation of the world. They greeted him with a cry of welcome as if he were the sun that would begin the melting of the snows. Had they been less illusioned, they might have read in the appointment signs of even sterner weather ahead.

Zimmermann appealed to Americans because he was what the *Times* fondly called "a man of the people," the first ever to be appointed to high office in the German foreign service, hitherto reserved for Junkers. He was a big, ruddy, good-humored, square-headed bachelor of fifty years with blue eyes, reddish blond hair, and bushy mustache, the very epitome of the German middle class, although his middle-class origin he had contrived partially to remedy by an approved dueling scar on his cheek. He had not a *von* to his name, and his training and early career had been in the consular service, realm of the non-*vons*. Had he stayed there, wrote former Chancellor Prince von Bülow in those four malicious volumes of posthumous memoirs that on their appearance in 1930 caused such agony in the ministries of Europe, or had he become a provincial bureaucrat, he would have been liked and esteemed and greeted every morning by the local populace as he came to take his apéritif on the terrace of the town's best hotel with a hearty "Good morning, good health, Your Honor!"

The fate thus patronizingly laid out for him Zimmermann escaped through sheer industry. He was transferred to the Foreign Office in 1902 and reached the rank of Under-Secretary by 1911. A story circulated in Berlin by the Dutch Ambassador of that day claims that Zimmermann might have had the top job in 1913 instead of Gottlieb von Jagow, but that neither wanted the responsibility which, in those days of the Kaiser's darting interferences, could be uncomfortable. Each deferred to the other, but Zimmermann won on the excuse that he was suffering from gallstones, and so "Herr von Jagow had to assume the responsibility although he had ten times as many gallstones."

Perhaps Zimmermann's initial reluctance was due to his being an outsider, a self-made man in the aristocratic ranks of the Foreign Office. This very attribute predisposed every American, bred to the automatic assumption that to be self-made is simultaneously to be virtuous, in his favor. In Imperial Germany it merely had the effect, as so often happens to the self-made in a society of exaggerated class distinctions, of making Zimmermann more Hohenzollern than the Kaiser. Because he wanted to be "one of them" he was the more anxious to be orthodox, the more easily taken into camp by the ruling elite. They did not appoint Zimmermann because they felt any necessity of liberalizing the government by bringing in a "man of the people," as the Americans imagined, but because they knew he was more amenable to the looming decision for full use of the U-boat than his predecessor, von Jagow, who was an insider by birth but, like Bernstorff, a believer in the necessity of a compromise peace. In America, Zimmermann's replacement of von Jagow was taken to be a softening of policy; actually it was the reverse, a logical sequel to a more momentous shift in command that had taken place two months earlier.

On August 29, 1916, the day after Rumania joined the ring of Germany's enemies, the two grand dragons of the Eastern Front, General von Hindenburg and General Ludendorff, had been elevated to the command of the General Staff. Hindenburg, the seventy-year-old hero of Tannenberg, became nominal chief, with Ludendorff, brains of the combination, as his quartermaster-general and in reality the active commander. In effect this was dictatorship; theirs was now the final word, although their ascendancy was not then as apparent in the daily shifts and balances of events as it is now through the telescope of hindsight. Chronically through 1916 they grappled with the civil government; the generals grimly fixed on fighting through to a victory that would fulfill the Pan-German dreams of expansion and annexation, the civilians convinced that to save even the *status quo ante* Germany must make peace soon. But after August 29 the civil government was losing. Kaiser Wilhelm still presided hollowly at General Headquarters, consulted but ignored, a mere mirror of a king. The Ministers of State still functioned; parliamentary opposition in fact increased; Chancellor Bethmann-Hollweg was still in authority. But the generals' prestige made them irreplaceable, and they knew it. Though the Kaiser longed to be rid of the "ugly mug of the top sergeant" as he called Ludendorff, he did not dare to do without him. By a threat of resignation the generals could prevail.

Zimmermann chose the generals. But he did not make his choice until he knew they were ready to force the issue. In March 1916 the war party's demand for ruthless use of the U-boat had been defeated, whereupon fork-bearded old Grand Admiral Tirpitz had resigned in despair. A lull had followed because the new grand admiral wished to wait until he had enough submarines on hand to give assurance of success. By fall he was ready. Again the fateful issue whether to risk American belligerency by releasing the U-boat or try for peace while there was still a chance of it came to a head. The military were prepared to take the risk; the Chancellor was not. Until now Zimmermann had supported the Chancellor because, as he told a secret session of the Reichstag early in the year, "Our situation is such that we cannot afford to have America as an enemy." In his conscience he knew this was still true, but in his heart he yearned to stand with the heroes of Blood and Iron. Moreover, like everyone else, he now believed that the Chancellor was on his way out and he did not propose to sink with Bethmann.

Bethmann was not the type of might-makes-right Prussian his most famous utterance has left him reputed to be. When he called Belgium's neutrality "a scrap of paper" he was not so much cynically affirming the worthlessness of treaties as expressing his despair that England would really go to war on this issue. No one had wanted a war, certainly not a two-front one, less than the tall, melancholy Chancellor who once, when the world was still at peace, had reminded Gerard of Abraham Lincoln. The resemblance was not very deep. True, Bethmann was tall and stooped and had sad eyes, like Lincoln, but in mind and spirit he was more like the premier of a later war, Neville Chamberlain. Well-meaning and serious but not forceful, inclined to trim when convictions were at stake, Bethmann, it was said, if he sat down across a treaty table with the English, would be lucky if he came away with Berlin.

For two years Bethmann had been holding out against unrestricted use of the U-boat, insisting that it would "inevitably cause America to join our enemies," pointing out that this would give the Allies enormous financial aid and lift in morale, plus use of all the German tonnage interned in American ports, and would influence other neutrals as well. The battle for the U-boat became a battle for Bethmann's head. The military party knew well enough, had known since 1915, that Germany could not win the war on land; therefore the only chance for victory lay in Germany's last weapon, the U-boat. But to be effective it must be used without restrictions, to the limit of its sinister capacity. Then, while the land war was kept going to drain the Allie's strength, the U-boat would finish them off by strangulation under the sea.

Pressure became intense. At an all-day conference Bethmann was described smoking one cigarette after another at a rate of five or six dozen a day. His hair had become white; his face was pale and lined; he looked to one observer "the personification of despair."

Everyone on the Right—military, Pan-Germans, conservatives—wanted Bethmann's removal. One thing saved him: no one could think of anybody who could take his place, and the Kaiser clung to him for fear that if he let go he might have to take back the suave and artful Prince von Bülow, who had so dreadfully wounded his feelings long ago. Meanwhile Bethmann clung to office, hoping that events would decide for him, in obedience to Bismarck's advice: "We can only wait until we hear the footsteps of God in history and then leap forward and try to catch on to His coat-tails."

Implacable Ludendorff, determined to free the U-boat one way or another, could not wait for God, but he could shift the weight in the civil government toward his side. If he could not get rid of Bethmann yet, he could at least get rid of one other opponent of the U-boat, Foreign Minister von Jagow. Hardly a formidable target, von Jagow was a puny rodent of a man whose Charlie Chaplin mustache and un-Teutonic look of an anxious rabbit caused him to be regarded by everybody, including himself, as inadequate for his post. But he had been listening to Bernstorff, who, from America, was furnishing the strongest arguments against use of the U-boat and pleading for time to allow Wilson, if he was re-elected, to get peace terms from the Allies. The military, still resolved to risk everything on victory by U-boat, wanted to hear no more of Wilson. Von Jagow, the voice of Bernstorff, must go. The Under-Secretary, that able, honest, industrious, excellent fellow Zimmermann must take his place. Bethmann, seeking always to maintain equilibrium and avoid a fracas, was prepared for the sacrifice, believing Zimmermann would work better with Ludendorff. "With Zimmermann," sadly wrote von Jagow after the war, "the fantical U-boat warriors thought they had a free hand. He was in his heart always pro-U-boat; that is, he always swam with the stream and with those who shouted the loudest. On that account he was considered 'strong.' "

In addition to his other virtues, Zimmermann was supposed to know all about America. Nearly twenty years before, he had returned from a consular post in China via San Francisco and New York, and ever since, as the result of his intimate knowledge of the American character gained while crossing the continent by train, he had fancied himself an expert on American affairs. Left by von Jagow to conduct the public affairs of the Foreign Office, he had carried on the personal contacts with Colonel House and Ambassador Gerard and had kept in close touch with Papen and Boy-Ed. He had also been receiving direct reports (bypassing Bernstorff) from the Consul-General in New York, who ridiculed Bernstorff's belief in the sincerity of Wilson's peace efforts and insisted Wilson was concerned only with getting favorable terms for the Allies. The Consul continually fed Zimmermann bloated estimates of the supposed success of German propaganda and of the fear of revolt by German-Americans that would keep the United States government from risking war. This became Zimmermann's hobby.

"In case of trouble," he warned Gerard when an argument over American arms sales to the Allies became heated, "there are half a million trained Germans in America who will join the Irish and start a revolution." A humorist himself, the Ambassador thought Zimmermann was joking but, on discovering he was serious, made his famous retort, "In that case there are half a million lampposts to hang them on."

Gerald liked the usually amiable Under-Secretary, admired his two-quart capacity for Moselle at lunch—but, he wrote the President, Zimmermann's talk was "largely ridiculous." Nevertheless Zimmermann, with the United States Census of 1910 on his desk showing a German-born population of 1,337,000 and an estimated 10 million of German descent, comforted himself in the belief that this formidable enclave would deter America from doing anything foolish. In 1916 when the American Ambassador to Turkey, Henry Morgenthau, came home by way of Berlin, Zimmermann treated him to his favorite discourse about how the German-Americans would "rise" in case of war.

Until the spring of 1916 he had gone along with the prevailing Foreign Office view that releasing the U-boat would cause America to join the Allies and that Britain could not be beaten once America was in the war. Except for the fire-eating Consul in New York, everybody with any knowledge of the United States held this opinion. It was what von Stumm, chief of the Foreign Office's American department, said, what the foreign news analysis bureau said, and of course what Bernstorff kept repeating day and night. But gradually, after the irritation of the *Lusitania* and the *Sussex* disputes, Zimmermann began to lose temper with the United States, almost to look forward to the event of war. He resorted more frequently to the German officials' *imponieren* habit, as Gerard called it when they wanted to be most imposing, of sinking their voices two octaves and "glaring at one like an enraged bullfrog." "I think Zimmermann hollered at the Colonel," reported Gerard when Colonel House came on one of his missions to discuss a basis for peace negotiations. "He certainly tried to scare me."

During the *Sussex* affair in May, when Wilson stated flatly he would break relations unless Germany pledged not to renew attacks on merchant ships without warning, Zimmermann hollered again—off the record—to a German press conference, "Gentlemen, there is no use wasting words about Mr. Wilson's shamelessness and impudence, but we have torn the mask from his face." From then on he regarded Wilson as a hypocrite who "feels and thinks English" and veered to the war party's view that, in any event, America was not a military power worth reckoning with. Now he listened with more sympathy to the pleas of the Navy, chained to its kennel in raging futility. Now he found more persuasive the Army's argument that America could neither train nor transport enough troops in time to affect the outcome and that before they could arrive in Europe in any number the U-boat, if let loose, would have beaten the British into surrender.

Listening to the drumbeat of military expediency, Zimmermann fell in step. Bethmann and von Jagow were still opposed; the Kaiser, bored by Bethmann but a little afraid of his generals, hesitated. Repeatedly the issue was thrashed out at high-level conferences. Admirals unrolled charts and graphs proving how many tons the U-boats could sink in a given time until they should have the British, as one of them put it, "gasping in the reeds like a fish." The struggle raged. In the Reichstag the Liberals and Social Democrats shouted, "The people don't want submarine warfare but *bread* and PEACE!" They exchanged pessimisms in the lobbies and told one another that another winter campaign was out of the question; peace had to come in the fall. But no one paid any attention to parliament or the people because, no matter how hungry they were, they remained obedient. "Here in Germany," said a deputy, "we don't have revolutions till things have got so bad that the revolution can be announced on official placards posted up on all street corners by the police."

By November the U-boats were being held back by barely a fingernail. Under the pounding of the military, the opposition had little grip left. Zimmermann had already gone over. On November 12, ten days before his elevation to von Jagow's place, he sent that telegram to Eckhardt in Mexico, hinting at an alliance in exchange for U-boat bases. Indeed it may have been some promises of his about a deal with Mexico and Japan that would keep America out of Europe altogether which brought about his promotion. On November 22 his appointment as Foreign Minister was announced.

Innocent of the real meaning behind the appointment, Americans greeted the new Foreign Secretary with a warmth born of a pathetic eagerness to find a friend in Germany. "Our Friend Zimmermann" was the title of a glowing appreciation in the New York *Evening Post*. "Liberalization of Germany!" proclaimed the *Literary Digest*. "One of the most auspicious omens for the future of German-American relations that have occurred since the outbreak of war," the *Post* added.

"All Americans like him," said the author of the

article, and in fact this was hardly an exaggeration. "I have had a conference with Zimmermann and he was exceedingly cordial and delightful," wrote Colonel House to the President early in 1915. "I have always liked him and I am glad we have resumed our friendly relations." Publicly he referred to him as "one of the biggest men in the Empire." Ambassador Gerard had been equally well disposed. "I get on very well with Zimmermann," he said and later spoke of him as "a fine type of man . . . my warm personal friend, just and friendly toward America, one of the ablest men in Germany today."

American journalists specializing in Germany rushed into print with rave notices. They contrasted Zimmermann's amiability with what they called the cold, haughty, Junker reserve of von Jagow (in reality no more than a disinclination to deal with people, born of a sense of inferiority that led him to leave personal diplomacy to his more extrovert Under-Secretary). They described Zimmermann as "frank, direct and jovial," as "having the best grip on world affairs of any man in the Foreign Office," as extremely popular with press, public, and parliament, as "reminding one strongly of a practical American politician," as "alert, keen, lucid and widely informed," as the first German to have adopted the American habit of talking freely to journalists, as one who met visitors rising with a smile of welcome, who was pleasant, helpful, and hearty, who understood American temperament and who never barked the Prussian official's favorite word, *ausgeschlossen*—"quite out of the question." They all made much of his bourgeois background, they found encouragement in the fact of his consular career which must have accustomed him to deal with businessmen, they said he was "believed" to belong to the liberal group advocating the democratizing of the German government, and they were curiously comforted by the legend of his being "essentially a man of the people."

They might have known, but not one said so, that it takes just such a man to become the most dangerously intoxicated by the fumes of grandeur he inhales upon entering the portals of royalty. Zimmermann traveling back and forth to Pless, doors bowed open for him by heel-clicking officers, Zimmermann amid the helmets and the Highnesses, Zimmermann having interviews with the All-Highest and conferences with Ludendorff, was not the man to champion a policy falling in any degree short of the extreme of military patriotism.

Having committed himself to the U-boat, he realized he must quickly prepare for the American belligerency that would follow. Now that the moment was in sight and his, on the civilian side, the responsibility, he no longer counted on anything so frivolous as a German-American revolt. He saw a brighter vision, conceived a greater coup, no less than a Mexican and Japanese alliance combined. For two years the polished Hintze, intimate of admirals and kings, had tried and failed to bring in the Japanese. He, Zimmermann, the outsider, would do it. He would be the first to bring Germany new allies. For years the bitterest criticism of the Junkers who staffed the foreign service had been their failure to win friends for Germany and their success in managing to lose those she had. The possibilities of triumph that Zimmermann foresaw excited him. He interpreted certain remarks of the Japanese Ambassador in Stockholm as indicating "the possibility of our coming to an understanding." He received assurances from Eckhardt of the close connections existing between Mexico and Japan. Further prompting evoked a flowery letter from President Carranza avowing his pro-German sympathies and his desire to seek closer economic and political ties with Germany, to strengthen his Navy with German help, and to acquire more arms. A supporting message from Eckhardt said that in spite of the British threat of reprisals, Carranza would nevertheless "help our submarines and eventually provide them with a permanent base on the Mexican coast."

Encouraged, Zimmermann began to plan for a military alliance that would carry Mexico's pledge to attack the United States in case of war between the United States and Germany. Casting about for the right inducement, he too remembered the Alamo; he would tempt Mexico with her own lost territory. He did not for a moment believe Mexico could win back Texas and the other states, but he did believe that Carranza would find the lure irresistible. He thought that Mexico, given the prospect of recovering her former frontiers, would do everything possible to gain Japan's assistance, and he was sure that once Mexico was bagged as an invasion base Japan would jump to the opportunity offered her.

One small but potentially serious difficulty bothered him. How to negotiate a project of such delicacy in the necessary secrecy? Most unfortunately the Mexican Ambassador to Berlin was absent in Switzerland, so negotiations had to be carried on through Eckhardt across the Atlantic. To assure extra secrecy of communications Zimmermann decided to make use of a certain channel made available to Berstorff for the express purpose of furthering his transmission of Wilson's peace proposals. Using this channel, to be sure, entailed the regrettable necessity of violating a pledged word, but this was no time for scruples. "Neither duplicity nor secrecy is in Secretary Zimmermann's lexicon of diplomacy," had gushed an American commentator, and the same verdict may be found in Prince von Bülow's opinion that Zimmermann "knew nothing of the art of diplomacy," meaning, one may infer, that he was too clumsily honest to deceive. That underestimated Zimmermann. He could practice deceit as well as Bülow himself, but in this case he would have been happier and history different had he not tried.

8

The Trap

     "The situation is developing very fast," wrote Wilson to Colonel House at the beginning of November. Unless he could bring about peace soon, he feared, "we must inevitably drift into war with Germany on the submarine issue."

Ambassador Bernstorff too could hear the hurrying of time's chariot at his country's back. From America he could see more clearly what would be the consequences of unleashing the submarine than could his superiors who were making the decision in Berlin. Temperament helped him. Having escaped, through birth and education abroad, the usual Prussian affliction of arrogance and delusions of grandeur, he did not believe Germany could crush the Allies by draconian use of the U-boat. The man who after the war devoted all his zeal to the League of Nations, who upon the advent of Hitler left Germany never to return, was wrestling now with his government for the fate of Germany. A year before, in the crisis over the sinking of the *Arabic,* he had, by exceeding his instructions and earning a reprimand, soothed America away from severing relations. Now that a new fleet of U-boats was ready and the U-boat warriors in Berlin drumming for action, Bernstorff was again straining to swerve Germany from the path he believed certain to lead to defeat. He had become convinced that the only way to stop the militarists was to stop the war itself first.

That was exactly the ambition of President Wilson, who had as great a reason for urgency as Bernstorff. War stifles reform and, if the United States was sucked in, all plans for the New Freedom would be thwarted. He was lured, too, by a vision of the New World, through himself, bringing to the Old the gift of peace and a league of nations to enforce peace, an old idea newly in vogue, which Wilson now embraced as his own. If he could stop the war he could save his own program and save Europe from itself. Ever since the war began he had been trying by exhortation and hints of pressure to persuade the belligerents to declare their peace terms, without a sign of success. At the end of 1916 two undertows sucking America toward war—economic involvement with the Allies and the submarine controversy with the Germans—were exerting such pull as to be almost impossible to resist. Wilson was bent on resisting; no man ever lived who was less willing to be the victim of events. He had made up his mind that if the November election confirmed him in office he would focus all his influence upon one last effort to substitute settlement for slaughter. He sensed, as Bernstorff knew, that little time, little room to maneuver was left.

Bernstorff pleaded with his government to postpone the decision of the U-boats until after the election and allow Wilson a chance to make his peace appeal. Germany's rulers were at this moment willing to allow Wilson to call off the war for them. They had known for some time that they could not win a decision on land and were ready to call quits if they could quit in possession of the spoils. They now bestrode Europe from the English Channel to the frontiers of Russia and from the Baltic Sea to the Black Sea. They occupied Poland, Rumania, Belgium, Alsace-Lorraine, and industrial France as far as Reims. Their allied empires were still intact. Austria-Hungary held the Balkans from Italy to Greece; Turkey was still sovereign from Baghdad to Jerusalem. Germany's idea of peace, according to a draft treaty circulating in the Reichstag at this time, was one that would partition Russia, annex three-quarters of Belgium, and "incorporate into Germany the French Coast from Dunkirk to Boulogne." And this modest document was drawn up by the Progressive People's Party! What the Germans wanted Wilson to do was not to make peace as he understood it, but to make the Allies stop fighting and seal the status quo plus a little

THE FATEFUL MESSAGE

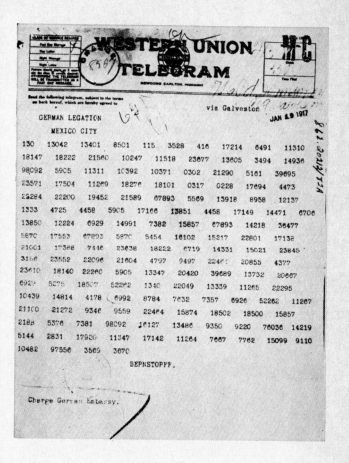

The telegram: the Western Union copy forwarded by
Bernstorff to Eckhardt.—*The National Archives*

Arthur Zimmerman.—*from Herbert Bayard Swope's*
"Inside the German Empire"

Rear-Admiral Sir William Reginald Hall.—*Russell,*
London

130	=	No. of Tel. No. 3
13042	=	No. of ciphers
13401	=	auswärtiges amt
8501	=	telegraphiert
115	=	Jan 16.
3528	-	Colm (?)
416	-	No: 1
17214	-	ganz geheim
6491	-	selbst
11310	-	zu
18147	-	entziffern
18222	-	Stop

F.W. 862.202 12/18½

The following pages reproduce the decode of the telegram in the copy made by Edward Bell of the American Embassy and forwarded to the State Department by Ambassador Page on March 2.—*from The National Archives*

21560	-	wir
10247	-	be absichtigen
11518		am
23677		ersten
18605		Februar
3494		un .
14913		eingeschränkt
98092		U boot .
5905		Krieg
11311		zu
10392		beginnen
10371		⊙
0302		es ~~(wünden)~~ wird
21290		versuchen
5161		werden
39695		V ereinigten Staaten v. Amerika
23571		trotz dem
1750.4		neutral

11269	= 3k
18276	erhalten
18101	⊙
0317	Für den Fall
0228	daß dies
17694	nicht
4473	gelingen
22284	sollte
22200	⊙
19452	Schlag – en
21589	wir
67893	Mexico.
5569	auf
13918	folgend
8958	grundlage
12137	Bündnis
1333	vor
4725	⊙
4458	gemeinsam
5905	Krieg
17166	führen
18551	⊙

4458	gemeinsam
17149.	Friedenschluß .
14471	⊙
6706	reichlich
13850	finanziell
12224	unterstützung
6929	und
14991	einverständnis
7382	unsererseits .
158'5)7	daß
67893	Mexico .
14218	in
36477	Texas
5670	⊙
17553	neu
67893	Mexico .
5870	⊙
5454	AR
16102	IZ
15217	ON
22801	A

The purloined snapshot: Count von Bernstorff on vacation. —*from "The Sketch," October 25, 1916*

extra. Unless Mr. Wilson could perform this service for them, the military were set to throw everything into a smashing decisive assault upon victory by U-boat.

But Germany was not united. Bethmann-Hollweg, Jagow, and others in the civil government desperately wished Wilson to stop the war before the military took to the U-boats. They believed Germany could never get a better peace than at this moment. They saw America looming on the brink. They saw the U-boat as a weapon of suicide. Yet the clamor for it was rising as from a lynch mob assembled beneath the Chancellor's window. In the mob were the military leaders, the court, the Junkers, the Right-wing parties, and a majority of the public, which had been carefully educated to pin its faith on the submarine as the one weapon to break the food blockade and vanquish England. The Chancellor trembled as he listened to their clamor. The issue was being fought out daily in secret sessions of the Reichstag. The Admiralty was preparing in feverish haste. All summer Bernstorff had been exhorting the Chancellor to stand fast until after the American election. Beleaguered Bethmann feared he could not wait that long. Unless Wilson acted quickly, he cried out to Bernstorff in September, the military would begin the U-boat war in "dead earnest." A week later Jagow asked Ambassador Gerard to go home and personally urge Wilson to hurry.

Gerard reached America on October 10 and was followed by a blustering memorandum, said to have been written by the Kaiser himself, which in effect told Wilson to make peace or else.

With his curious distaste for hearing first-hand reports, Wilson refused even to see Gerard for ten days. When he did, under Lansing's urging, he made no mention of the peace proposal but merely instructed his ambassador to be friendly and "jolly the Germans" and convince them of the wrongfulness of firing on armed merchant ships without warning. When Gerard said he would try, the President banged his fist on the desk and said, "I don't want you merely to support my view; I want you to *agree* with it."

The fact was that he did not think highly of Gerard and habitually treated his ambassadors as if they were office boys who were asked merely to transmit his views without being informed of the policies behind them. And he did not wish to be hurried on the peace proposal; he felt he could not make a move of such importance in the midst of a political campaign and, if he won, could speak with more effect after the election.

The initiative almost passed from him when for two days the election teetered upon the returns from California, then fell at last in Wilson's lap. Even then he hesitated. He did not know how near Bethmann's hourglass was to running out. On November 7 Joseph C. Grew, left in charge of the Berlin embassy, wired that an unknown number of submarines had suddenly left Kiel with fuel and stores sufficient for three months at sea. It was a portent, but still Wilson hesitated. On November 22, Grew was summoned to see the Chancellor, who seemed to him to be trying to ask America to act. Bethmann gave an impression of great weariness and discouragement. "He seemed like a man broken in spirit, his face deeply furrowed, his manner sad beyond words." He had cause, for November 22 was the day of Jagow's dismissal and replacement by Zimmermann, a further portent of danger to America, if anyone had had the wit to read it. Instead it was interpreted as "liberalization," and Wilson allowed himself more time. Bernstorff tried to press for action. Wilson sent him a message saying he intended to move for peace "at the first opportunity." Peace, replied the German Ambassador, was "on the floor waiting to be picked up." That was wishful thinking and had as little effect on Wilson as any other form of persuasion.

The truth was that Wilson was afraid to make the test. Anxious not to fail, he was waiting for some sign of encouragement from the Allies. None was forthcoming. On the contrary only signs of hardening intransigence. Lloyd George had already told the world in September that Britain would not "tolerate" intervention by neutrals but would fight till she could deliver the "knockout blow" that would break Prussian military despotism beyond repair. Briand had denounced the very idea of a negotiated peace as an "outrage" upon the memory of the fallen heroes of France. That was before the election. Now, from his pontificate on Fleet Street, Lord Northcliffe issued a bull proclaiming that "the suggestion that Great Britain should consider peace can only be regarded as hostile. . . . There will be no peace discussion while Germany occupies any portion of Allied territory."

In fact the Allies' position was too poor to negotiate. Their Western Front strategy was bankrupt. Into the Moloch of the Somme they had poured thousands upon thousands of lives while for three months under the autumn rains, forgotten in the planning, General Haig shouted, "Attack!" to men mired in the mud and shattered by exploding shells. By the end of November the offensive was over, for a total gain in depth of seven miles and a total casualty list, on both sides, of one million. In January, 1916, final failure of the Dardanelles expedition had been sealed; in December the Allies' new recruit, Rumania, had surrendered; the Czarist regime was beginning to split at the seams and whispers of Russian readiness for a separate peace to seep through. On December 5 the dispirited Asquith government gave way to one headed by the militant Lloyd George, who would as soon negotiate as capitulate.

The facts would have forced themselves upon anyone but Wilson, but the armor of fixed purpose he wore was impenetrable. He chose two main principles—neutrality for America, negotiated peace for Europe—as the fixed points of his policy and would allow no realities to interfere with them. He no longer read the long, informative letters which Ambassador Page wrote him week after week from London, the nerve center of the war, because he considered Page hopelessly pro-Ally. Although no two men in any one period of history were more unlike, Wilson shared one characteristic with the Kaiser—he would not listen to opinions he did not welcome. Wilhelm was afraid of them, but Wilson considered opinions which opposed his as simply a waste of time. Intent upon saving Europe, he ignored the mood of the Europeans. Just as he was determined to confer democracy upon Mexicans, ready or not, he was determined to confer peace upon Europeans, willing or not. He had no idea how like condescension his attitude appeared to them. He listened to himself rather than to them. He seemed unaware that two and a half years of fighting a war that was taking the best lives of nations had welded the combatants into a frame of mind in which compromise was impossible. He refused to recognize that each side by now wanted tangible gains to show that the pain and cost had been worth while, and each had aims—Alsace-Lorraine was only one, but it would have been enough—that were permanently irreconcilable.

Wilson could see only expanding violence. Turks were killing Armenians with a savagery that, if the facts were told, reported the American Ambassador, "would make men and women weep." Poland, trampled beneath the tremendous clash of armies, was a wasteland of wandering skeletons with snow falling and not a head of livestock or a stick of firewood left. Belgians were being shipped like cattle into Germany for slave labor. The belligerents after the Battle of the Somme were as helpless in the war's vortex as ever and as powerless to find a way out. Wilson saw the world caught in a berserk carnage endlessly continuing unless stopped by a disinterested outsider—himself. The question of rights and wrongs he would not look at or professed, at this time, not to see. He recognized that a triumph of German militarism "would change the course of civilization and make the United States a military nation," but he believed that the way to prevent this disaster was not to join the Allies but to stop the war. He felt obliged to be, or at least to act, impartial if he was to have any chance of getting both sides to listen to him. He was convinced that only a negotiated peace could endure, that a dictated peace forced upon the loser "would be accepted in humiliation, under duress, at an intolerable sacrifice, and would leave a sting, a resentment, a bitter memory upon which the terms of peace would rest, not permanently, but only as upon quicksand."

"Only a peace between equals can last," a "peace without victory"—this was the wisdom that made him great, but it was a long-distance wisdom that ignored realities underfoot. The combatants were in no mood for it. Shivering in trenches in blood and mud and stench, they resented advice from a man in a far-off white mansion who said he was "too proud to fight." Wilson thought he saw the better path, but Europe would not take it. Had all the world been a school and Wilson its principal, he would have been the greatest statesman in history. But the world's governments and peoples were not children obliged to obey him. The world was a little group of willful men who would not and could not be made to behave as Wilson told them they ought to. He was a seer whose achievements never equaled his aims. In the few years left to him he was to become the symbol of the world's hope and of its failure. He was one of those few who formulate the goals for mankind, but he was in the impossible position of trying to function as seer and executive at the same time. He held political office and would not acknowledge that politics is the art of the possible. He obeyed the injunction that a man's reach should exceed his grasp; it was his tragedy that he reached too high.

On December 9, a month after the election, while Wilson was still hesitating, Bernstorff received a warning from the Foreign Office: "We cannot wait any longer." He tried to convey the urgency but was handicapped because the President trusted "neither his accuracy nor his sincerity" and considered him an "astute and unscrupulous man." House, on the other hand, admired Bernstorff as the only envoy in Washington with a sense of proportion. Lansing detested him. He suspected Bernstorff of planting rumors against him in the newspapers in an effort to have him supplanted. Washington diplomatic circles, on the whole, were not characterized by mutual high regard. Jusserand, the polished and scholarly French Ambassador, was eyed warily because he had been an intimate member of Theodore Roosevelt's tennis cabinet. Bakmetieff, the Russian Ambassador, was regarded as "a reactionary of the worst type and a little less than mad," while Spring-Rice of Britain was considered a super-sensitive individual too emotional for his job who would be much better off recalled. Wilson paid no attention to any of them, any more than he did to his own ambassadors. He preferred to rely for his information upon Colonel House, and that individual was not always as well-informed as he thought he was.

Bernstorff could not get Wilson to hurry and he could not get his own government to wait. With Jagow gone and Bethmann weakening fast, his influence at home had waned. And just at this moment the celebrated Bathing Beauty episode depleted it further.

During a weekend in the Adirondacks at the home of a lady who often entertained him, Bernstorff had been photographed in a bathing suit with his arms intimately encircling two ladies similarly outfitted. One of his fellow guests obtained a copy of the snapshot and showed it at a subsequent weekend party on Long Island where a member of the group was a British agent. After dinner the agent felt the picture being slipped surreptitiously into his hand. Taking the hint, he sent it off by chauffeur to New York, where it was copied, and the original was returned before daybreak. Shortly afterward an enlarged copy was delivered to the Russian Ambassador, Count Bakmetieff, who "seemed very happy about it." He displayed it, elegantly framed, upon his mantelpiece where all the diplomatic corps of Washington could see it and whence it soon made its way into the newspapers.

The effect was to undermine Bernstorff's influence in Germany at a crucial time. The Kaiser, who was only amused when his Chief of Military Cabinet, General Count von Hülsen-Haeseler, dressed as a ballerina in short tulle skirt and rose wreath, danced for his entertainment,* was deeply offended in his delicate sense of decorum by Bernstorff's peccadillo. The U-boat warriors, who hated Bernstorff because of his efforts to prevent the use of their

---

*The incident took place in 1909. "Everybody found it most entertaining, for the Count danced beautifully," reported the Court Chamberlain. Upon retiring, the Count fell down dead of exhaustion.

cherished weapon, seized upon it to show that his gallantries somehow proved the unreliability of his political judgments.

Even though they had succeeded, to their own satisfaction, in discounting Bernstorff's advice, Germany's rulers were not yet ready to risk the submarine without a demonstration to the German public and the world at large that they had no other recourse. They wanted to hear no more of that long-awaited peace offer from Mr. Wilson, who, they were now convinced, was deliberately procrastinating in the interests of the Allies. By now it was clear enough to them that no peace he could arrange would be acceptable to them. The only peace that the Allies would accept —a peace of renunciation and indemnity by the Germans —would mean the end of the Hohenzollerns and the governing class. Conquest was necessary to them—they had to make someone else pay for the war, or go bankrupt. A compromise peace bringing no aggrandizement to Germany would require enormous taxes after the war to pay for years of fighting that had proven profitless. It would mean revolution. "The German people wish no peace of renunciation," stormed Ludendorff when the faltering Austrians were urging peace, "and I do not intend to end being pelted by stones. The dynasty would never survive such a peace." The longer the war lasted, the clearer it became to the court and its cohorts, the land-owing Junkers, the industrialists, and the military, that only a war ending in gains offered any hope of their survival in power. This might have been clear to Wilson had he been a little less concerned with his own motives and a little more concerned with the nature of the regime he was dealing with. Zimmermann had once stated the case quite frankly to Colonel House when he said that if peace parleys were begun "on any terms that had a chance of acceptance," it would mean the overthrow of the government and the Kaiser. In such a peace, an "American" peace, the German rulers had no interest. All they had wanted of Mr. Wilson was for him to make the Allies stop fighting, not to arbitrate issues. For the sake of world opinion, as well as to eliminate Mr. Wilson as mediator, they now determined upon a dramatic gesture of their own.

The Reichstag was suddenly convened for December 12, no one knew why. Berlin buzzed with speculation. On the twelfth, all the neutral diplomats were summoned to the Chancellor's office, to which they were admitted one by one. As Grew, still American chargé d'affaires in Gerard's absence, waited in the anteroom, the Swiss Minister on his way out whispered, *"Friedens Antrag"*—"Peace offer"—and the Danish Minister, following after, muttered, "If it fails, look out for our ships."

At the same hour Secretary Zimmermann was holding an off-the-record press conference in which he remarked jovially that, as Germany was "threatened by a peace move by Mr. Wilson, we would fix it so this person would not have his finger in the pie."

The startling news that the Central Powers were proposing peace was somewhat dampened by their carelessness in omitting to mention terms. The offer was, of course, designed to fail, as its phraseology made certain. It opened with a harangue upon Germany's "invincible power" and closed with the threat that if it was rejected Germany would carry on the war to a victorious conclusion but would "solemnly decline all responsibility therefor before Humanity and History." Explaining the offer to his troops, the Kaiser tactfully added that he was proposing to negotiate with the enemy "in the conviction that we are the absolute conquerors." He couldn't help the German swagger from showing through the dove's clothing.

As expected, Allied scorn poured down. Wilson, robbed of his thunder, did not know whether to be more annoyed or encouraged by the German move, but one thing was certain: there was no use waiting any longer for the psychologically right moment to make his own peace proposal; it was now or not at all.

On December 18, a week before Christmas, announcing himself "the friend of all nations engaged in the present struggle," he asked them for a declaration of their war aims from which a settlement of issues could proceed and, ultimately, peace be guaranteed through "the intelligent organization of the common interest of mankind." The document was Wilson at his best, eloquent in sincerity, incontrovertible in logic, and welcomed by none to whom it was addressed. One phrase, equating the objectives of both sides as "virtually the same," caused King George to weep and Clemenceau to remark that the war aim of France was victory.

Nevertheless it was out at last. The German reply arrived first and proved to be a rebuff. Still Wilson refused to give up until the Allies' answer too should come through. They might slam the door shut or they might offer a toehold for negotiation, but until they replied he felt bound to keep the opportunity for parley open. No one else in any of the governments retained a shred of hope in the possibility of bringing the belligerents together on any terms. Only Bernstorff was still trying. He had abandoned the luxury of hope but not the eleventh-hour fight to keep his country from the suicide's plunge. To him as to Wilson the vital thing was to keep the talk going with Berlin, in the belief that as long as some groping toward peace was in progress Germany would not release the submarine. Pressing ahead in that effort, the President and the Ambassador used a channel that was to prove a trap for war. Its architect was Colonel House.

On the morning of December 27, 1916, Bernstorff visited House to discuss a new offer from the President: if Germany would submit her basic terms to him confidentially, he would limit himself to bringing the enemies together around a peace table and would not insist on taking part himself except for final shaping of a league of nations. House had talked over the idea with Wilson on the telephone that morning. When Bernstorff came in he was anxious to carry it out but told House he did not think his government would be willing to submit confidential terms through the State Department "because there were so many leaks there." This was Bernstorff's way of saying that he did not want to go through Lansing, who, he knew, had no sympathy with the President's peace scheme. If some means could be arranged, he said, of permitting his government to communicate directly with Wilson through

House, there would be greater opportunity for a full and frank discussion. House agreed. Privately he had no faith in the peace plan, which, like Lansing, he regarded as a disservice to the Allies, but he reasoned, as he told the President, that "the more we talk with Germany just now the less danger there will be of a break because of submarine activity."

The method House had in mind for helping Bernstorff had already been in use before with the President's consent. Depending on the President's answer, House told the Ambassador, he would let him know whether or not to go ahead. The next day, December 28, the President's sixtieth birthday, on receiving a code message from Wilson, House informed Bernstorff that the answer was yes.

What he had arranged and what the President authorized was permission for the German government to send messages in its own cipher between Bernstorff and Berlin, in both directions, over the State Department cable. It was an American version of the Swedish Roundabout, but quicker, for the Swedish route took a week for message and reply. Accepted neutral practice would have required a belligerent's messages to be submitted in clear for transmission in American code. In fact House, with the President's consent, committed the American government to the irregular, not to say simple-minded arrangement of transmitting a belligerent's message in a code not known to itself.

Secretary Lansing, who had to be informed because his department would be required to play the role of post office, was shocked to the cell of his legal soul, even to rebellion, and each time the method was used he had to be personally ordered by the President, who was conscious only of the rectitude of his goal and careless of his methods, to comply. Wilson was perhaps less sensitive to a neutral's duties than to a neutral's rights. He considered himself justified in ignoring the obligations of neutrality because his mind was fixed on stopping the war. Aware that this object was noble, he did not imagine that anyone in Germany might make ignoble use of the channel he had opened up for them. Lansing's objections to the procedure as unneutral he brushed aside as petty and legalistic. Besides, he had exacted Bernstorff's promise to confine the messages strictly to the issue of peace terms. Sharing the general impression of Bernstorff's new chief, Zimmermann, as a great liberal, honest broker, and friend of America, he apparently assumed that Bernstorff's pledge would cover Zimmermann's replies. In this impression he was strengthened by Colonel House, who assured him that the German government was at this moment "completely in the hands of the liberals." To err may be human, but to be that deep in error was dangerous.

House had conceived the method as far back as September 1914. In an early effort toward negotiating a settlement, he had then proposed to invite the German and English Ambassadors, Bernstorff and Spring-Rice, to an intimate dinner meeting at his home and, on his own authority and according to his own diary, had promised Bernstorff, if anything came of the conversation, "permission from our government for him to use code messages direct to his government." Nothing did come of it because Spring-Rice refused to meet Bernstorff, but the offer was characteristic of the colonel's illusion that he could manipulate history by an exchange of personal civilities. He was an aficionado of backstairs diplomacy with front-office people. Twice before the war he had toured the European capitals to propose disarmament and promote a relaxing of tension among the powers. The centuries of rivalry, the plethora of issues, the ancient bitternesses intricately rooted in Balkan wars, Moroccan crises, Pan-Slavism, naval expansion, reinsurance treaties, balance of power, dual alliances, and triple ententes, in the Black Hand of Serbia and in the black-draped statues of Alsace and Lorraine on the Place de la Concorde—all this Colonel House proposed to oil away by intimate chats with statesmen in front of fireplaces. Though regarded as a shrewd man of the world, a complement of Wilson the idealist, he was, if anything, more unrealistic about Europe than the President. On July 3, 1914, a week *after* the assassination at Sarajevo, House, writing from Europe to Wilson of his encouraging talks with sovereigns and ministers, concluded, "So you see things are moving in the right direction as rapidly as we could hope."

Such misjudgments left him unembarrassed. He lived as in a moving picture of himself reflecting a trim, panama-hatted figure flitting suavely from smoke-filled room to White House sanctum, equally at home lunching with the Kaiser in what Gerard called "the ugliest room in Europe" or dining with King George or cosily closeted with Sir Edward Grey—and always, daily, in personal touch with the most important man in the world, whom he unfailingly addressed as "Dear Governor," an affectation designed to show his intimacy as one of the original Wilson-before-Baltimore men. He looked, acted, and fancied the role of gray eminence, indeed in character and performance fitted the role so neatly as to deserve to become its modern prototype. He mistook fraternization with rulers for influence upon them and quite overestimated the amount he exerted. He supposed because Sir Edward Grey gave up hours to chatting privily with him that he was carrying his point with England's Foreign Secretary and never understood that he was being stalled. Why the President listened to and depended upon this self-conceived, if naïve, Machiavelli for so long is an enigma. But the lonely eminence of power requires a confidant, and House played the role expertly, telling Wilson he would be able to do the "most important world's work within sight" because "God has given you the power to see things as they are," telling him that each speech would "live" as if his every utterance were a Gettysburg Address, purveying worldly advice and undertaking as confidential emissary all those unofficial contacts the President could not make and had no taste for.

Superficially it would seem that Wilson, who dealt in principles and disliked details, was perfectly seconded by such a man as House, who loved the minutiae of deals and personalities. But this was not so. If Wilson had too much contempt for men, House had too little respect for principles. He became so immersed in his wire-pulling, in playing one personality against another, in keeping everyone conciliated and all wheels turning that this became an end in itself. The goal of negotiation became lost in the procedure.*

House's maneuver of giving the Germans access to the State Department cable grew out of his penchant for personal diplomacy. During a mission to Europe in 1915, he had arranged to have reports in cipher from the embassies cabled directly to him, bypassing the State Department. The arrangement, begun on his own behalf, was merely extended, when the moment seemed to call for it, to Bernstorff. The privilege was first given to the German Ambassador in midsummer 1915, during the *Lusitania* crisis, when war was gaping between the United States and Germany. According to Bernstorff's version in his memoirs, "From that day forward, the American government agreed to allow me to send dispatches in cipher to my government in Berlin through the State Department and the American embassy," but this may be an overstatement of what was probably an intermittent arrangement.

The reverse process made equal use of American good offices; telegrams for Bernstorff were handed in by the German Foreign Office to the American embassy and forwarded by it, without knowledge of their contents, to the State Department, which in turn delivered them, however reluctantly, to Bernstorff. Grew, two months before the peace offer, mentions a long telegram in code sent by the Germans "through us." And Bethmann-Hollweg in postwar testimony confirmed that the American government "permitted us to make use of their embassy here for the purpose of correspondence in cipher." Zimmermann on the same occasion added that the privilege was used sparingly for fear of attracting British attention. That was a wasted precaution, for British attention, needless to say, once caught by the appearance of the German code on the American cable, was focused upon the exercise with fascinated interest. Although entitled to protest against a neutral's transmission of belligerent messages in code,

---

*Eventually this became evident to Wilson when, at Paris, he returned after an absence to find that House's skill at conciliation had conciliated away the main principles he had been sticking for. This was one cause of the final break between them.

the British forbore, preferring to eavesdrop upon the enemy rather than to stand upon their rights.

Before December 1916, Colonel House's diary is judiciously silent on the whole procedure. Each night, with a careful eye upon posterity, he dictated a diary of the day's doings to his secretary, corrected her copy, and returned it for retyping. Omission of the cable privilege given to the Germans could not have been accidental. But he did not reckon with another diarist who was giving posterity equally careful attention. Each day in Washington, Secretary Lansing was recording neat, almost hourly entries in his desk diary every time his door closed upon a visitor. Twice in 1916, once in January and once in May, appears the notation, "W.W.S. [initials of the code clerk] with cipher message for the German Ambassador," and on the second occasion he adds his private rebellion: "Directed him to refuse to deliver it." These entries are the evidence that defeated House's careful silence.

Pretending to disapprove, House once recorded a story going around Washington:

"Do you know the new spelling of Lansing?"

"No. What is it?"

"H-O-U-S-E."

Methodically recording the appearances of W.W.S., Secretary Lansing unconsciously had his revenge.

But at the time, House prevailed, for there was validity in the joke about the spelling of the Secretary of State's name. During those last days of the peace effort, while history's bloodiest year was dying out and no one knew what the new year or even the next morning would bring, House insisted that the Germans be allowed uncensored use of the American cable. Each time a message came through, Lansing balked, until the colonel became really quite exasperated. On December 30, Bernstorff reported to House that Lansing had refused to transmit his cipher message. Some days later Lansing refused again, provoking Bernstorff to lament that he was really at a loss to comply with the President's peace suggestions "if the State Department takes this attitude." Lansing, he complained, would never accept his messages routinely but only when each carried instructions from the President. Lansing had no way of knowing what might be the gist of all this German loquacity; he was simply objecting on principle and because he privately believed it was in America's interest to join the Allies in a war for democracy against autocracy rather than make a peace that would leave the German Empire unbeaten.

On January 12 the Allies' answer to Wilson's peace offer came through, rejecting firmly any possibility of compromising with the enemy. They stated their aims and reaffirmed their immovable purpose to accept nothing less, and to fight on until they won unconditional victory. There was not a line or a sentence that could possibly be construed as leaving a loophole for negotiation. Upon Wilson their refusal to allow him to intervene had no more effect than a human sigh might have upon Olympus. He simply ignored it. What process of thought he followed that allowed him to do so was his own secret. Perhaps he felt he had no alternative but to go on trying. He kept the Bernstorff talks going, but after this Lansing, on being presented with an unusually long message, refused once more, demanding to know whether there was now any reason for its going through. Assistant Secretary William Phillips, whose uncomfortable office it was to be go-between, telephoned House to ask what to do and was informed with some asperity that the German government was talking to the President "unofficially through me" with the President's approval. Certainly the message must go through, House said, and he might have added the Roman judge's words, "though the heavens fall," for they were about to.

Still for a few days more the President stubbornly and Bernstorff despairingly pursued the goal of a peace parley. The messages kept going and coming, Lansing kept balking, Phillips kept telephoning House. Addicted to his wire-pulling and to the sense of power it gave him, House was far more concerned with keeping open the private wire he had so cleverly strung than with achieving the object for which it was intended. Deep down he had little sympathy with Wilson's peace effort, yet, perhaps from a habit of telling the President what he wanted to hear, he went on saying that "if we can tie up Germany in a conference so that she cannot resume her unbridled submarine warfare it will be a great point gained." When he wrote this it was already too late, but House was happily ignorant of what was going on in Germany. He was too absorbed in the game of playing the Germans along to suspect that they might be playing him, too occupied in oiling the machinery to question whether the Germans' use of it might have some purpose other than peace.

It was not he but Lansing who at last succeeded in inserting some cautionary doubts in the President's mind. Annoyed by one more call from Phillips saying that Lansing had again refused to forward a long Bernstorff telegram, House suggested that Lansing see the President personally and get the matter settled once and for all. Lansing immediately went to the White House, and his deep distrust must have been persuasive, for the next day, January 24, Wilson warned House by letter that if the State Department continued to forward Bernstorff's messages, "we should know that he is working in this cause [peace] and should in each instance receive his official assurance that there is nothing in his dispatches which it would be unneutral for us to transmit."

By the time the President came to have these doubts they were focused on the wrong person. Neither he nor anyone else seems to have asked at any time for assurances that the incoming telegrams *to* Bernstorff should also be confined to the subject of peace. Wilson presupposed honest intentions on the part of the German Foreign Office. With the barometer needle quivering close to war, that was incautious. But Wilson was his own barometer. "There will be no war," he told House early in January. "This country does not intend to become involved in war. It would be a crime against civilization for us to go into it." No country would then be left, he meant, with enough influence to make peace.

The Telegram Is Sent

On January 9, 1917, at the castle of Pless on the edge of Poland, where Supreme Headquarters was maintained in three hundred rooms served by liveried footmen, a momentous meeting was called—not to reach a decision but to seal one already made. A month earlier the Supreme High Command had reached their own decision to use the U-boat even if it brought America in against them. They calculated on the U-boat's bringing victory within six months and on the impossibility of America's recruiting, organizing, training, and transporting an army within that time. Secretary of the Navy Admiral von Capelle had flatly stated their article of faith: "From the military point of view, the assistance which will result from the entrance of the United States into the war will amount to nothing." That the moral effect of America's entrance would encourage the Allies to hold out long enough to upset the German time table was a possibility which everyone was conscious of but no one mentioned.

Field Marshal von Hindenburg, despite a vague uneasiness stirring the heavy processes of his mind, had allowed himself to be persuaded by his demonic colleague, General Ludendorff. Together they persuaded the Kaiser, who, whatever his own doubts, had not the courage to appear less resolute than his commanders. All that remained was to bring round the Imperial Chancellor, who was at that moment on his way to Pless. Lugubriously the general, the field marshal, and Admiral von Holtzendorff, Chief of Naval General Staff, waited for him and discussed the prospects while a staff colonel sat recording in a corner.

Holtzendorff: The Chancellor arrives here tomorrow.

Hindenburg: What's troubling him now?

Holtzendorff: He wants to control the diplomatic presentation of the announcement in order to keep the United States out of it. . . . The Foreign Office is worried about what South America will do and our relations with them when the war is over.

Hindenburg: We must conquer first. . . .

Holtzendorff: Later today I will read my memorandum to His Majesty, who even this morning had no real understanding of the situation.

Hindenburg: That is true.

Holtzendorff: What shall we do if the Chancellor does not join us?

Hindenburg: That is just what is bothering me.

Holtzendorff: Then you must become Chancellor.

Hindenburg: No, no. I cannot do that. I won't do it. I cannot talk in the Reichstag. I refuse.

Ludendorff: I would not try to persuade the Field Marshal . . .

Hindenburg: Well, we shall hold together anyway. We have to. We are counting on the probability of war with the United States and we have made all preparations to meet it. Things cannot be worse than they are now. The war must be brought to an end by whatever means as soon as possible.

Holtzendorff: His Majesty doesn't understand the situation.

Ludendorff: Absolutely not.

Holtzendorff: People and Army are crying for the unrestricted U-boat war.

Ludendorff: Quite so.

Holtzendorff: Secretary of State Helfferich said to me, "Your plan will lead to ruin." I said to him, "You are letting us drift into ruin."

Hindenburg: That is true.

In this sparkling mood they reassembled next day in the presence of His Majesty, attended by the triumvirate known as the Hydra's Head—von Valentini, Baron von Lynckner, and Admiral von Müller, chiefs of civil, military, and naval cabinets respectively—whose duty was to keep the Supreme War Lord in good humor. On this day they had not been notably successful; His Majesty was pale, irritable, and excited. Admiral von Müller himself looked "melancholy as an owl"; Valentini, who was to be rapporteur, far from cheerful.

Driving up the long avenue between leafless trees to the white castle of Pless, Bethmann-Hollweg, huddled in his cloak, smoked cigarette after cigarette. The famous lawns, laid out to rival the best in England, were patched with snow; the sky was leaden. He entered the gigantic reception hall hung with boars' heads embedded in red damask, wearily climbed the marble staircase, and was shown into the conference room, formerly the state dining room, where once the Kaiser, unburdening his feelings to Princess Daisy, had wept into his cigar.

Admiral von Holtzendorff took the floor and proved beyond dispute that in unrestricted warfare, "in the course of which every enemy and neutral ship found in the war zone is to be sunk without warning," his U-boats could sink six hundred thousand tons a month and force England to capitulate before the next harvest. It was all there on the table before him in the massive two-hundred-page memorandum drawn up by the Admiralty, complete with charts of tonnage entering and clearing British ports; tables showing freight rates, cargo space, rationing systems; comparisons with last year's harvest; statistics on everything from the price of cheese and the calorie content of the British breakfast down to the yardage of imported wool in ladies' skirts. With mathematical precision the German Admiralty had worked out the month, almost the day, when England would be forced to give in. It had designated February 1 as the day when the U-boat war was to start.

"If we fail to make use of this opportunity, which, as far as can be foreseen, is our last," concluded the admiral, "I can see no way to end the war so as to guarantee our future as a world power. On its part I guarantee that the U-boat will lead to victory." He looked around him. "I shall need three weeks' notice," he said and sat down. February 1 was precisely three weeks off.

Bethmann pulled himself to his feet and spoke for an hour, the ghastly spectacle of a man knuckling under to ruin and knowing it. He repeated what he had been saying for the past year: that United States' entrance into the war would give Germany's enemies new and enormous moral support and unlimited financial resources, revive their confidence in victory, and strengthen their will to endure. He cited the opinions of all the German envoys who knew the United States at first hand—Bernstorff, Dr. Albert, Counselor Haniel, Major von Papen—who were unanimous and emphatic in declaring that American belligerency would be Germany's defeat and that none of the arguments used at home to minimize it were valid; the German-Americans would *not* rise, ships and troops *would* get across, a united country *would* back the war. He reiterated the conviction in which he now stood alone, that Mr. Wilson's offer to bring about a settlement was genuine and should be pursued to its last shred before making a choice that cut off all chance for peace and, if it failed to bring victory, would bring certain defeat.

He paused. He knew the choice had been made. The Kaiser, who hated to listen to anyone for more than ten minutes consecutively, was making grunts of impatience and grimaces of disapproval. The moment of Bethmann's Gethsemane was at hand. He could either bow to a course he believed fatally wrong or he could stand by his convictions and resign. Slowly and painfully he stumbled toward his choice. Yes, it was true the last harvest had been bad for the Allies. True, the increased number of U-boats now on hand offered a better chance of success than when he had opposed their use last summer. On the whole, perhaps, the prospects were favorable. Of course, it must be admitted that the prospects were not capable of proof. Certainly the situation was better than it was in September. . . . But we must be perfectly certain. . . . The U-boat was the "last card." . . . A very serious decision. "But if the military authorities consider the U-boat

war essential I am not in a position to contradict them."
On the other hand, America . . .

Admiral von Holtzendorff jumped up. "I guarantee on
my word as a naval officer that no American will set foot
on the Continent!" The Field Marshal rose too. "We can
take care of America," he said. "The opportunity for the
U-boat war will never be as favorable again." The three
commanders, the three secretaries, and the Kaiser looked
at the Chancellor. The Chancellor looked out the french
window to the frozen pond in the park below. In a familiar
nervous gesture he rubbed a hand over his clipped gray
hair and summoned his voice.

"Of course," he said, "if success beckons, we must
follow."

The meeting was over. The Kaiser affixed his signature
to the document already drawn up and ready: "I order
that unrestricted submarine warfare be launched with the
utmost vigor on the first of February. . . . Wilhelm I R."
Followed by the High Command, he marched out to lunch.
A moment later von Reischach, a court functionary who
had served the Kaiser's father and grandfather before
him, entered the room and found Bethmann slumped in a
gilt chair looking utterly broken. Shocked, he asked,
"What's the matter? Have we lost a battle?"

"No," answered Bethmann, "but *finis Germaniae.*
That's the decision." He told what had taken place. Von
Reischach said simply, "You should resign." Bethmann
shook his head. He could not resign in Germany's crucial
hour, he said, for that would sow dissension at home and
let the world know he believed Germany would fail. In
the nakedness of lost dignity he wrapped himself in the
cloak of duty. An officer must carry out a superior's command, even against his own judgment, he said, and as
Chancellor he could do no less. From that moment von
Reischach ceased to believe in victory. Von Valentini, who
was present, went upstairs and wrote Bethmann's *finis
Germaniae* in his diary. Bethmann went back to Berlin to
face the final humiliation of carrying the decision through
the Reichstag, to which he was responsible for the political
conduct of the war. Vice-Chancellor Helfferich, when he

heard that the "last card" had been played at Pless, commented, "If it is not trumps, Germany is lost for centuries." He too struggled with his conscience and emerged no less loyal to office than Bethmann. With admirable Teutonic subservience to military dictate, no one in the civil government resigned.

For Zimmermann the three weeks of notice were busy ones. Announcement of the U-boat war was not to be made to the neutrals until the evening of January 31, the last moment before the torpedoes would be let loose. Meanwhile, to keep the Americans from suspecting what was in store, he had to keep them talking peace while at the same time taking his own measures to prepare for America's entrance. He had been called down to Pless himself ten days earlier to confer on these measures with Hindenburg and Ludendorff, with whom he got on very well. As the expert on America, he had supplied them with comforting reasons why America could be discounted. He no longer talked so much about an uprising of German-Americans, for he had a new hobby that offered more exhilarating prospects of trouble—Mexico and Japan. He had worked up this hobby into a system of logic that was unassailable. Except for the Eastern seaboard, he argued, the United States was against war. Wilson did not want war, he had been re-elected on an anti-war platform, and he owed his election to the Western states. He could not declare war without the approval of Congress, where, according to Zimmermann, the Western and Middle Western states held a majority. The Western states, he declared, "will not wage war against us because of Japan." Zimmermann had been talking up the Yellow Peril to the Americans for so long he had convinced himself. He had gone out of his way to impress this peril and the need "for solidarity of the white race against the yellow" upon Gerard, and he believed, as he told the Reichstag, that in this matter he "knew just the right tone to adopt with the American Ambassador to make him respond."

Since then he had given much thought to the possibility of enticing Mexico and Japan to attack the United States. He was sure that America could never become importantly active in Europe if her existing entanglement in Mexico were swollen into full-scale war and if her fear of Japan's attacking from behind were given new reason for urgency. He intended to see to it that both these things happened. He proposed his plan of an alliance to his government colleagues and to the Supreme Command at Pless. He felt sure, he told them, that Mexico, given the prospect of recovering her lost territory, would do everything possible to get help and would persuade Japan to join. He argued that Japan, having seized all the loose pieces currently available in the Far East, would be looking for further loot. He was very convincing, and he was told to go ahead.

While working out the terms to be offered Mexico, he was also busy trying to keep Germany's ally, Austria-Hungary, as well as America, from the knowledge that the U-boat decision had been taken. Gasping for peace, Austria was even more frightened of the U-boat than Bethmann and dispatched a special emissary to Berlin to plead against it. Zimmermann told this gentleman that the matter was still under discussion (although it had already been decided six days earlier) and not to worry because America was not likely to go further than severing relations. She was unprepared for war, too entangled in Mexico, and too fearful of Japan. Japan would certainly jump upon her if she entered the war, and in any event America would not be ready to fight for six or eight months and by that time England would be beaten. Later he told the Austrians that information he was receiving convinced him more and more that "America would very probably *not* allow it to come to a breach with the Central Powers."

While juggling the Austrians and Mexico, he had also to keep teasing the American peace talk along, but not too fast. "We are convinced that we can win," he telegraphed Bernstorff. "You must therefore be dilatory in stating our conditions." These last moments called for a delicate touch, but he felt confident he could handle the simple Americans. A magnificent dinner at the Hotel Adlon was arranged by the German-American Trade Association at which Zimmermann, Vice-Chancellor Helfferich, and an impressive mustering of business, government, and military tycoons was assembled in honor of the return of Ambassador Gerard. Toasts were drunk, hours of fulsome afterdinner speeches unreeled, mutual expressions of confidence and amity exchanged. Zimmermann and Gerard, each engaged in lulling the other, outdid each other in purring.

"Our personal friendship encourages me in the assurance that we can continue to work in a frank, open manner, putting all our cards upon the table, and subdue every difficulty together," said the Secretary.

As long as his friends Bethmann, Helfferich, and, last but not least, his good friend Zimmermann remained at the head of affairs, "relations between our two countries are running no risk," graciously replied the Ambassador. That was carrying out instructions and jollying them to the limit, he told Grew after the dinner.

From this farcical feast of good fellowship Zimmermann went straight to the drafting of his instructions to Eckhardt to propose an alliance with Mexico and Japan for the purpose of attack upon the United States.

He intended to send them in a letter by way of Washington to Mexico aboard the merchant submarine *Deutschland* which had made a much admired trip to the United States in the previous July and was scheduled to depart again on January 15. But at the last moment its trip was canceled; the instructions would have to go by telegram. Zimmermann decided that the telegram should go by the most direct way possible, and what more direct than the channel put at his disposal by the Americans themselves? The idiotic Yankees, as Papen called them, had given it to him to use for peace, but that was simply more of Mr. Wilson's humbug. Germany was not to be fooled by such cant. If Wilson chose to hand them a key it would serve him justly—and struck Zimmermann as entirely fitting—to use the Yankee key to rob the Yankee roost.

When Zimmermann decided upon this stroke, America was not an enemy. The U-boat decision risked making her one, but Zimmermann himself, as well as many of the High Command, believed there was a good chance that Wilson might swallow this challenge with no more than an angry note or two, as he had done before. At this moment it was of the utmost importance to Germany to refrain from doing anything further to provoke America. Zimmermann's choice of telegraph route could hardly have been more inappropriate, under the circumstances, yet it was perhaps predestined by the German character. The fatal German assumption of superiority, superior right, superior cleverness, led him straight into it. To the superior person it is permitted to deceive fools; it is not ungentlemanly of him, it is expected, it is nature, it is law. A U-boat commander once remarked to an English merchant-ship captain whose ship, which had not carried concealed weapons, the German had just torpedoed, "You British will always be fools, and we Germans will never be gentlemen."

Zimmermann did not know that Room 40 had broken the German code, but had the Germans been less given to underestimating the enemy he might have thought twice before using the American cable route to propose a military alliance against America—just in case someone might be listening. Messages from the American embassy in Berlin went by overland telegraph to Copenhagen, and thence via the Atlantic cable, which touched at England. Zimmermann, however, did not think twice.

On January 16 he sent the telegram to Bernstorff for his information and for forwarding to Eckhardt in Mexico. He attached it to a longer telegram addressed by Bethmann-Hollweg to Bernstorff, conveying the final decision about the U-boats. Bethmann's telegram was numbered 157. Following it came Zimermann's instruction to Bernstorff, numbered 158: "Most secret. For Your Excellency's personal information and to be handed on to the Imperial Minister in Mexico by a safe route." Following this came the message to Eckhardt. It was headed "No. 1" and the full text read:

WE INTEND TO BEGIN UNRESTRICTED SUBMARINE WARFARE ON THE FIRST OF FEBRUARY. WE SHALL ENDEAVOR IN SPITE OF THIS TO KEEP THE UNITED STATES

NEUTRAL. IN THE EVENT OF THIS NOT SUCCEEDING, WE
MAKE MEXICO A PROPOSAL OF ALLIANCE ON THE FOL-
LOWING BASIS: MAKE WAR TOGETHER, GENEROUS FI-
NANCIAL SUPPORT, AND AN UNDERSTANDING ON OUR PART
THAT MEXICO IS TO RECONQUER THE LOST TERRITORY
IN TEXAS, NEW MEXICO, AND ARIZONA. THE SETTLE-
MENT IN DETAIL IS LEFT TO YOU.

YOU WILL INFORM THE PRESIDENT [OF MEXICO] OF
THE ABOVE MOST SECRETLY AS SOON AS THE OUTBREAK
OF WAR WITH THE UNITED STATES IS CERTAIN AND ADD
THE SUGGESTION THAT HE SHOULD, ON HIS OWN INITIA-
TIVE, INVITE JAPAN TO IMMEDIATE ADHERENCE AND AT
THE SAME TIME MEDIATE BETWEEN JAPAN AND OUR-
SELVES.

PLEASE CALL THE PRESIDENT'S ATTENTION TO THE
FACT THAT THE UNRESTRICTED EMPLOYMENT OF OUR
SUBMARINES NOW OFFERS THE PROSPECT OF COMPEL-
LING ENGLAND TO MAKE PEACE WITHIN A FEW MONTHS.
ACKNOWLEDGE RECEIPT.

ZIMMERMANN.

To make sure of its arrival Zimmermann dispatched the
telegram in code over three different routes: by the "main
line" wireless from Nauen to Sayville, where, owing to
the American censorship, it might or might not get
through; by the Swedish Roundabout; and finally, dutifully
tapped out by an American embassy clerk, over the State
Department cable, courtesy of Colonel House. It passed
through the State Department on January 17 and was
delivered by the Department, with Lansing's usual mis-
givings, to Bernstorff on the eighteenth. Ten days later
Secretary Lansing, impatient for the Germans to do something to awake America to the peril of a German victory,
wrote in his diary, "I hope those blundering Germans will
blunder soon." He did not know it, but the blunder had
just passed through his hands.

In England Room 40 was "highly entertained" to discover Zimmermann's telegram passing quietly over the
American cable. In fact Room 40 intercepted the telegram
along all three of its routes. First they picked the Nauen
wireless message out of the air and subsequently found the

same message coming in on the American cable and the Swedish Roundabout.

In Washington Ambassador Bernstorff, on receiving his copy from the State Department, forwarded the instructions, still in the same code, to Eckhardt on January 19 via Western Union. He struck out the instructions to himself beginning with "No. 158 . . ." and ending ". . . by a safe route," and substituted his own number of telegram, 130, plus the additional line, "Foreign Office telegraphs January 16, No. 1, Most Secret, decode yourself." At the end, he added, "End of telegram, Bernstorff." These differences in text were to be of the utmost importance. As far as is known, Bernstorff's responsibility ended there. The Zimmermann telegram was left, like a spark dropped in a forest, to smolder in secret while more public matters raced to a climax.

Bernstorff now knew the worst, yet continued trying desperately to convince Berlin that Wilson would be an honorable mediator and that some way must be found to accept his peace offer. If Germany accepted it, Bernstorff said, he was sure she would emerge with her world position maintained in full measure. No one in Germany believed him. Zimmermann believed that Wilson "would exert all his influence against us" because "he feels and thinks English"; Helfferich insisted there was a "trick of some kind" behind Wilson's offer, and the Kaiser placed "absolutely no reliance" on it. But Bethmann, suffering the pains of remorse, replied that he was still looking for "any possible means likely to diminish the danger of a break." Having swallowed the cake, he hoped to avoid the stomach ache.

It was at this moment that Wilson made his last and most moving appeal. He delivered the famous "peace without victory" speech before the Senate on January 22 but addressed it, in his mind, to the peoples of the world over the heads of their governments. The phrase "peace without victory" infuriated the Allies, but Bernstorff picked up hope. Still using the State Department cable, he begged Berlin for at least a period of grace for neutral ships, in which case he believed that Wilson would redouble his efforts for peace. Bethmann seized upon the idea but was curtly told by the Admiralty that it was too late; many of the U-boats were already at sea and could not be reached for a change of orders.

Only a week now was left for Bernstorff to work in. One more plea went out from him, imploring Berlin to answer Wilson's last request for peace terms and then, if the Allies rebuffed Wilson, Germany would have put herself in a position to use the U-boat without, perhaps, provoking American retaliation. "In spite of all statements to the contrary, American war resources," he warned, "are very great."

When Bernstorff's last-minute message came through on January 28, Zimmermann was at Pless, conferring with the High Command. Hours counted now. At the Foreign Office they called in a trusted friend of Zimmermann's, Jacob Noeggerath, a German-American who had long been his adviser on American affairs. All day Noeggerath tried to get Zimmermann on the telephone, and, when he did, passionately pleaded with him to ask the High Command to postpone the U-boats. And Bethmann, armed with Bernstorff's telegram, took the night train for Pless, where on the following day, January 29, another meeting was held. It was brief and formal with Hindenburg, Ludendorff, Bethmann, Zimmermann, and the Kaiser present. No question of postponing the U-boats was raised because the Navy had emphatically stated they were beyond recall. All Bethmann could get was a decision to add a statement of Germany's peace terms to the announcement of the U-boat war, plus a pious hope that the American government would continue its efforts toward peace and a promise that Germany would call off the submarines as soon as it became evident that the President's efforts would lead to a peace "acceptable to Germany."

On January 31, at the last possible moment, allowing less than eight hours' notice, at the end of the working day, notice of the U-boat war was given to the American government. Bernstorff presented it to Lansing at four o'clock, and Zimmermann informed Gerard at six o'clock.

Washington was taken by surprise. Despite many warnings, the administration, believing the North Sea and North Atlantic too difficult for submarines in winter, had not expected the Germans to take this step until spring. For Bernstorff it was the end of his eight years' embassy in America, the debacle of his long labor to keep the United States out of the war. Looking unnatural minus his customary smile, he presented the document to an amazed and angry Lansing, saying, "I know it is very serious, very. I deeply regret that it is necessary." He managed a wan smile, murmured, "Good afternoon," bowed, and departed. Later, when besieged by the press, he uttered what was perhaps the only impulsive remark he ever made in America—"I am finished with politics for the rest of my life."

In Berlin the question everyone asked him and his neighbor was, what will the United States do? Zimmermann, hearty with false courage, had for days been working to convince himself and everyone else that America might not come in after all. A Danish journalist who called to interview him found him on tenterhooks waiting for news. "If only the United States will keep hands off," Zimmermann blurted out, "and leave us alone, two or three months will be enough." On February 1, defending the U-boat decision before the Reichstag, he urged all the reasons—the Western states, the anti-war feeling, the menace of Japan—why the United States would not go to war. He was like a boy who, aghast at having opened a dam, tries to tell himself the water will somehow not rush through.

In London expectancy was equally tense; in Washington it was highest of all. The long-awaited challenge, fended off so often, had suddenly been flung in America's face. Freedom of the seas, commented one American paper, would henceforth be enjoyed "by icebergs and fish." Eighty correspondents crowded Lansing's press conference on the morning of February 1 and were still swarming in the corridors when he returned from the White House at five o'clock. For three days they and the country waited while President Wilson wrestled with himself. The President told Colonel House, who came down from New York, that he felt as if the world had suddenly reversed itself and was now going from west to east instead of east to west, and that he could not get his balance. He still insisted he would not allow German provocation to lead to war if it could possibly be avoided. He still said it would be a "crime" for his government to go to war, closing to itself all possibility of becoming peacemaker.

The fear of Japan that Zimmermann counted on was immediately manifest. With nice appreciation of a delicate moment, the Japanese Ambassador called at the State Department to protest two Alien Land Bills then up for passage in Idaho and Oregon. The senators of those states, summoned to an urgent conference by Under-Secretary Polk, were sufficiently impressed, though both Republicans, to telegraph their home legislatures not to embarrass the administration "at this critical hour." Responding admirably, Idaho and Oregon withdrew the bills.

On February 2 the regular Friday Cabinet meeting was called at half past two. "What shall I propose? I must go to Congress. What shall I say?" the President asked almost pleadingly. Restively the Cabinet members, of whom all but one or two were by now certain that America should join the Allies, spoke their minds. Which side did he want to see win? one of them asked the President. Neither, answered Wilson; he still wanted a peace without victory for either side. With startling effect, he then advanced upon his listeners a new argument for not going to war. The Boswell of the Cabinet, Secretary of Agriculture Houston, recorded it. In order "to keep the white race strong against the yellow—Japan for instance, in combination with Russia and dominating China—" it would be wise, Wilson said, to do nothing; indeed he *would* do nothing but would submit rather to any imputation of weakness or cowardice. The Cabinet was stunned. Next the President, still searching for an alternative, suggested a united demand for peace by all neutrals, something which, while intent upon his own role as mediator, he had not before considered. Then he adjourned the meeting to make up his own mind privately, as usual.

Next day, February 3, he decided. Bernstorff was to

be given his passports, diplomatic relations with Germany broken off—but without malice. "I refuse to believe," he told Congress that afternoon when he went up to the Hill to announce his decision, "that it is the intention of the German authorities to do in fact what they have warned us they will feel at liberty to do . . . only actual overt acts on their part can make me believe it even now."

While he was talking it was dinnertime in Europe. In London, Ambassador and Mrs. Page, First Secretary Laughlin and his wife, and the Ambassador's secretary, Mr. Shoecraft, had been sitting all day in one room, hardly speaking, while they waited for news of Wilson's decision. Suddenly they heard the front doorbell ring. The private secretary hurried downstairs and met Admiral Hall, the first man in Europe to hear the news, coming up. "Thank God!" said the admiral as he marched into the Ambassador's room and pulled from his pocket a telegram from Captain Gaunt which read, "Bernstorff goes home. I get drunk tonight."

In Berlin that same evening Ambassador and Mrs. Gerard were enjoying after-theater supper in the company of Secretary Zimmermann and a lady friend. "You will see," Zimmermann told them, "everything will be all right. America will do nothing because Wilson is for peace and nothing else. Everything will go on as before."

When he got the news next morning he showed great emotion, and his language to newspapermen was violent. To the Germans he said that it was a good thing—"At last we have gotten rid of this person as peace mediator." When it came to saying good-by to Gerard and Grew, he had recovered enough to part "in the warmest way possible" and to convince the two diplomats that the break had come to him as a complete surprise for which he was genuinely and profoundly sorry.

It was not war yet, but Zimmermann, feeling the seat grow hot, decided not to wait. Although he had originally told Eckhardt not to broach the alliance with Mexico until the war with the United States was certain, he now on February 5 telegraphed him to make the offer "even now." As Bernstorff was now cut off, this second telegram in the same code as the first, was sent direct to Eckhardt, probably via the Swedish Roundabout. Zimmermann was fully conscious that he was handling explosives, for his telegram began: "Provided there is no danger of secret being betrayed to United States, Your Excellency is desired to take up alliance question without further delay with the President." Zimmerman added that Carranza "might even now on his own account sound out Japan." He concluded: "If the President declines from fear of subsequent revenge, you are empowered to offer him a definitive alliance after the conclusion of peace, provided Mexico succeeded in drawing Japan into the alliance." Like its predecessor, this telegram was headed, "Most secret, decipher personally," and signed "Zimmermann."

A little bit earlier, and he would have caught Carranza in a more receptive mood. But just before Eckhardt received his instructions to go ahead, President Carranza's bellicosity toward America was deprived of its chief stimulus by the sudden withdrawal of the Pershing expedition. Truculent to the end, Carranza had just rejected a formula for withdrawal beaten out in months of wrangling by a Joint High Commission of Mexicans and Americans. Helpless, the Commission had adjourned on January 15, 1917, leaving Wilson no choice but to flounder even deeper into Mexico or withdraw unconditionally. He had never come well out of his contests with Mexican dignity, he had had a surfeit of this one which he had disliked from the start, American reputation was dwindling every day the bootless chase continued, and his advisers, uneasy over Germany, were strongly urging retrieving the Army now. Wilson agreed to back out. The withdrawal, ordered January 25, was completed by February 5, the same day Eckhardt was instructed to offer Carranza alliance "even now."

Crowing over Pershing's withdrawal as his personal triumph, Don Venus felt mollified, and to that extent less inclined to succumb to the German offer than he might have been two weeks earlier. Meantime Germany's carefully prepared plans for Mexico were gaining momentum. American agents began picking up a fresh spurt of rumors.

From Laredo on February 5: "A German captain arrived in Nuevo Laredo today for the purpose of organizing Mexicans to raid United States territory." From El Paso on February 12: "The German Consul in Chihuahua has brought his wife across the border and left her there while he has returned and is running back and forth to Juárez buying unusual supplies of merchandise." From San Salvador on February 13: "Large numbers of Germans are spreading through Mexico. The hotels of Torreón, Mexico City, and Monterey are full of them and they associate mostly with Carranzista officers. They are working up feeling against Wilson as anti-Catholic." Other reports told of an influx of Germans from the United States into all parts of Mexico, of Germans buying up ship coal on Mexico's west coast, and of a German businessman who reported that Mexicans on the streets had suddenly taken to embracing him, saying, "It is high time Germany was getting after the schoolteacher."

Wilson, having refused to go beyond breaking relations, was shut up in the White House, where, as Ambassador Page fumed in his diary, "He engaged in what he called 'thought' and the air currents of the world never ventilated his mind." The comment was that of a hurt and frustrated man but not without justice. Wilson still would not heed the plain fact that the belligerents did not want him to mediate and would fight to the end rather than settle for less than victory. In his speech to Congress announcing the break with Germany, he had said that Americans were sincere friends of the German people and would not believe that "they are hostile to us unless and until we are obliged to believe it." He was still determined to keep the United States free of the struggle, in a position to make peace, withstanding all provocation short of the "overt act." He did not expect one to come out of Mexico.

"The Most Dramatic Moment in All My Life"

Zimmermann's overt act still lay, like an unthrown hand grenade, inside Admiral Hall's safe. When the DNI read the terms of Wilson's speech announcing the break with Germany, he realized that his heartfelt "Thank God!" on first hearing the news had been premature. The Americans were not coming in after all. Their President was still clutching neutrality with his eyes squeezed shut against Germany's explicit hostility. "Unless and until we are obliged to believe it." Was it possible the man could still be in doubt? It looked as if it might be up to Admiral Hall to oblige him to believe it. All he had to do was pull the pin on the hand grenade and toss it in the American lap—yet he did not. He could not move until certain arrangements he was making to conceal Room 40's possession of the code were complete.

Meanwhile Britain's situation was daily growing worse. U-boats were making a cemetery of the sea approaches to the British Isles. The limit of Britain's financial resources had already been reached. Having used up her negotiable securities, she could now offer only government credit to finance the $10,000,000 a day of war supplies she was purchasing in the United States. Would the American government allow loans on that basis? America's economy was now deeply tied to British purchases, but Wilson's attitude was disquieting. He showed signs of wanting to use Britian's indigence to force her into a negotiated peace. Only if the United States entered the war could that danger be dispelled and credit unlimited and ships unlimited be obtained.

After Wilson's discouraging speech Admiral Hall no

longer felt justified in keeping the existence of the Zimmermann telegram a secret from his government. On February 5 he unlocked his safe, took out the telegram, marched across the Horse Guards Parade to the Foreign Office, where he handed the fateful document to Lord Hardinge, Permanent Under-Secretary. It was still incomplete and garbled in places because Montgomery and de Grey had not entirely succeeded in solving the variations of the code, but enough was available to show that Room 40 had got hold of the greatest coup of the war.

Lord Hardinge did not like it. As a civil servant trained to proceed according to protocol, he could not help regarding a decoded intercept as something slightly shady and the idea of the British government's using such an instrument to influence a neutral state as distasteful. Admiral Hall explained that he was not ready to use it until certain requirements had been satisfied and the decoding perfected, but he wished Mr. Balfour to know of the telegram's existence so that he might in the meantime consider how best to handle it.

The requirement Admiral Hall had set himself was to secure a copy of the telegram as sent by Bernstorff to Mexico. This, he reasoned, would have small but significant differences in dateline, address, and signature from the original as sent by Zimmermann to Bernstorff. If such a copy were the one to be published, the Germans would spot the differences and infer from them that the interception had been accomplished somewhere on the American continent. Cocksure of the inviolability of their code, they would persuade themselves that an already decoded copy of the telegram had been betrayed or stolen *after* reaching its destination. They would blame it on carelessness or perfidy or spies inside their own embassies in Washington or Mexico. Room 40's role would remain unsuspected. This predicted behavior the Germans were obligingly to carry out to the last step.

Casting about for a way to obtain a transatlantic copy of the telegram, Hall had thought of the indispensable Mr. H. in Mexico, the man who had tracked Herr Cronholm. Some three weeks later Mr. H. was able, through a most fortuitous set of circumstances, to supply Hall with what he needed.

It happened that an Englishman who operated a printing press in Mexico City had returned to his shop unexpectedly one Saturday afternoon when his Mexican workmen were taking their half-day off. On the workbench he noticed some unfamiliar plates and upon examining them found to his horror that they were plates for printing forged currency. Near them was neatly stacked a pile of forged *cartones,* a form of substitute currency which had come into use in Mexico during the successive revolutions when each new regime declared the currency of its predecessor valueless and issued one of its own. So many forgeries flourished under this system that President Carranza had recently decreed the death penalty for forgers.

Understandably the English printer was terrified. If there was one thing the Mexicans were proficient at, it was ordering executions and carrying them out. The printer scooped up the evidence, locked it in his safe, slipped out of his office as inconspicuously as he could, and dashed to a friend's house for advice. In his absence the workman who had made the forgeries returned and, finding his plates and *cartones* gone, became terrified in his turn. He too saw himself facing a firing squad at dawn and decided to clear himself by accusing his employer, who, he rightly guessed, had found the forgeries. He went to the authorities, who promptly arrested, tried, and convicted the printer, all on the same Saturday, and condemned him to be shot on Monday.

Rescue arrived in the person of Mr. H. He was an acquaintance of the friend whom the printer had consulted before his arrest. On being told of the affair, Mr. H. went to the British Minister, who, although it was Sunday, obtained a reprieve for the unfortunate printer and eventually, when the real forger was found out, his release. The printer was happy to have his life, the friend was happy to be freed of suspicion, and Mr. H. was happy because he had acquired a grateful ally in the heart of the Mexican Telegraph Office. That, it turned out, was where the printer's friend worked. He was only too glad to produce copies of any telegrams in which his benefactor, Mr. H., might be interested.

There was one in particular, and it was found. On February 10, Admiral Hall received from Mexico a copy of the Zimmermann telegram as received by Eckhardt from Bernstorff. It contained just those small textual differences he had hoped it would.

Meantime Room 40 had intercepted and decoded Zimmermann's second telegram, instructing Eckhardt to contract the alliance, including Japan, "even now." Japan's possible infidelity had been troubling the Allied consciousness like an aching tooth for some time. Besides this, Britain had reason enough of her own to worry about Mexico. Without Tampico's oil the British Navy would soon come to a halt. Protection of the foreign oil properties was in the hands of the Indian Pelaez, a kind of bandit war lord who sold protection on the squeeze principle, but a determined German-led assault might break through his guard. Or Carranza, once under the German thumb, might, as he was always threatening, cancel the foreign concessions and take back the subsoil oil rights on behalf of Mexico. So far, it had paid Mexico better to accept the foreign royalties than to kill the goose that laid them, but it was impossible to say what the capricious Carranza might do with a German alliance to nerve him.

On February 13, Carranza revealed his closeness to the Germans when he issued a call to all the neutrals to embargo war supplies to the belligerents. This, in effect, would have cut off supplies to the Allies, since Germany was already blockaded. Newspaper cartoons pictured Carranza as a wooden puppet manipulated by a spike-helmeted Prussian who chortled with sinister glee as he made the puppet squeak, "Embargo everything!" Next day a German-inspired revolt in Cuba broke out, and the continued influx of German reservists from North and South America into Mexico was becoming alarming. Agents reported them active in the Tampico area, and three hundred German officers were said to have gathered in Mexico in recent weeks. When the German embassy in Washington closed down, two of its personnel, instead of returning to Germany, went to Mexico. One of them was the Japanese expert Baron von Schoen, who long ago had annoyed Wilson with his tactless prediction that America would have to fight Japan. His reassignment to Mexico was apparently in pursuit of the same goal. At the same time the Mexican Minister to Berlin, Rafael Zubaran, came home, reportedly bringing with him the draft of Carranza's embargo proposal, which was generally believed to have been written in Berlin. All this converging of Germans and German influence upon Mexico City pointed to some imminent and remarkable development.

In London, Balfour had seized upon Hall's news of the Zimmermann telegram with eagerness. Untroubled by Lord Hardinge's compunctions, he was impatiently awaiting the moment when the telegram could be discreetly leaked to stimulate the Americans. How to present it so as to convince the Americans, without revealing its source, was a dilemma which was still being thrashed out at the Foreign Office in almost daily conversation with Admiral Hall.

From the beginning the greatest fear—and one that was to prove valid—was that the Americans would pronounce it a hoax unless full information about how Britain had obtained it was given them. And then there was that question of the intentions of the inscrutable ally in the Far East. If Japan were really to join the enemy, nothing would so certainly induce the Russians to back out and make a separate peace—a calamity that the Allies were straining to prevent. With this on his mind, Balfour requested the honor of a visit from the Japanese Ambassador. Politely he endeavored to sound him out on Japan's relations with Mexico, and as suavely the Ambassador replied that there were no relations of any interest. Japan was only anxious, the Ambassador said, to quiet American suspicions and had no ambitions in Mexico. Mr. Balfour did not come away greatly enlightened.

Three days later, on February 19, the men in Room 40, after working for five weeks on a solution of the code for the missing passages, completed their decryptment of Zimmermann's telegram. Admiral Hall informed Balfour that the moment had come, and it was decided between them that Hall himself should make the revelation to the American embassy.

In the embassy at that moment the mood was despairing. "I am now ready to record my conviction that we shall not get into the war at all," Ambassador Page wrote in his diary on February 19. The President, he went on, had no understanding that the Allies could not accept a peace without victory without becoming vassals of Germany. "He is constitutionally unable to come to the point of action. That much seems certain to me."

To Page the let-down after Wilson's break with Germany was almost more agonizing than the years of frustration before it. He had thought that at last he was going to be able to shed the official mask of neutrality he had so unwillingly worn, but that wonderful moment which he had anticipated, when he could face his English friends with pride, had never come. Instead Wilson had backed away again. Page could not understand him. He had known Wilson since they were both in their twenties. As editor of the *Atlantic Monthly* and later as founder and editor of *World's Work,* he had invited and published Wilson's articles, encouraged his bent toward politics, told all his friends to "Watch that man!", believed in his destiny as a leader of a new era in public life. But from the beginning of the war he believed the policy of neutrality to be pernicious. How could Wilson, whom he knew to be as steeped in England's literature and constitutional traditions as he was himself, fail to see that the principles they both believed in were dependent on an Allied victory? Yet Wilson persisted in trying to pressure the Allies into what he called a "peace between equals."

To represent a policy that equated the Allies and the enemy was a torment to Page. The duty of conveying complaints against British blacklists, the pain and humiliation of acting for a country that hung back from the fight, caused him genuine suffering. Sir Edward Grey thought him the most convinced believer in democracy he had ever known, and democracy to Page was so unmistakably the central issue of the war that neutrality seemed to him almost like treason. His heart was with the Allies, and the heart of this warm, impressionable, winning man was concealed from no one. It spoke out in his vivid, illuminating letters, letters that were like eager talk, letters that, before they disagreed with him, Wilson described as "the best I ever read."

But Wilson was Chief Executive and Page his envoy, and the President had soon become irritated by Page's constant criticism of his declared policy and even more by Page's tendency to blunt its edges when transmitting it to England. He stopped reading the Ambassador's letters, discarded him mentally, and left it to Colonel House to concoct all sorts of clever tricks to bypass him. In the summer of 1916 they had decided to bring Page home on leave to "get some American atmosphere in him," but when he arrived Wilson refused to talk to him about the war. Only when Page stubbornly declined to go away did Wilson finally consent to a serious discussion. Although they talked all one morning, they were worlds apart and the interview was empty and sad. As he left, Page put a hand on the President's shoulder and saw Wilson's eyes fill with tears. They parted and never met again.

Page had returned to London, and after the President's reelection in November he offered to resign. His offer remained unanswered for some months, and only when he pressed for a reply was he told to stay on, while, behind his back, the President offered the post to Cleveland H. Dodge, who turned it down. The offer, made on February 6, three days after the break with Germany, is evidence of how seriously the President still intended to pursue neutrality.

Ignorant of the effort to supplant him, Page was happy enough to continue as Ambassador, despite his total lack of sympathy with the policies he was supposed to represent, for the hope would not down that events would sooner or later force Wilson to abandon neutrality. He continued alternately pouring out brave accounts of the Allies' struggle and succumbing to fits of depression.

Back home, in February 1917, although the country was apathetic as a whole, impatience equal to Page's was being voiced by many, most vociferously of all by former President Theodore Roosevelt. Writhing like a bound Prometheus against the confines of American pacificism, he raged against Wilson's failure to "lead" and to "act."

"I don't believe Wilson will go to war unless Germany literally kicks him into it," he burst out in a letter to Senator Lodge on February 12. Even kicking Wilson wouldn't be enough, he decided a few days later. "If anyone kicks him he brushes his clothes and utters some lofty sentence." And again a few days after that: "He is evidently trying his old tactics; he is endeavoring to sneak out of going to war under any conditions." "Yellow all through" was at this time Roosevelt's favorite epithet for the man who reigned in his place. It seemed to him the only way to explain Wilson's failure to fight against the menace of a German triumph. He believed that if Germany won she would move into the Caribbean, invade Cuba, threaten the Panama Canal, and probably enter into alliance with Japan, thus making possible simultaneous attacks on both coasts of the United States. Elihu Root, who had been Roosevelt's Secretary of State, believed a victorious Germany would take Britain's colonies and dominions, including Canada, and America would find herself staring at the Kaiser across her northern frontier.

Inside the administration, Lansing felt "depressed and anxious" at the President's inaction, believing, as he fervently did, that "we can no longer refuse to play our part . . . in favor of Democracy against Absolutism." The situation in Washington, wrote home the British Ambassador in that last week of February, was like a bottle of champagne after the wire has been cut but before the cork has been exploded.

In England, Admiral Hall was in the process of exploding the cork in conversation with Mr. Edward Bell of the American embassy. Bell, whose job was to maintain liaison with the various intelligence offices of the British government, was well known to the DNI. It was to him Hall had given the Archibald papers in 1915 when, mistrusting the slow bureaucracy of his own Foreign Office, he wanted to make sure of their exposure in the United States. When Bell came to Room 40 and was shown a copy of Zimmermann's telegram (in the text obtained in Mexico with Bernstorff's alterations), he became the first of a long line of Americans whose immediate reaction was to pronounce the thing a fraud out of simple disbelief that anyone in his right mind would dare propose giving away a slice of the continental United States. Upon his receiving Hall's assurances, his reaction changed to fury and then slowly to satisfaction as he realized the possibilities. Publication of the telegram, he told Hall, would certainly mean war.

Warned by Bell's initial incredulity, Hall was anxious to reveal the telegram in a way that would combine the greatest assurance of authenticity with the least exposure of Room 40. Without having agreed upon a method, he and Bell moved over to Grosvenor Square to inform the Ambassador. How Page took the news we do not know, because for some reason—maybe Hall enjoined secrecy even upon diary writing—he kept no record of it. We do know he spent the rest of the day in conference with Hall and Bell and Irwin Laughlin, First Secretary of the embassy, trying to work out a foolproof method of handling the decoded dynamite. As a first step they decided that Mr. Balfour should officially give the telegram to Ambassador Page, because, as Page put it, "that would be the British government giving it to our government." Page would cable the text to Washington—but then, what if Wilson demanded proof? After prolonged wrestling with this problem, they hit upon a scheme which they hoped, rather nervously, would be proof against unexpected pitfalls. The Americans would be told that they could locate in their own files the incoming cable to Bernstorff or his forwarding telegram sent via Western Union to Eckhardt. This would of course still be in German code, but the code groups could be wired to Bell in the London embassy, where, on what was technically American soil, he could personally decode it with the help of de Grey, who would be allowed, for that occasion only, to bring over the code book from Room 40. Through this maneuver the American government, if challenged, would be able to say that the telegram had been decoded by Americans on American territory. Exhausted but relieved, the four gentlemen congratulated one another and went to bed.*

The next day, Friday, February 23, the Secretary of State for Foreign Affairs formally presented the Zimmermann telegram to the American Ambassador. Balfour, on the authority of one who knew him, was "unusually excited"—a rare occasion. "Lofty" was a word people often used of him, as they did of Wilson. Like Wilson, he had a certain aloofness from the arena—Wilson because he felt superior to it, Balfour because he was casual and detached. As a thinker Balfour was Wilson's match, with a passion for philosophy in place of Wilson's passion for reform. Wilson was an American Gladstone who practiced politics on moral principles. Balfour was an English Jefferson who practiced politics as a gentleman's occupation and applied himself equally to science, metaphysics, aesthetics, lawn tennis, early sports cars, and social celebrity. Philosophers read him on logic and doubt; sportsmen read him on golf; ladies found him "the most delightful of men"; Churchill found him "the most perfect of men"; and no one who met him failed to respond to his charm, to be warmed by his sympathy, to be dazzled by his conversation, to be relaxed by his ease, if occasionally irked by what a French friend called his "seraphic equanimity."

From the beginning of the war, first at the Admiralty,

---

*In a letter to President Wilson a year later, Page wrote that he had made up his mind to live twenty years more in order to be present at the opening of Admiral Hall's papers, for "the man is a genius—a clear case of genius," and writing his story would be "the shortest cut to immortality for him and for me that has yet occurred to me." The hope was not to be fulfilled. Illness brought Page home a month before the Armistice, and a month after it he died. "I loved that man," said Balfour, who was among the large group that came to say good-by to Page at Waterloo Station. "I almost wept when he left England."

Admiral Hall lived to see the Second World War and died in 1943 at the age of seventy-three.

later as Foreign Secretary, Balfour had felt as deeply as Page the fundamental bond between England and America and the fundamental issue of the war as one in which "I cannot doubt that America is no less concerned than the British Empire." The question as to when America would come to acknowledge this herself, had become a matter of urgency for Britain. From his place in the War Cabinet, Balfour knew that England could not afford the luxury, which most Englishmen would have preferred, of fighting the war without the Americans. Since the day he first learned of the Zimmermann telegram, he had been waiting tensely—or as tensely as his character permitted—for the moment when it could be disclosed. His anticipation of its effect upon the United States was particularly keen because his first duty upon taking over the Foreign Office two months before had been to compose England's own reply to accompany the joint Allied note answering Wilson's peace offer. In it he had made plain his conviction of the error and futility of Wilson's proposal to treat with the enemy.

So long as Germany remains the Germany of aggressive aims and barbarous methods, he had said, so long as her aims and methods have not fallen in disrepute among her own peoples, no state could feel secure. No peace treaty made with such a Germany could prevent her from once again setting out to dominate the world. "Those who think," he wrote, with an eye on the White House, "that for this disease international treaties and international laws may provide a cure . . . have ill learned the lessons so clearly taught by recent history." Taking direct issue with Wilson's thesis that only a peace between equals could endure, he notified America that "the people of this country do not believe that peace can be durable unless it is based on the success of the Allies."

Untouched, unpersuaded, Wilson gave the document no notice. Now, in the Zimmermann telegram, Balfour had another document to send to America, which this time the President could not ignore. Balfour would not have been human if he had not felt an extra zest in the opportunity. The moment when he handed Page the sheet of paper containing the decoded message was, he later confessed, "the most dramatic in all my life."

Page took the paper back to the embassy and sat down to draft a covering message explaining to Wilson how the telegram had been obtained. Because of the difficulty of saying just enough, but not too much, the task took him all night. Hardly able to wait till it was finished, he alerted the State Department at 2 A.M. on the twenty-fourth with a cable saying, "In about three hours I shall send a telegram of great importance to the President and Secretary of State."

Finally satisfied with his covering note, he telegraphed it, together with the Zimmermann text, at 1 P.M. on February 24. The explanation he gave the President was somewhat ingenuous and not entirely in conformity with the facts, either because Hall had not given him all the facts or because he had prevailed upon Page to disguise them. Wilson was told that the British government was so greatly exercised by Zimmermann's proposal that "they have lost no time in communicating it to me to transmit to you . . . in view of the threatened invasion of United States territory." Warning Wilson that what he was about to tell him was strictly confidential, Page said that the British government possessed the German code used in the message and had made it their business to secure Bernstorff's telegrams to Mexico which had been sent back to London and deciphered there. This, he said, accounted for the delay since January 19, the date the message had reached Eckhardt. The British government earnestly requested Wilson to keep the source of his information profoundly secret but they put, added Page with marvelous gravity, "no prohibition on the publication of Zimmermann's telegram itself." He suggested to Wilson that "you can probably obtain a copy of the text relayed by Bernstorff from the cable office in Washington." The British copy, he said, had not been obtained in Washington but "bought in Mexico."

Exhausted by the effort and emotion, Page felt more depressed than elated when his task was done and the message on its way to Washington. Though it seemed to him that such a bomb had seldom before been thrown, he was not sure that even this would budge Wilson. "This would precipitate a war between any two nations," he wrote that night in his diary; "Heaven knows what effect it will have in Washington."

11

The Telegram in Washington

At nine o'clock Saturday morning, February 24, the State Department received Page's first telegram, saying a message of "great importance" would follow in about three hours. What could it mean? Could the British be thinking of negotiating after all? At the end of three hours nothing further had come in. At the end of the afternoon, still nothing. The suspense was tantalizing. In the absence of Lansing, who was away for a three-day weekend, Acting Secretary Polk felt it keenly. At last, at eight-thirty in the evening, the code room sent word that a long telegram from Page had been received. While it was being put into clear, an Assistant Secretary hovered at the door, snatched the finished copy, and hurried upstairs to deliver it to Polk. With astonishment the Acting Secretary read the revelation, and with anger, as he read on, learned that the German plot upon American territory had been launched five weeks ago while its authors were talking peace to Wilson. This could not wait for Lansing— nor for morning. Wilson must be informed at once. Polk used the private wire to ask the President to expect him and, taking Page's telegram with him, walked across the street to the White House.

The only record we have of what Wilson thought or said when he first saw the Zimmermann telegram is Polk's report that he showed "much indignation." Whatever his feelings about Page, Wilson seems not to have questioned the telegram's authenticity for a moment. He was so aroused that, without even taking time to think, he wanted to release it right away. Polk suggested waiting until Lansing could be consulted upon his return, and on second thought the President agreed as he began to realize the potentialities of the telegram. It had come at a moment of peculiar delicacy, for, in fact, that weekend the President was facing an urgent decision.

Ever since the German declaration of unrestricted U-boat war, American ships, unwilling to sail, had been clogging the ports. Cargoes of wheat, cotton, and all manner of supplies were piling up, and unless authority was given to put Navy gunners on merchant ships with orders to shoot on sight, the sacred right to the high seas would go by default, with serious economic consequences. The administration and the public of the Atlantic seaboard states were in a furor over the armed-ship issue. A National Pacifist Congress of five hundred people was meeting at the Biltmore in New York. The Association of German-American Pastors had named the coming Sunday a day of prayer to destroy "all evil counsel and base machinations which are at work to plunge our nation into war." Ship owners were demanding arms. Preparedness societies were marching. The Roosevelt cohorts were railing at "the general paralysis of Wilsonism." These groups were of one mind, but the pacifists were divided, the majority against arming the ships but some in favor of it as a deterrent to war.

Wilson's position was so far his own secret. On Friday, the day before the telegram came, the Cabinet erupted in a stormy meeting during which some of the members, who denounced German methods, were accused by the President of "trying to push us into war." That afternoon the Senate Republicans held a caucus from which the pro-war group, led by Senator Lodge, and the pacifist faction, led by Senator La Follette, emerged in unprecedented unanimity. Congress was due to adjourn automatically at noon on March 4, leaving the President free for nine months to follow his own counsel without benefit of Congressional advice. None of the Senators knew what the President planned to do, but all were agreed they were not going to let him do it alone. The Lodge group was afraid he would find a way to back out of war, and the La Follette group was afraid he would drag the country into war, so they had agreed at the caucus to prolong debate on a pending revenue bill in order to force an extra session.

When the Senators filed back into the chamber, reporters were astonished to see Republicans who had not spoken to La Follette in years consult him on the floor, offer amendments at his nod, and demand delaying roll calls. The word "filibuster!" hissed through the halls and reached the White House that evening. These were only slowdown tactics so far, but by morning all Washington knew that if an armed-ship bill was introduced in Congress the pacifist faction was planning a true filibuster to defeat it.

Yet Wilson now made up his mind to ask Congress for the bill, not as a step toward war but as a warning to the Germans, which he hoped might deter them from the "overt act." He decided upon it as a last buttress of America's crumbling neutrality. He had the executive right to arm the ships on his own authority, but the use of arms was a step of awful portent for which he wanted Congress's seal of approval. There was nothing he wanted less than an extra session, for he would have preferred to remain "alone and unbothered," as one of his Cabinet privately remarked. He knew the filibuster forces were gathering, but when he smelled opposition his will became steely, and in the Zimmermann telegram he believed he had a means to dissolve a filibuster. It is not the least irony of this history clogged with ironies that Wilson's wish to force the Armed Ship Bill through Congress, as a last resort against war, led him to publish the gravest incitement to war in the history of America before Pearl Harbor.

Wilson saw the telegram Saturday night; he spent Sunday composing a speech on the Armed Ship Bill, which he proposed to deliver to Congress in person on Monday. Polk spent Sunday trying to get Bernstorff's telegram forwarding the Zimmermann message to Eckhardt, out of the files of Western Union. He was blocked by adamant refusal. Standing upon a federal law protecting the contents of telegrams, the company would not let its files be searched. Balked by the lower echelons, Polk set about bringing government pressure on Western Union's president, Newcomb Carlton. By this time it was Monday, and the President was due in Congress at one o'clock. In the morning he had sent a copy of the Zimmermann telegram to Colonel House with the cryptic comment that it was "astounding." He said nothing of what he intended to do about it nor asked for any opinion from House (unnecessary, because House always gave an opinion anyway, which he would immediately enter in his diary so that in a later entry he could impress upon posterity how the President took such and such action "as I suggested"). Wilson let the telegram lie over Monday, probably less because he was waiting for Lansing, who was not due back until next day, than because he wished to test the mood of Congress before making it public.

There is no evidence that he ever thought of withholding it. Indeed, when Polk that same day informed Ambassador Fletcher in Mexico of Zimmermann's proposal, he said the American government did not believe that the telegram could properly be withheld from the public. Expecting that its publication would cause "great consternation" and "intense feeling," he instructed Fletcher to get a statement from President Carranza of Mexico's "disinterestedness." Washington suspected that Carranza might well be interested in a German alliance, but was trying to give him an opportunity to declare himself out. Carranza did not take it. A telegram sent that very day, February 26, by Eckhardt to Zimmermann indicates why. "Most Secret," it was headed. "Beginning negotiations . . . (indecipherable) . . . Could WE provide munitions? Request reply."

At one o'clock the President, "looking well and trim in a cutaway of fashionable cut," took his stand on the Speaker's rostrum to ask a joint session of Congress for arms to protect American ships and people "in their legitimate and peaceful pursuits on the seas." While he was talking, the news tickers suddenly began clacking a bulletin announcing the sinking of a small Cunard liner, the *Laconia,* which had been torpedoed twice without warning, with the loss of two American lives. The news passed verbally through the chamber as the President was still speaking. It hardened both parties in their already assumed positions: the pacifists against letting American ships sail to the same fate, and the pro-Allied group in favor of arming the ships to show they would not be frightened off the seas by German *schrecklichkeit*.

On Tuesday morning Lansing returned and was shown Zimmermann's "amazing message" by Assistant Secretary Phillips as soon as he reached his office. Here was the very blunder he had been hoping those blundering Germans would make. From Polk he learned that the Bernstorff copy had still not been obtained, but Western Union was weakening and early results were expected. At eleven Lansing went to the White House to see the President. He went armed with something Polk had found for him in the State Department's own files—evidence of "an exceptionally long message of some one thousand groups" that had come through for Bernstorff over the State Department cable on January 17. It was the proof of Zimmermann's sardonic twist of humor in using America's good offices for his plot against America. The President, like Queen Victoria, was not amused.

"Good Lord! Good Lord!" he exclaimed, outraged to the point of intemperate language when confronted by the full effrontery of the Germans. Conscious of his own share in having unneutrally lent the cable privilege to Germany—and of the embarrassing fact that the British must know about it—he felt peculiarly sensitive on the point. And when Wilson was touched personally, as by Madero's murder or Huerta's defiance, he could become very angry.

Lansing, whom Daniels called "mousy" and Page, in one of his more disgusted moments, disparaged as a "library lawyer," was in truth a correct and careful soul whose contribution to the flood of postwar memories revealed little of his feelings at dramatic moments. But a surge of I-told-you-so satisfaction must have warmed even that proper bosom when he informed Wilson how Zimmermann had sent the telegram. For once he was in the position of having to hold back the President. He cautioned against giving out the telegram officially lest it look like an attempt to influence Congress, and advised waiting at least until Polk should secure the confirmatory copy from Western Union. Angry as he was, Wilson could see the force of this argument and agreed to wait. But so deeply did he feel the German insult that he actually asked Page to thank Balfour for information of "such inestimable value" and to convey his very great appreciation of "so marked an act of friendliness on the part of the British government." Neutrality had begun to slip.

Lansing returned to the State Department, a happier man than he had been in months, and there found Polk in proud possession of Bernstorff's telegram from the files of Western Union. From Mexico an answer came through from Ambassador Fletcher, saying Carranza was absent from the capital but that Foreign Minister Aguilar had denied any knowledge of Zimmermann's proposal. In fact Aguilar knew all about it, for Eckhardt had begun negotiations with him in Carranza's absence. And Aguilar had already taken it up with the Japanese. This was reported to Zimmermann by Eckhardt in a telegram dated March 2, in which he said that, a visit to Carranza at Querétaro being inopportune, he had sounded out the Foreign Minister on February 20. "He willingly took the matter into consideration and thereupon had a conversation which lasted an hour and a half with the Japanese Minister, the substance of which is unknown to me. He subsequently went away to see the President, where he was staying at the time." This was, of course, unknown in Washington.

Late Tuesday night it became known that La Follette had rounded up ten Senators to filibuster against the Armed Ship Bill. Wilson had precipitated a fight, and now he had got it. Next morning, Wednesday, he decided that the Zimmermann telegram must be made public and called Lansing to tell him so. He said he wanted a conference with two other members of the Cabinet, McAdoo and Burleson, to discuss the best method of releasing it. Later he called back to say they were up at the Hill and could not be reached, another way of saying he preferred to act alone, for it can hardly be supposed a Presidential summons could not reach two Cabinet members in the Senate visitors' gallery.

While the President was conferring with himself, the State Department wired the text obtained from Western Union to the American embassy in London for confirmation. Now word came down from the Capitol that Senator Stone of Mississippi, Democratic Chairman of the Foreign Relations Committee and therefore the administration's captain in charge of the Armed Ship Bill, had come out against the bill and declined to lead it through Congress. Next in seniority was Senator Hitchcock of Nebraska, who was so uniformly pacifist as to be classed as pro-German. He had in fact voted against the bill in committee.

At 4 P.M. Wilson telephoned Lansing to say he wanted the telegram released for the morning papers and suggested that Senator Hitchcock be invited to come down and look it over first. Twenty minutes later Hitchcock arrived at the Department and listened while Lansing read him the intercepted German message. It was at this moment, about four-thirty in the afternoon of February 28, that the chemistry of the Zimmermann telegram began acting upon the American public in the person of the Senator from Nebraska. It shocked Senator Hitchcock as it was to shock the whole body of neutralist, pacifist, and pro-German sentiment into a sudden realization of German hostility to America. He confessed that it was a "dastardly plot" and would certainly cause a tremendous sensation. In answer as to whether it was authentic, Lansing replied he would vouch for it and asked Hitchcock to inform Senator Stone of its contents. Hitchcock then consented to undertake leadership of the Armed Ship Bill, which, like the President, he hoped might help to keep the country out of war.

The next immediate problem was to release the telegram to the press as the President had directed, but the question was, who was to sponsor it? Lansing was still anxious to keep it from appearing too obviously a move to influence Congress, so it was decided to release the news unofficially through the Associated Press. At six that evening E. M. Hood of the A.P. was called to Lansing's home, where he was given a paraphrase of the text and a briefing of the circumstances, and pledged to secrecy as to where and how he had obtained the greatest scoop of the war.

The story broke in eight-column headlines in the morning papers of Thursday, March 1. The *Times* proclaimed:

GERMANY SEEKS ALLIANCE AGAINST U.S.
ASKS JAPAN AND MEXICO TO JOIN HER;
FULL TEXT OF HER PROPOSAL MADE PUBLIC

The *World* offered a symphony of subheads that extended halfway down the page:

MEXICO AND JAPAN ASKED BY GERMANY
TO ATTACK U.S. IF IT ENTERED THE WAR;
BERNSTORFF A LEADING FIGURE IN PLOT

President Had Note of January 19 in which Foreign Secretary Zimmermann Told of Coming Ruthlessness and Sought Alliance with Mexico; Texas, Arizona and New Mexico to be Reconquered. Carranza to Convey German Proposals to Japan—Bernstorff, as Chief of Diplomats Concerned, Believed to Have Directed Conspiracy—Was to Have Kept U.S. Neutral if Possible—This Plot the Culmination of German Secret Activity and Discovery of It Is Believed to Explain Peculiar Policy of Mexican Government in Seeking to Promote Embargoes. Public Will Be Amazed if All Evidence of Plots Is Made Public by Government.

"Profound sensation," Lansing noted, and it was nationwide. Not even Admiral Hall could have asked for more. The public might have been even more angered if it had been told by what channel Zimmermann transmitted his instructions, but that embarrassing fact never leaked out. One reporter got near enough to write that the telegram had been sent by a secret means which the government now knows, "but does not care to disclose"—an understandable reluctance.

The A.P.'s story had given no hint how the telegram had been obtained. It began simply, "The A.P. is enabled to reveal . . ." gave the facts of Zimmermann's proposed alliance, stated that a copy was in the possession of the government, and went on to recall the history of German machinations in Mexico. It contained only one error, but one that was to cause a lot of trouble. In briefing the A.P. correspondent, Lansing inherited the difficulty that hampered Page and Hall before him—of saying enough to convince but not so much as to give away the arch-secret of the deciphered code. Either through a misunderstanding or in the hurry of putting together the story, Hood wrote that the Zimmermann telegram had been in the President's hands since he broke off relations with Germany, that is since February 3, when, in fact, he had not learned about it until February 24.

When Congressmen came to the Capitol on Thursday morning, newspapers screaming the German plot were in every hand. Congress "is stirred to its depths today," reported the New York *Sun*. The House erupted in patriotic oratory and passed the Armed Ship Bill, 403 to 13. Not so the Senate. Debate on the bill having been postponed by a maneuver, the Senators plunged into a rhetorical orgy on the authenticity of the Zimmermann telegram. It was precipitated by one among them whose steel-trap mind instantly perceived, on reading his morning paper, that Wilson and war were delivered into his hands. This was Senator Henry Cabot Lodge of Massachusetts, the friend and ally of Theodore Roosevelt, spokesman of preparedness and pro-Allied sentiment, despiser of Wilson, whose unrelenting goad he had been for two years.

"As soon as I saw it," Lodge confided to Roosevelt, "I felt it would arouse the country more than anything else that has happened." If the President could be got to say it was authentic, at one stroke he would be "tied up." He would have given the country a national reason to be enraged at Germany and be unable to dissociate himself from the result. He had provided, gloated Lodge, the very instrument that would be of "almost unlimited use in forcing the situation."

Immediately upon reaching the Senate, Lodge introduced a resolution asking for a statement by the President on the Zimmermann telegram. Then he sat back and watched the play unfold exactly as he could have wished. All the pacifist Senators promptly voiced the most sinister suspicions as to the origins of the telegram, and the more they argued the more, of course, they were forcing upon Wilson the necessity of publicly vouching for it. How had it been obtained? from whom? when? Senator Stone wanted to know. He fastened upon the one error in the A.P. story and attached the worst motives to Wilson's supposed suppression of the telegram for four weeks and his release of it at this particular time. He darkly suggested that an interested belligerent government was behind the affair and proposed an amendment demanding to know if this in fact was the case.

"Did this information come from London? Was it given to us by that government? . . . That is all I am asking at this time," he said. His voice and manner clearly stated that, if the answer was yes, the whole Zimmermann story must be regarded as nothing but a British trick.

Other Senators were more impressed by the German threat. "The public mind has been inflamed by this publication like a bolt," declared Senator Thomas of Colorado, his wrath getting the better of his grammar, "and we share that excited condition." How it was obtained is irrelevant, said Senator Williams of Mississippi; the only question should be, does the telegram exist and is it authentic? Up jumped Irish Senator O'Gorman from New York to renew the charge that it could all be traced to perfidious Albion. He was supported by another Democrat, Senator Tillman of Arkansas, who said the telegram was a lie. Senator Smith of Michigan said it was "a forgery and a sham born in the brain of a scoundrel and a tool." There was no lack of senior statesmen to thus rush in who were soon to wish they hadn't.

While the uproar continued, down at the State Department the sophisticated gentlemen of the press, determined not to be taken in, were hurling questions at Secretary Lansing. He told them firmly that the American government was satisfied that the telegram was authentic, and hinted that their insistence on further revelations might endanger the life of the agent responsible. He left the impression that a daring spy had got hold of the telegram in Mexico or Washington or possibly even in Germany. The reporters went off happily to a carnival of cloak-and-dagger tales that burgeoned in the press for weeks, until every newspaper had its favorite story of the provenance of the telegram and readers followed earnestly the adventures of reporters who galloped off in all directions to track down clues.

On its first day in public, however, the telegram was getting some bad notices. When Lansing, after the press receded, learned of the Lodge Resolution, he realized that some further official statement could not be avoided. He sent off a message, hurriedly drafted in pencil by Polk, to Page in London, saying it was most urgent, in view of attempts to discredit the telegram, that Page or someone else in the Embassy personally decipher the Western Union text in order "to strengthen our position and enable us to state we had secured the Zimmermann note from our own people." Then he went to work to draw up a report for the President to sign, in readiness for the Lodge Resolution.

It was now afternoon, and up on the Hill horrid suspicions were still flooding the Senate air. It was unfortunate that the President's warmest defender should have been the not very savory Senator Fall of New Mexico, the oil magnate of future Teapot Dome fame, who made an impassioned speech declaring he had never heard of such insinuations against a President since the impeachment proceedings against Andrew Johnson. Actually Senator Fall loathed Wilson—because of his Mexican policy—but as his one function as Senator was to bring about intervention in Mexico, he perforce welcomed the Zimmermann telegram toward that end. After him Senator Oscar Underwood of Alabama defended Zimmermann on the ground that he was merely instructing his envoy in Mexico what to do in case the United States should declare war on Germany, a perfectly proper procedure taken with no "unfriendly intention" (!) toward the United States.

Much was to be made of this point by pacifists in America as well as by Zimmermann himself and others in Germany. The argument could have been exploded at once by publication of Zimmermann's follow-up telegram of February 5 instructing Eckhardt not to wait for war with America but to contract the alliance "even now," which proved that Zimmermann had not made his proposal contingent upon America's entering the war but had asked for action while she was still neutral. But the "even now" telegram was, for some reason that is even now unclear, never made public during the war. Possibly Hall forbade mention of it because it had been sent directly to Eckhardt and its publication would have given the Germans a valuable clue in locating the point where access to their secret had been had. Possibly the American government—if it knew about the "even now" message at all—refrained from using it from a desire to give Carranza leeway to repudiate the very idea of joining Germany against the United States. If so, the hope was vain. Carranza never obliged. Whatever the reason for withholding Zimmermann's second telegram, the fact is, its existence did not come to light until the postwar Investigating Committee of the German Republic published it in 1920.

At six in the evening the Lodge Resolution, amended so as to ask the President for all information he could safely give instead of, as originally, asking for his opinion of the telegram's authenticity, was voted unanimously. The change did not matter to Lodge, who was satisfied with anything that would publicly tie the President to the telegram. With adjournment only three days off, the Senate was working late, and before that night was over they were to have the President's answer.

Whether Wilson did not see the implications of the Lodge Resolution, or whether he was so angry at Zimmermann's perfidy and at the opposition to his Armed Ship Bill that he did not care, is a question no one can answer. Whether Lansing understood the implications is another matter. Probably he did. He had his German blunder at last and he certainly had no wish to let the President or the country escape its effect. He did not wait for confirmation from Page and he certainly hurried the President along. He tells in his memoirs how he had to leave the Department before the reply to Lodge was completed, how he arranged to have a clerk bring it to him at the Italian embassy, where he was dining that night, how he left the table to sign it, how he arranged by telephone to have the clerk passed by the White House guards to bring it without loss of time to Wilson. For once Wilson did not retire to think. He read over the report, which stated that the government was in possession of evidence establishing the telegram as authentic, that it had been "procured by this Government during the present week," and that no further information could be disclosed. He signed it and sent it off to the Senate, where it was received at 8 P.M. Lodge's trap had snapped shut.

"We have tied the German note to Wilson," reported Lodge triumphantly to Roosevelt. "This, I think, is a great thing. One would think the note would make the whole country demand war. . . . We have got Wilson in a position where he cannot deny it."

And Lodge, his greatest enemy, added the fairest statement made then or since on Wilson's terrible dilemma: "He does not mean to go to war but I think he is in the grip of events."

Next day, Friday, March 2, was Cabinet day. The Cabinet, which had not been consulted at any point in the affair up to this time, now discussed in anxiety what steps to take if Zimmermann disavowed the telegram. Stunned and incredulous at the publication of the message, Germany had up to now maintained a blanket of silence behind which frantic questioning was going on.

In America Wilson's statement had satisfied many minds but by no means all. It had had no effect whatever on Senators Stone and O'Gorman and the rest of the eleven willful men who, at that moment, led by La Follette and Norris of Nebraska, were well into their filibuster against the Armed Ship Bill, with only forty-five hours to go. They were to succeed and provoke Wilson's most memorable remark. Other powerful voices were equally unimpressed. Hearst instructed his editors, *after* the President verified the telegram, to treat it as "in all probability a fake and forgery." George Sylvester Viereck, editor of *The Fatherland,* leader of pro-German sentiment and secretly a German agent, unhesitatingly pronounced it a "brazen forgery planted by British agents," a "preposterous document, obviously faked."

Nor was it only German sympathizers and pacifists who were disinclined to believe it. On March 2 the distinguished gentlemen of the Round Table Dining Club, a gathering of the intellectual cream skimmed off the social and professional elite of New York, were discussing the Zimmermann sensation between oysters and port at the Knickerbocker Club. Elihu Root was present, and Joseph H. Choate, former Ambassador to England, former Attorney General Wickersham, Nicholas Murray Butler, and assorted bishops, bankers, editors, and lawyers. Members were allowed to bring guests but only such as other members "would be glad to greet." A guest that evening was Captain Guy Gaunt. Obviously this was no gathering of pro-Germans or neutralists. Yet, Gaunt reported to Admiral Hall, "they all went for me." Choate, as warm an Anglophile as any in America, "openly said that the Zimmermann note was a forgery and was practically unanimously supported by the whole bunch." When the Round Table Club wanted proofs, Captain Gaunt looked grave and asked if they really wanted details "where men's lives were at stake." When they asked him point-blank if he knew anything about it, he expressed surprise that "they should cross-examine me instead of accepting the word of their President." That silenced them.

When such a group as the Round Table was incredulous, it was no wonder the Cabinet was worried about the problem that had haunted the telegram from the beginning—how to authenticate it. Lansing had received a telegram from Page saying they were at work decoding the Western Union text and their results would follow soon. Edward Bell was indeed working without pause, with the help of de Grey and Room 40's code book, and his decryptment, confirming the original text, came in at the end of the day. Even the expectation of this, however, was no comfort, for while it would silence any remaining doubts in the government, supposing any to exist, it could not be used publicly without compromising Room 40. An unsolicited and unexpected confirmation arrived from the indefatigable Agent Cobb in El Paso, who wired that General Villa had recently left Parral with three thousand men, proclaiming that he was going "to help the Germans whip the United States and obtain Texas, Arizona, and California back for Mexico." The coincidence of the wording with that of the Zimmermann telegram was too striking to be missed and indicated that the Germans must have made a similar proposition to Villa or that he had learned of it somehow.

But this did not help the Cabinet in their problem of how to deal with a German denial, which they expected at any minute. Already the Mexicans, the Japanese, and Eckhardt had denied the telegram. Foreign Minister Aguilar lied flatly: "Up to today [March 2] the Mexican Government has not received from the Imperial German Government any proposition of alliance." The Japanese chargé d'affaires, who had recently spent an hour and a half discussing it with Aguilar, expressed his utter ignorance of the matter. Eckhardt's denial lacked a little something of the others' firmness, perhaps because he was nervously wondering where the betrayal had taken place. "If you must say something you may say the German Minister knows nothing about all this," he told newspapermen. Then he thought it might be a good idea to implicate Bernstorff. "You must go to Washington for your information," he added.

If, on top of these denials, Zimmermann challenged the United States to prove the authenticity of the telegram, the American government, restricted by its pledge of secrecy to Great Britain, would be unable to do it. The Cabinet could only agree to assert emphatically that they possessed conclusive evidence, and unhappily disperse.

Unbelievably, next morning, to the "profound amazement and relief," in Lansing's words, of everyone concerned, Zimmermann inexplicably admitted his authorship.

It was a second blunder, wrote Lansing, almost bemused with relief, of a most astounding kind. He thought it showed Zimmermann to be not at all astute and resourceful, for in admitting the truth he not only settled the question in American minds but threw away an opportunity to find out how we had obtained the message.

What led Zimmermann, who, despite Lansing, was both astute and rsourceful, to commit this historic boner, is not known. That he was too stunned to think clearly is unlikely, for the Germans had had two days to consider their answer and Germans do not issue official statements off the cuff. Probably he reasoned that since the Americans had somehow acquired a true version of the message they were likely also to have acquired some documentary proof of its authorship; therefore denial could only make him look foolish. This was logical but as not infrequent with logic, wrong.

At Zimmermann's press conference, just before the fatal words were spoken, William Bayard Hale, who was in Berlin as Hearst correspondent, tried to head him off. Hale was at this time and had been for two years a paid German agent, under actual contract to the German government at $15,000 a year as propaganda adviser to the German embassy in America, but this status was not known at the time and did not become known until much later.

"Of course Your Excellency will deny this story," Hale urged in a frantic signal to Zimmermann to toss back the grenade upon the United States. The Foreign Minister failed to take the hint. "I cannot deny it," he said. "It is true."

Obliged to Believe It

Zimmermann's admission shattered the indifference with which three-quarters of the United States had regarded the war until that moment. The nation sat up and gasped, "They mean us!" Nothing since the outbreak of war had so openly conveyed a deliberately hostile intent toward Americans, and nothing had so startled opinion across the country. Back in 1915 the *Lusitania* had shocked the nation, but that shock was humanitarian, not personal. This was different. This was Germany proposing to attack the United States, conspiring with America's neighbor to snatch American territory; worse, conspiring to set an Oriental foe upon America's back. This was a direct threat upon the body of America, which most Americans had never dreamed was a German intention. It penetrated to the midpoint of the continent, even to Omaha, Nebraska, a thousand miles from either ocean and a thousand miles from Mexico. "The issue shifts," soberly stated the Omaha *World Herald,* "from Germany against Great Britain to Germany against the United States."

Wilson had said the American people would not believe that Germany was hostile to them "unless and until we are obliged to believe it." And, in judging the submarine issue to be no cause for believing it, the American people, on the whole, agreed with him. Torpedoings of merchant ships and loss of noncombatant lives, including American, convinced Americans of German frightfulness but not of German hostility to themselves. Despite Washington's concentration on neutral rights and freedom of the seas, the mass of Americans, who never saw a seacoast, could not be worked into war fever over an international lawyers' doctrine nor aroused to a fighting mood over persons who chose to cross the ocean on belligerent boats in wartime. Besides, they had got used to maritime atrocities, had grown accustomed to official crises over ship sinkings. The *Lusitania,* the *Sussex,* the *Arabic* had followed one after another, provoking Wilson's notes, Bryan's resignation, endless correspondence in incomprehensible diplomatic language, even some quite comprehensible threats and ultimatums, all mixed up with similar eruptions vis-à-vis the British over contraband and blacklisting. It was all very confusing and—to the majority of the country—remote.

But the Prussian Invasion Plot, as the newspapers labeled the Zimmermann telegram, was clear as a knife in the back and near as next door. Everybody understood it in an instant. When Germany plotted attack upon United States territory there could no longer be any question of neutrality. Overnight the Midwest isolationist press acknowledged it. The Chicago *Daily Tribune* warned its readers they must realize now, "without delay, that Germany recognizes us as an enemy," and the United States could no longer expect to keep out of "active participation in the present conflict." The Cleveland *Plain Dealer* said there was "neither virtue nor dignity" in refusing to fight now. The Oshkosh *Northwestern* said the note had turned pacifists, critics, and carpers into patriots overnight. The Detroit *Times* said, "It looks like war for this country." All these papers had been ardently neutral until Zimmermann shot an arrow in the air and brought down neutrality like a dead duck.

His admission exploded the disbelief in the telegram which the pacifists and pro-Germans had clung to when the blow first fell upon them. George Sylvester Viereck said it ended pro-Germanism in the United States. Nothing the American government could have said could have convinced the doubters, but when Zimmermann said, "It is true," he himself silenced the talk of forgery and British trick. The German-Americans, of whom he had such fond hopes, retreated across their hyphen to take their stand, somewhat sullenly, on the American side. In Minneapolis, where large numbers of them were concentrated, the

Journal admitted it was no longer possible for German-Americans to be loyal to both their native and their adopted countries, and the *Tribune* said Germany's bid to bring in Japan against us was "equivalent to an act of war." In Milwaukee, home of the German brewing industry, that city's *Journal* feared that Zimmermann's act would cause a "revulsion of sentiment" among Germany's many friends in the Middle West, and this proved to be the case. Such papers as the Chicago *Staats-Zeitung,* the Detroit *Abend-Post,* the Cincinnati *Volksblatt* and *Freie Presse,* and the St. Louis *Amerika,* several of which had earlier pronounced the telegram a fraud, were now sheepishly silent or hurried to proclaim their loyalty to America.

Midwest sentiment paled beside the outraged indignation of the Pacific Coast and the roar that came out of Texas. The San Antonio *Light* asserted with "quiet modesty and simple truth" that if a German-Mexican-Japanese army overran Texas, not a Texan would be left alive unless he was across the border fighting his way back. The El Paso *Times* grew purple at the spectacle of Prussian militarism "writhing in the slime of intrigue," and out in California the Sacramento *Bee* echoed its outrage at Germany's "treacherous enmity, underhanded, nasty intriguing."

Editors from Vermont to Florida to Oregon expressed a sense of Zimmermann's having crystallized feelings everywhere. The Springfield (Massachusetts) *Republican* said that nothing else but this threat of hostile action to American territory could have so solidified the American people, and the Los Angeles *Tribune* said it extinguished all differences. These were overstatements, because editorial opinion never truly reflects the diversity of private opinions. Pacifism was not extinguished, but it was outweighed by a sense that America was now involved and, willing or not, would have to fight.

In the already Anglophile East the press tended to regard the Zimmermann note as a blessing that would awaken the rest of the country to an awareness of the German threat, and the Eastern papers did their best to warm up that awareness. The Buffalo *Express* let itself go in a horrendous imaging of "hordes of Mexicans under German officers, sweeping into Texas, New Mexico and Arizona." The New York *American* on its own authority added Russia to the proposed combination of Germany, Mexico, and Japan, and depicted this unholy quadruple alliance overwhelming and carving up our country: Mexico, it said, would retake the Southwest and restore it to barbarism; Japan would take the Far West and "orientalize" it; Germany and Russia would enslave generations of Americans in the payment of vast war indemnities. "Citizens, prepare!" it commanded. "The hours are short, the days are few . . ."

By the middle of March, when the Zimmerman telegram had had two weeks to take effect, the American people, by and large, realized they would have to face up to war. The press was already ahead of the President. Individual pacifists were still vocal, but the majority of the people were mentally (if not militarily) prepared. They were not calling for war; they were simply waiting—waiting for Wilson. Far in the van, Theodore Roosevelt was bugling for action. If Germany's plot to get Mexico and Japan to join her in "dismembering" this country was not an overt act of war, he told a public meeting, then Lexington and Bunker Hill (rather an odd comparison) were not overt acts of war. If Wilson does not go to war now, he wrote to Lodge, "I shall skin him alive."

Meanwhile discovery had not stopped Zimmermann's efforts to bring Mexico into the war. In their urgent need of a cause to keep America occupied on her own side of the Atlantic, the Germans increased, if anything, their efforts to set off an explosion in Latin America. Alarming reports kept coming in of German activity in Guatemala, on Mexico's southern frontier, and in Salvador, just below Guatemala. Eckhardt and the German Minister in Guatemala, Herr Lehmann, were reported to have Carranza's support in a design to ignite a train of revolutions down through the little republics of Central America. Regimes friendly to the United States were to be turned out and a federated state of Central America, stretching from Mexico to Panama, set up with a pro-German president.

In Mexico itself German propaganda campaigned to provoke anti-Yankee incidents of the Villa variety that would precipitate American intervention and the long-sought war with Mexico. *El Democrata,* the German legation's organ, published a series on American aggression against Mexico, past, future, and imaginary. Monterey, a railroad junction of lines connecting with Tampico, Mexico City, and the Pacific Coast, suddenly found itself host to an influx of German's from southern Mexico. German agents were surveying Mexico's west coast for submarine and air bases. General Pershing's headquarters reported a German junta at Cordoba near Veracruz. Agent Cobb wired, "My men on track of big German-Villa combination." Consul Canada reported Germans and Mexican officials thick at Veracruz—"They have secret meetings every night."

American pressure upon Carranza to repudiate the Germans availed no more than Wilson's efforts had once done upon General Huerta to make him salute the flag. Even when Ambassador Fletcher journeyed to see the Mexican President personally at Guadalajara, Carranza remained truculently uncooperative. He would only say that no German proposition had been made to him and avoided answering the question of what he would do if it were. He kept returning, reported the Ambassador, to the embargo proposal.

This was far from satisfactory, but Zimmermann had no more success. He was frantically trying to find out how the telegram had been betrayed and at the same time trying to gain Carranza's consent to become a German ally. He pelted Eckhardt with telegrams, of which the improbable fact may be recorded that they were all sent in the same code as the one already betrayed. Admiral Hall had rightly judged the Germany character. It did not permit them even to consider the possibility that a code devised by Germans could be solved by lesser minds. As Hall had counted upon, they decided that, through someone's carelessness, a decoded copy must have fallen into the enemy's hands and either Bernstorff or Eckhardt would have to be the scapegoat. The circumstance that Bernstorff was aboard a twelve-day boat crossing the Atlantic on his way home when the telegram was published gave Eckhardt that much time in which to shift the blame, and he lost none of it. Protesting his blamelessness even before anyone had time to accuse him, he rushed off a telegram to Zimmermann on March 1: "Treachery or indiscretion here out of the question; therefore apparently it happened in U.S.A., or cipher 13040 is compromised." Eckhardt had the wit to see that Zimmermann's second telegram, the "even now" order, was crucial and he hurried to assure Zimmermann that it had not been published, adding, "I denied everything here."

Zimmermann's answer began, "Please burn compromising instructions," surely the most futile closing of a stable door in history. Equally unnecessarily he reported his admission of "No. 1," the original telegram, and added, "In connection with this, emphasize that instructions were only to be carried out after declaration of war by America. Dispatch No 11" (the second telegram) "is of course being kept strictly secret here also." It is not often that arrogance is the mother of naïveté, but only the Germans' arrogant confidence in the superiority of their code can explain their naïve belief that No. 11 could remain secret after No. 1 was known.

Never had the cryptographers of Room 40 so enjoyed their work as when they followed the increasingly agonized exchanges between Berlin and Eckhardt. Still using the same code to inquire how the code was betrayed, the German Foreign Office cabled Eckhardt on March 21, "Most secret. Decipher personally. Please cable in same cipher who deciphered Nos. 1 and 11, how the originals and decodes were kept and in particular whether both dispatches were kept in the same place." Eckhardt, recognizing the scapegoat maneuver, replied that both dispatches had been deciphered by his secretary, Magnus, and were kept from the knowledge of other legation officials. The originals were "burned by Magnus and the ashes scattered," and until they were burned had been kept "in an absolutely secure steel safe procured especially for the purpose and installed in Magnus's bedroom."

Even the steel safe and the scattered ashes did not satisfy Berlin. "Various indications suggest that treachery was committed in Mexico," they told Eckhardt. "The greatest caution is indicated." And he was again ordered to "burn all compromising material."

Eckhardt angrily retorted that greater caution "than is always exercised here would be impossible." All telegrams were read to him by Magnus "at night, in a low voice." (Hilarity in Room 40.) His servant slept out and did not understand German. No one had the combination of the safe but himself and Magnus. Then he added some hints about Bernstorff. Kinkel, one of the Washington embassy officials who had joined Eckhardt's staff after Bernstorff left, had told him that in Bernstorff's embassy "even secret telegrams were known to the whole staff," and two copies were always made. This raised the possibility of carbon copies and waste paper, he hinted. As a final protest he said that if he were not officially exculpated, he and Magnus would insist on a "judicial investigation."

Berlin did not like the sound of that at all, for no one knew what an investigation might turn up. They quickly reversed themselves. "Hardly conceivable that betrayal took place in Mexico," they mollified Eckhardt. "No blame rests on either you or Magnus."

Now the onus shifted to Bernstorff and the famous mystery of the Swedish trunk. Already he was the obvious villain in American minds. They knew little of Zimmermann and nothing of Eckhardt, but the elegant Count was a familiar figure whose complicity in the sabotage activities of Papen, Boy-Ed, and Rintelen was already known. Indeed, in the popular mind, Count Bernstorff was the Dr. Moriarty of the plot. Headlines had proclaimed him the "chief agent" and called the telegram the climax of his embassy's "intrigues in this hemisphere." In the days between the breaking of relations and the publication of the telegram, the papers had been full of stories about the elaborate arrangements for his departure with all his staff, consuls, wives, families, and retainers. Negotiations with Britain for his safe conduct, his farewell reception in the Red Parlor of the embassy, his last words to the press, his departure, "snugly buttoned in fur coat and spats," from Union Station in Washington, his embarkation on the Danish liner *Frederik VIII* at New York with a party totaling two hundred persons, and a last-minute two-day delay before sailing were all chronicled in detail.

The British had agreed to grant safe conduct to the German party only if the ship halted at Halifax for search. Upon her arrival at Halifax on February 16 the *Frederik VIII* was instantly covered by a swarm of Canadian contraband officials who instituted a search of epic proportions into the baggage, cabins, clothing, and persons of every passenger. After it had gone for a week, during which none of the German party was allowed ashore, speculation and protests mounted. The British blandly said that the "marked partiality" of the German passengers for quantities of cotton pajamas and extra pairs of rubber heels necessitated extra care in view of the contraband on cotton and rubber. A hint that phonograph records, which the Germans were said to be taking home in remarkable numbers, might contain messages in code, required the search to be extended further. In all, the *Frederik VIII* was held up in Halifax for twelve days.

The truth was that Admiral Hall, who had been a constant reader of Bernstorff's passionate efforts to keep his government from provoking America into war, was taking no chances with the Ambassador's powers of persuasion. Once home, and in personal contact with the German leaders, he might even yet persuade them to accept Wilson's peace mediation. Hall wanted the Zimmermann telegram to take effect first. It was he who arranged matters to delay Bernstorff's homecoming. Not until after the telegram was sent off to Washington and had had three days to gestate was the *Frederik VIII* allowed to leave Halifax, on February 27.

Bernstorff was on the high seas all during the uproar. On his arrival at Christiania, where the ship was diverted by storm, he expressed surprise at the sensation and, with the habitual insouciance with which he always greeted revelations of German intrigues and sabotage in America, said, "It's news to me." Hurriedly briefed by the German Minister to Norway, who was on hand to meet him, he was able, when he reached Berlin two days later, to fall in with Zimmermann's prepared defense—that the proposal was a perfectly correct preliminary which had never been communicated to the Mexican government. He conferred with Bethmann and Zimmermann the same day and was said to be working on a report on how the telegram might have been discovered.

The whole German press had obediently taken the line that Mexico would never have heard about the alliance if the United States had not obtained the telegram by "treachery" and disclosed it, in a typical piece of Wilsonian hypocrisy, to influence Congress. In fact, according to them, the affair was an American "plot," not a German one. Doubtless Zimmermann told as few people as possible —if any—about the existence of his "even now" order and Eckhardt's replies. Whether Bernstorff was told or not, he subscribed to the official story and smoothly denied that the German government had ever attempted to influence Latin American countries "in any sense hostile to the United States." All those tales of German intrigues in Haiti, Cuba, and Colombia, he said—omitting Mexico —were "fairy tales."

Among the many friends to welcome Bernstorff at the station were several ladies who, according to reporters, screamed with delight upon his arrival. His circle of adorers was evidently as extensive at home as in America. But the German press greeted the returning Ambassador coolly, and for this the story of the Swedish trunk was responsible. The story came out of London, where, it was said, the Foreign Office was interesting itself in the contents of a trunk full of Swedish diplomatic papers which had been taken off the *Frederik VIII*, where it had been placed among Count Bernstorff's luggage by the Swedish Minister in Washington. The implication was that the trunk contained Bernstorff's most secret papers layered between Swedish documents and locked up under the Swedish seal. On the ground of this alleged violation of neutrality, the British had seized the trunk and were examining it. They let it be known that, before they had taken possession of it, its seals had been broken, somewhere between New York and Halifax, that is, between February 9 and February 16. The dates fitted; the press leaped to the bait. Here was the answer to the question of the hour—how the telegram had been obtained. Some clever American agent must have got at the trunk in New York harbor and extracted the original from among Bernstorff's papers. The atmosphere of espionage and intrigue already woven about the *Frederik VIII* added verisimilitude.

A Swedish trunk did, in fact, exist, and the British, remembering how obliging the Swedes had been in the matter of the cable Roundabout, had, in fact, seized it. But the hints about the broken seals were a plant by Admiral Hall to encourage the belief that the telegram had been discovered in America.

Bernstorff was the victim. Together with Eckhardt's insinuations about careless carbon copies, the Swedish trunk convinced the Kaiser, among others. Although Bernstorff requested an immediate audience, the Kaiser refused to received him, and despite his arrival from America, with eight years' experience of that country, at a time when war with America was expected at any moment, the Kaiser delayed seven weeks before consenting to talk to him at all. Later in the war, when Chancellor Bethmann-Hollweg fell from office and Bernstorff was mentioned as a possible successor, the Kaiser's aversion was said to be one factor that eliminated him.

To Zimmermann, not yet entirely off the hook, the appearance of a scapegoat was fortuitous. He had been questioned on March 5 at a secret session of the Reichstag steering committee. After a six-hour debate, and despite some rumblings by the Socialists, the members dutifully and unanimously endorsed his proposal to Mexico and Japan, while expressing "regrets" that it had been revealed. The press, on his behalf, scolded the public for criticizing him. Had they not always complained of German diplomats' failures to make friends and allies? Here was Herr Zimmermann energetically rounding up allies; certainly he should not be condemned for it. Premature disclosure, though unfortuante, was not his fault but a mean American trick.

Even so, Zimmermann's position was not a happy one. He still had to face a public debate in the Reichstag, which took place on March 29. He had not taken his own advice to Eckhardt to "burn compromising instructions," and the critical second telegram remained in his files to be discovered after the war. But he remained sublimely confident that the betrayal of the original one was a fluke and the second one unknown. Carranza, he lied to the Reichstag, would have heard nothing of the alliance up to the present if the United States had not revealed it. How the Americans obtained the dispatch, "which went to America in a special code," we do not know, he said. That was a misfortune, but to seek allies was natural, and the Americans were "not at all justified in getting so excited about our action." Nor could his proposal be considered far-fetched, based as it was on ancient feuds between the United States and Mexico and on well-known anagonism between the United States and Japan. "I maintain," he said stoutly, "that these antagonisms are stronger than those which, despite the war, exist between Germany and Japan" (and who shall say he was wrong? As an Axis designer, Zimmermann was merely ahead of his time). Who better, he asked, could persuade the Japanese to change sides than the Mexicans, who were on good terms with them and of "a like race"? The Reichstag gave him a vote of confidence.

Nevertheless Zimmermann knew success would be his best defense. He continued exerting every effort to turn Mexico into an active ally. "Please state sums necessary to carry out our policy," he wired Eckhardt on April 13. "Arrangements are being made on this side to transfer considerable sums. If possible include amount required for arms, et cetera."

Even the lure of those "sums" was not enough to reassure Carranza. The hullabaloo had scared him off. On April 14 it was Eckhardt's sad duty to telegraph Zimmermann that the President of Mexico had decided to stay neutral. "He says the alliance has been wrecked by premature publication but might become necessary at a later stage." He promises that, if he is drawn into the war despite his desire to stay neutral, "we can discuss the matter again."

Zimmermann, planning the coup that would keep America out of Europe, had dreamed of a hero's welcome for himself when he should bring off a Mexican alliance. Upon Carranza's refusal, his hopes crashed—the doors of Valhalla banged shut. His career did not long survive the disappointment. Four months later he lost office, along with the Chancellor, and never held it again. He died in 1940 at the age of eighty-one.

While Zimmermann was still trying to draw in Mexico, events in America were hurrying toward the brink. On March 4, Congress, gagged by the Senate filibuster, had gone out of session without passing the Armed Ship Bill. Wilson raged at the American government's being thus rendered "helpless and contemptible" by "a little band of willful men representing no opinion but their own." An extra session, required by the Senate's refusal to vote the appropriation bills, was scheduled to convene on April 16 so that the country would not be left, as Lodge said, "alone with Wilson" for nine months. Until it met again, the President held the helm alone. On March 9, using his executive authority, he gave the order to arm the ships anyway. He did not, however, take any action on an urgent message from Page warning that, failing a United States government loan, Britain could not buy another gun or crate of goods from America.

On March 18 three American ships were sunk without warning by U-boats. On March 19 occurred the most significant event of the war prior to America's entrance— the preliminary revolution in Russia that overthrew the Czar and established the parliamentary Kerensky government. With the disappearance of the Czar, the black sheep vanished from the democratic herd and the war could now be safely said to be a war to save democracy. On March 20 the President met the Cabinet and heard them unanimously declare for war, even including the pacifist Daniels, who was close to tears. As was his habit, Wilson left the room without declaring himself. That night he must have made up his mind. The next day, March 21, he reconvened Congress for April 2, two weeks earlier than scheduled, to hear a message concerning "grave matters of national policy."

The night before he spoke the public words that were to mark a chasm in our history, he spoke other words to a friend, Frank Cobb, the liberal editor of the New York *World,* whom he asked to visit him at the White House. They have the quality of last words, like Sir Walter Raleigh's poem before his execution. He could see no alternative, Wilson said, although he had tried every way he knew to avoid war. He said that once the American people entered the war, freedom and tolerance and level-headedness would be forgotten. Moreover, a declaration of war would mean "that Germany would be beaten and so badly beaten that there would be a dictated peace, a victorious peace. . . . At the end of the war there will be no bystanders with sufficient power to influence the terms. There won't be any peace standards left to work with." And even at this moment the cry broke from him, "If there is any alternative, for God's sake, let's take it!"

But there was none. At eight-thirty next evening he drove up to the Capitol through the rain and went in to face a joint session. "With a profound sense of the solemn and even tragical character of the step I am taking," he advised Congress to "declare the recent course of the Imperial German Government to be in fact nothing less than war against the government and people of the United States," and to "formally accept the status of belligerent." Neutrality, he said, is no longer possible or desirable under the menace that lies "in the existence of autocratic governments backed by organized force which is controlled wholly by their will and not by the will of the people." He dwelt on the submarines as outlaws against the law of nations and on other proofs of the German government's intention to act against the security of the United States, referring specifically to the Zimmermann telegram. "That it [the German government] means to stir up enemies against us at our very doors, the intercepted note to the German Minister at Mexico is eloquent evidence. We accept this challenge of hostile purpose. . . ."

Packed into the chamber, the members of both Houses, the Supreme Court, the Cabinet, the diplomatic corps, the press, and the visitors who filled the gallery listened with every nerve. The peroration mounted to the phrases that everyone knows, as the speaker declared that the German government was a "natural foe of liberty," that "the world must be made safe for democracy," that "the right is more precious than peace," that America must fight "for the principles that gave her birth," that, "God helping her, she can do no other."

"A roar like a storm" greeted the President's address, wrote one reporter. Overseas the Allies heard it, in their moment of extremity. England, the fulcrum of the Allies, was bending; France was weakened to the point of exhaustion. Stalemated in the trenches, torpedoed on the seas, emptied of funds, they heard the sound of a huge, fresh, new ally coming to join them with ships and money and goods and men. The sound brought them the promise of victory. To an English historian, R. B. Mowat, the event was "one of the most dramatic in history."

To Americans it was the beginning of unwilled wedlock to the rest of the world. The question, what brought it about? has been asked ever since. Why did Wilson, who three months earlier had said it would be a "crime against civilization" to lead the United States into war, who cried out for an alternative even on the eve of war, decided at last that "the right is more precious than peace"? His April 2 summary of the nature of the enemy as "the natural foe of liberty" was equally true three months or six months, a year or two years earlier. The man who made the April 2 speech was the same man who wished to settle for peace without victory in January, who refused to believe that the Germans were hostile to us in February. Ambassador Page, writing in his diary, asks the inevitable question, "What made him change his mind? Just when and how did the President come to see the true nature of the Germans?" Was it Germany's declaration of unrestricted U-boat war on February 1 or was it, Page wondered, the Zimmermann telegram?

Certainly it was not the former, for the President had refused to believe that the Germans meant to do what they declared they would until they should prove it by an "overt act." This came on March 18, when the three American merchant ships were sunk with heavy loss of life. Within the next three days followed the solemn Cabinet meeting and the President's summons to Congress, which marks the point when he made up his mind. Would he have decided as he did without the telegram with its earlier revelation of Germany's overt hostility to America? Only Wilson can answer that, and he never did. One answer has been offered by a man whom the President trusted and made the recipient of all his papers. When Wilson, in the last letter he ever wrote, a week before his death, asked Ray Stannard Baker to write his official biography, he said, "I would rather have your interpretation than that of anyone else I know." Baker's judgment of the Zimmermann telegram is that "no single more devastating blow was delivered against Wilson's resistance to entering the war."

This is not to say that Wilson wanted neutrality the day before the telegram, and belligerency the day after. The telegram was not the only deciding factor upon the President. It was, rather, the last drop that emptied his cup of neutrality.

There were other factors too, not the least "the wonderful and heartening" overturn in Russia, which, he told Congress, now made that great nation "a fit partner for a League of Honor." Probably the nearest one can approximate the truth about what moved Wilson is to say that a combination of events brought him to a point where he had no alternative. As Lodge said, he was in the grip of events. As England's outspoken Lord Chancellor, Lord Birkenhead, said, "The United States were in fact kicked into the war against the strong and almost frenzied efforts of President Wilson."

The kick that did it, to the people whether or not to the President, was the Zimmermann telegram. It awoke that part of the country that had been undecided or indifferent before. It transformed, Lansing said, the apathy of the Western states into "intense hostility to Germany" and "in one day accomplished a change in sentiment and public opinion that otherwise would have required months to accomplish." It was not a theory or an issue but an unmistakable gesture that anyone could understand. It was the German boot planted upon our border. To the mass of Americans, who cared little and thought less about Europe, it meant that if they fought they would be fighting to defend America, not merely to extract Europe from its self-made quarrels. It put them in a frame of mind willing to accept Wilson's statement in April of the necessity of war.

Would they have been ready without the telegram? Probably not. Before it was published, the dominant feeling inspired by the war—always excepting pro-Ally New England—was the stubborn, if inglorious, slogan that elected Wilson four months before—"He kept us out of war." Afterward, so far as public organs of opinion can reveal it, the mood changed to one of recognition that war could no longer be evaded. Wilson knew this when he drafted his speech for the meeting of Congress on April 2. He knew that what he had to say would be accepted; that, in fact, he no longer had any excuse for not saying it. Until then he could afford to ignore all the goading of the Lodge and Roosevelt forces because he knew the country as a whole was not with them. After the public reaction to the Zimmermann telegram, even that excuse was taken from him. On March 17 the *Literary Digest* published a résumé of nationwide press comment on the telegram under the heading, "How Zimmermann United the United States." That was a fair estimate of published opinion, even if it ignored the unswerving LaFollettes and Norrises and Villards and that mute opinion which can never be weighed. It left Wilson bereft of the prop of public opinion which had so far sustained his struggle to keep the United States neutral. After the middle of March there was nothing to hold him back.

Had the telegram never been intercepted or never been

published, inevitably the Germans would have done something else that would have brought us in eventually. But the time was already late and, had we delayed much longer, the Allies might have been forced to negotiate. To that extent the Zimmermann telegram altered the course of history. But then, as Sir Winston Churchill has remarked, the course of history is always being altered by something or other—if not by a horseshoe nail, then by an intercepted telegram. In itself the Zimmermann telegram was only a pebble on the long road of history. But a pebble can kill a Goliath, and this one killed the American illusion that we could go about our business happily separate from other nations. In world affairs it was a German Minister's minor plot. In the lives of the American people it was the end of innocence.

Code Text of the Telegram

Edward Bell's copy of the decode made at the American embassy (National Archives, Foreign Affairs Branch, State Department Decimal File, 862.20212/81½. English translation added by the author).

This is the text with Bernstorff's slight alterations at the beginning, which Bernstorff forwarded to Eckhardt, and is the same as the text obtained by Admiral Hall in Mexico City which he gave to Ambassador Page.

130	(number of telegram)	—
13042	(code identification number)	—
13401	*Auswärtiges Amt*	Foreign Office
8501	*telegraphiert*	telegraphs
115	*Januar 16*	January 16
3528	*colon(:)*	colon(:)
416	*number 1*	no. 1
17214	*ganz geheim*	strictly secret
6491	*selbst*	yourself
11310	*zu*	to
18147	*entziffern*	decipher
18222	*stop(.)*	stop(.)
21560	*Wir*	We
10247	*beabsichtigen*	intend
11518	*am*	from the
23677	*ersten*	first
13605	*Februar*	February
3494	*un-*	un-
14963	*eingeschränkt*	restricted

98092	*U-boot*	U-boat
5905	*Krieg*	war
11311	*zu*	to
10392	*beginnen*	begin
10371	*stop(.)*	stop(.)
0302	*Es wird*	It will
21290	*versucht*	attempted
5161	*werden*	be
39695	*Vereiningten Staaten*	United States
23571	*trotzdem*	nevertheless
17504	*neutral*	neutral
11269	*zu*	to
18276	*erhalten*	keep
18101	*stop(.)*	stop(.)
0217	*Für den Fall*	In the event
0228	*dass dies*	that this
17694	*nicht*	not
4473	*gelingen*	succeed
22284	*sollte*	should
22200	*comma(,)*	comma(,)
19452	*schlagen*	offer
21589	*wir*	we
67893	*Mexico*	Mexico
5569	*auf*	on
13918	*folgender*	following
8958	*Grundlage*	terms
12137	*Bündnis*	alliance
1333	*vor*	(prefix of verb vorschlagen— to offer)
4725	*stop(.)*	stop(.)
4458	*Gemeinsam*	Together
5905	*Krieg*	war
17166	*führen*	make
13851	*stop(.)*	stop(.)
4458	*Gemeinsam*	Together
17149	*Friedenschluss*	peace
14471	*stop(.)*	stop(.)
6706	*Reichlich*	Generous
13850	*finanzielle*	financial
12224	*unterstützung*	support
6929	*und*	and
14991	*einverständnis*	understanding
7382	*unserer seits*	our part
15857	*dass*	that
67893	*Mexico*	Mexico
14218	*in*	in
36477	*Texas*	Texas

5870	*comma(,)*	comma(,)
17553	*New*	New
67893	*Mexico*	Mexico
5870	*comma(,)*	comma(,)
5454	*AR*	AR
16102	*IZ*	IZ
15217	*ON*	ON
22801	*A*	A
17138	*früher*	former
21001	*verloren*	lost
17388	*Gebiet*	territory
7446	*zurück*	back
23638	*erobern*	conquer
18222	*stop(.)*	stop(.)
6719	*Regelung*	Settlement
14331	*im*	in the
15021	*Einzelnen*	details
23845	*Euer Hoch-*	Your Excel-
	wohlgeboren	lency
3156	*überlassen*	to be left
23552	*stop(.)*	stop(.)
22096	*Sie*	You
21604	*wollen*	will
4797	*vorstehendes*	of the fore-
		going
9497	*dem*	the
22464	*Präsident*	President
20855	*streng*	in strictest
4377	*geheim*	secrecy
23610	*eröffen*	inform
18140	*comma(,)*	comma(,)
22260	*sobald*	as soon as
5905	*Kriegs*	war's
13347	*Ausbruch*	outbreak
20420	*mit*	with
39689	*Vereinigten*	
	Staaten	United States
13732	*fest*	certain
20667	*steht*	is
6929	*und*	and
5275	*Anregung*	suggestion
18507	*hinzufügen*	add
52262	*Japan*	Japan
1340	*von*	by
22049	*sich*	himself
13339	*aus*	from
11265	*zu*	to
22295	*sofortig*	immediately
10439	*beitretung*	join

14814	*einladen*	invite
4178	*(setze infinitiv mit zu—i.e., einzuladen)*	(form the infinitive—i.e., to invite)
6992	*und*	and
8784	*gleichzeitig*	at the same time
7632	*zwischen*	between
7357	*uns*	us
6926	*und*	and
52262	*Japan*	Japan
11267	*zu*	to
21100	*vermitteln*	mediate
21272	*stop(.)*	stop(.)
9346	*Bitte*	Please
9559	*den*	the
22464	*Präsident*	President
15874	*darauf*	of this
18502	*hinweisen*	point to
18500	*comma(,)*	comma(,)
15857	*dass*	that
2188	*rücksichtslos*	ruthless
5376	*Anwendung*	employment
7381	*unserer*	our
98092	*U-boote*	U-boats
16127	*jetzt*	now
13486	*Aussicht*	prospect
9350	*bietet*	offers
9220	*comma(,)*	comma(,)
76036	*England*	England
14219	*in*	in
5144	*wenigen*	few
2831	*Monat-*	month-
17920	*en*	s
11347	*zum*	to
17142	*Frieden*	peace
11264	*zu*	be
7667	*zwingen*	compelled
7762	*stop(.)*	stop(.)
15099	*Empfang*	Receipt
9110	*bestahigen*	acknowledge
10482	*stop(.)*	stop(.)
97556	*Zimmermann*	Zimmermann
3569	*stop(.)*	stop(.)
3670	*Schluss der Depesche*	End of dispatch
	BERNSTORFF	

Sources

Notes

Index

Sources

Titles marked with a single asterisk were particularly useful; those with a double asterisk were indispensable.

1 Manuscript Sources

National Archives; Foreign Affairs Branch, State Department Decimal File, 1910–1929:

> File No. 701.6293—Diplomatic Representation of Germany in China
>
> > 712.94—Relations between Mexico and Japan
> > 763.72—European War
> > 812.00—Political Affairs; Mexico
> > 812.001—Chief Executive of Mexico
> > 812.113—Fire arms, ammunition, explosives, etc.; Mexico
> > 812.74—Wireless Telegraph in Mexico
> > 862.20212—Germany Military Activities in Mexico
> > 894.20212—Japanese Military Activities in Mexico

Library of Congress: Diary of Chandler P. Anderson, Robert Lansing Desk Diary and Papers, Woodrow Wilson Papers.

Houghton Library, Harvard University: Joseph C. Grew Papers, Walter Hines Page Diary and Papers, William Phillips Papers.

Yale University Library: Edward M. House Diary and Papers, Frank L. Polk Papers.

2 Printed Official Sources

**Germany: *Official German Documents Relating to the World War. The Reports of the First and Second Subcommittees of the Committee Appointed by the National Constituent Assembly to Inquire into the Responsibility for the War.* 2 vols. New York, Oxford: Carnegie Endowment for International Peace, 1923. (Includes 1300 pages of testimony given in 1919 by Bethmann-Hollweg, Helfferich, Zimmermann, Bernstorff, Papen, Hindenburg, Ludendorff, Capelle, Holtzendorff, and others, as well as correspondence, records of High Command conferences, the Admiralty memorandum on submarine warfare, the text of the Zimmermann telegrams of January 16 and February 5, and other documents.)

Great Britain: Foreign Office. *Austrian and German Papers Found in the Possession of Mr. James F. J. Archibald, Falmouth, August 30, 1915.* Command 8012: London, Harrison, 1915.

United States:

Department of State. *Papers Relating to the Foreign Relations of the United States,* 1911, 1913, 1914, and *Supplements, World War, 1914–18.* Washington: G.P.O., 1928–34. (Referred to in Notes as U.S. Foreign Relations.)

———. *Papers Relating to the Foreign Relations of the United States; The Lansing Papers, 1914–20.* 2 vols. Washington: G.P.O., 1939. (Referred to in Notes as U.S. Lansing Papers.)

*Senate Documents. Foreign Relations Committee. *Investigation of Mexican Affairs, Report and Hearings.* 2 vols. 66th Congress, 2nd Session, Senate Document 285, Washington, 1920. (Referred to in Notes as Senate, Mexican Affairs.)

———. Judiciary Committee. *Hearings on Brewing and Liquor Interests and German and Bolshevik Propaganda.* 2 vols. 66th Congress, 1st Session, Senate Document 62, Washington, 1919. (Referred to in Notes as Senate, Propaganda.)

Congressional Record. *Senate Debate March 1, 1917.* 64th Congress, 2nd Session, vol. 54, part 5, pp. 4569–4605.

Mixed Claims Commission. *U.S.A. on behalf of Lehigh Valley Rr. et al. against Germany.* Docket 8103, vol. 1, exhibits 53, 192, 320. (Contains an affidavit on Code 13040 and other material put in evidence by Admiral Hall.)

3 Contemporary Works

Ackerman, Carl. *Germany, the Next Republic?* New York: G. H. Doran, 1917.

———. *Mexico's Dilemma.* New York: G. H. Doran, 1918.

Aston, Sir George. *Secret Service.* New York: Cosmopolitan, 1930. (The author served in British Intelligence.)

Baker, Newton D. *Why We Went to War.* New York: Harper, 1936.

**Baker, Ray Stannard. *Woodrow Wilson, Life and Letters.* 8 vols. New York: Doubleday Doran, 1927–39.

Balfour, Arthur James, Earl of. *Essays, Speculative and Political.* London: Hodder and Stoughton, 1920.

Balfour, Arthur James, Earl of. *Chapters of Autobiography.* London: Cassell, 1930.

Bernhard, Georg. "Le Comte Bernstorff et le Kaiser," *Europe Nouvelle,* November 4, 1939.

*Bernstorff, Johann Heinrich, Graf von. *My Three Years in America.* New York: Scribner's, 1920.

*———. *Memoirs of Count Bernstorff.* New York: Random, 1936.

Bethmann-Hollweg, Theobald von. *Reflections on the World War.* 2 vols. London: Butterworth, 1920.

Bright, Charles. "Telegraphs in War Time," *Nineteenth Century and After,* April 1915.

Bullitt, Ernesta Drinker. *An Uncensored Diary of the Central Empires.* New York: Doubleday Page, 1917.

Bülow, Bernhard, Fürst von. *Memoirs.* 4 vols. Boston: Little, Brown, 1931–32.

*Churchill, Winston Spencer. *The World Crisis, 1911–1918.* 4 vols. New York: Scribner's, 1923–27.

———. *Great Contemporaries.* New York: Putnam, 1937.

Corbett, Sir Julian, and Newbolt, Henry. *History of the Great War, Naval Operations.* 5 vols. (Official history, published by Committee of Imperial Defence.) New York and London: Longmans, 1920–31.

*Czernin, Ottokar, Graf von. *In the World War.* New York: Harper, 1920.

*Daniels, Josephus. *The Life of Woodrow Wilson.* Chicago: Winston, 1924.

*———. *The Wilson Era,* vol. 1. *The Years of Peace, 1910–1917.* Chapel Hill: University of North Carolina Press, 1944–46.

Dearle, N. B. *An Economic Chronicle of the Great War for Great Britain and Ireland* (Economic and Social History of the World War, British Series). London, Oxford and Yale, 1929.

Diez, Hermann. "Einige Worte über Admiral von Hintze," *Deutsche Revue,* July–September 1918.

Dugdale, Blanche E. C. *Arthur James Balfour.* 2 vols. New York: Putnam, 1937.

**Ewing, Alfred Washington. *The Man of Room 40, the Life of Sir Alfred Ewing.* London: Hutchinson, 1939. (By his son.)

**Flynn, William J. "Trapped Wires," *Liberty,* June 2, 1928.

*Gerard, James W. *My Four Years in Germany.* New York: G. H. Doran, 1917.

*———. *Face to Face with Kaiserism.* New York: G. H. Doran, 1918.

Goltz, Horst von der. *My Adventures as a German Secret Agent.* New York: McBride, 1917. (Would be invaluable if the reader could persuade himself to believe it.)

Grew, Joseph C. *Turbulent Era.* 2 vols. Boston and New York: Houghton Mifflin, 1952.

Grey, Edward, Viscount. *Twenty-five Years.* 2 vols. New York: Stokes, 1925.

*Guzman, Martin Luis. *The Eagle and the Serpent.* New York: Knopf, 1920. (A first-hand account of revolutionary days and personalities under Carranza and Villa.)

Gwynn, Stephen, ed. *The Letters and Friendships of Sir Cecil Arthur Spring-Rice.* 2 vols. Boston: Houghton Mifflin, 1929.

Hagedorn, Hermann, *The Bugle That Woke America* (selected letters and speeches of Theodore Roosevelt). New York: John Day, 1940.

Hall, Admiral Sir William Reginald, Interview with *Daily Mail,* reprinted in *World's Work,* April 1926.

**Hanssen, Hans Peter. *Diary of a Dying Empire.* Bloomington:

Indiana University Press, 1955. (By the leader of the Danish minority in the Reichstag and first published in Danish in 1924, this book is among the most valuable of all published German contemporary sources.)

Harris, Frank. *Latest Contemporary Portraits*. New York: Macaulay, 1927. (Contains a chapter on Bernstorff.)

Hazen, David W. *Giants and Ghosts of Central Europe*. Portland, Oregon: Metropolitan Press, 1933. (Includes accounts of interviews with Zimmermann and Eckhardt in 1933.)

**Hendrick, Burton J., ed. *Life and Letters of Walter Hines Page*. 3 vols. New York: Doubleday Page, 1923–26. (First, best, and most careful account of the circumstances in which the Telegram was intercepted.)

*Hirsch, Gilbert. "Our Friend Zimmermann," New York *Evening Post*, November 25, 1916.

*Houston, David F. *Eight Years with Wilson's Cabinet, 1913–1920*. 2 vols. New York: Doubleday Page, 1926.

**James, Admiral Sir William. *The Eyes of the Navy; a Biographical Study of Admiral Sir Reginald Hall*. London: Methuen, 1956.

Jones, H. P., and Hollister, P. M. *The German Secret Service in America, 1914–18*. Boston: Small Maynard, 1918.

Keynes, John Maynard. *Economic Consequences of the Peace*. New York: Harcourt, Brace, 1920. (Invaluable for a first-hand portrait of Wilson and analysis of his limitations in diplomacy.)

La Follette, Belle Case and Fola. *Robert M. La Follette*. 2 vols. New York: Macmillan, 1953.

Landau, Captain Henry. *The Enemy Within*. New York: Putnam, 1937.

Lane, Franklin K. *The Letters of Franklin K. Lane*, ed. A. W. Lane and L. H. Wall. Boston and New York: Houghton Mifflin, 1924.

**Lansing, Robert. *War Memoirs*. Indianapolis and New York: Bobbs-Merrill, 1935.

Literary Digest, March 17, 1917, "How Zimmermann United the United States." (A survey of nationwide press opinion on the telegram.)

Lloyd George, David. *War Memoirs*. 6 vols. Boston: Little, Brown, 1933–37.

Ludendorff, Erich, *Ludendorff's Own Story, August 1914–November 1918*. 2 vols. New York: Harper, 1920.

MacAdam, George. "German Intrigues in Mexico," *World's Work*, September 1918.

*Maximilian, Fürst von Baden. *Memoirs*. 2 vols. New York: Scribner's, 1928.

*McAdoo, William Gibbs, *Crowded Years*. Boston and New York: Houghton Mifflin, 1931.

Moats, Leone B. *Thunder in Their Veins*. New York and London: Century, 1932. (Mexico during the revolutionary decade, by an observer.)

*O'Shaughnessy, Edith (wife of Nelson O'Shaughnessy, First Secretary and later Chargé d'Affaires of the American Embassy in Mexico City, 1911–14). *A Diplomat's Wife in Mexico; Letters from the American Embassy at Mexico City*. New York and London: Harper, 1916.

———. *Diplomatic Days*. New York: Harper, 1917.

*———. *Intimate Pages of Mexican History*. New York: G. H. Doran, 1920.

Papen, Franz von. *Memoirs*, tr. by Brian Connell. London: A. Deutsch, 1932.

Phillips, William. *Ventures in Diplomacy*. Boston: Beacon, 1953.

Pless, Mary Theresa Olivia, Fürstin von. *Daisy, Princess of Pless, by Herself*. New York: Dutton, 1929.

Pooley, A. M. *Japan's Foreign Policies*. London: Allen and Unwin, 1920.

Providence Journal, pub. *A Few Lines of Recent American History*. Pamphlet, 23 pp., 1917.

Rathom, John R. "Germany's Plots Exposed," *World's Work*, February 1918.

Redfield, William C. *With Congress and Cabinet*. New York: Doubleday Page, 1924.

*Reinsch, Paul S. *An American Diplomat in China*. New York: Doubleday Page, 1922.

Reischach, Freiherr von. *Unter Drei Kaisern*. Berlin: Verlag für Kulturpolitik, 1925.

*Rintelen von Kleist, Franz. *The Dark Invader*, intro. by A. E. W. Mason. London: Lovat Dickson, 1933.

———. *Return of the Dark Invader*. London: Dickson and Thompson, 1935.

*Rintelen von Kleist, Franz. Foreword to *Errant Diplomat, The Life of Franz von Papen*, by Oswald Dutch (pseud.). London: E. Arnold, 1940.

Roosevelt, Theodore. *Fear God and Take Your Own Part*. New York: G. H. Doran, 1916.

———. *Letters*, ed by Elting E. Morison. 8 vols. Cambridge, Mass.: Harvard University Press, 1954.

*———, and Lodge, Henry Cabot. *Selections from the Correspondence of* . . . 2 vols. New York: Scribner's, 1925.

Round Table. *The Roster of the Round Table Dining Club*. New York: privately printed, 1926.

Saturday Evening Post. "War Propaganda," by One of the War Propagandists, Anonymous. Series of five articles, beginning June 22, 1929. (Internal evidence indicates that the author was George Sylvester Viereck.)

Scott, Hugh L. *Some Memories of a Soldier*. New York: Century, 1928.

Scott, James Brown. *A Survey of International Relations between the United States and Germany, August 1, 1914–April 6, 1917. Based on Official Documents*. New York: Oxford, 1917. (Especially Chapter IV, "Censorship of Communications.")

*Seymour, Charles. *The Intimate Papers of Colonel House.* 4 vols. Boston and New York: Houghton Mifflin, 1926–28. (Referred to in Notes as Seymour, IP.)

Sims, Joseph P., ed. *Three Wars with Germany.* New York: Putnam, 1944. (Correspondence of Admiral Hall and Amos J. Peaslee.)

Somerville, Boyd. "The *Frederick VIII* at Halifax; story of an epic search," *Living Age,* series 8, vol. 16, 1919.

Steed, Henry Wickham. *Through Thirty Years.* 2 vols. New York: Doubleday Page, 1924.

Strother, French. *Fighting Germany's Spies.* New York. Doubleday Page 1918.

———. " 'The *Providence Journal* Will Say This Morning,' " *World's Work,* December 1917.

Swope, Herbert Bayard. *Inside the German Empire in the Third Year of the War.* New York: Century, 1917.

Thwaites, Lieutenant-Colonel Norman. *Velvet and Vinegar.* London: Grayson and Grayson, 1932. (By the agent who obtained the Bathing Beauty photograph.)

Times, The (London). *History of the War.* 22 vols. London, 1921.

Tompkins, Colonel Frank. *Chasing Villa.* Military Service Publishing Co., 1934.

Treat, Payson Jackson. "Japan, America, and the Great War," *A League of Nations,* No. 8, December 1918.

Tumulty, Joseph P. *Woodrow Wilson as I Know Him.* New York: Doubleday Page, 1921.

Viereck, George Sylvester. *Spreading Germs of Hate.* New York: Liveright, 1930.

———. *The Strangest Friendship in History; Woodrow Wilson and Colonel House.* New York: Liveright, 1932.

*Voska, Emanuel Viktor, and Irwin, Will. *Spy and Counterspy.* New York: Doubleday, 1940.

Weale, Putnam (pseud. of Bertram Lenox Simpson). *An Indiscreet Chronicle from the Pacific.* New York: Dodd, Mead, 1922.

*Wilhelm II. *Letters from the Kaiser to the Czar,* ed. by Isaac Don Levine. New York: Stokes, 1920. (Referred to in Notes as Willy-Nicky letters.)

Wilson, Henry Lane. *Diplomatic Episodes in Mexico, Belgium and Chile.* New York: Doubleday Page, 1927.

Yardley, Herbert O. *The American Black Chamber.* Indianapolis: Bobbs-Merrill, 1931.

Young, George, and Kenworthy, Joseph M. *Freedom of the Seas.* New York: Liveright, 1929. (Sir George Young became, after Ewing left, the chief cryptanalyst of the political division of Room 40.)

*Zedlitz-Trützschler, Robert, Graf von. *Twelve Years at the Imperial German Court.* New York: Doran, 1924. (A particularly revealing study of the Kaiser by his unhappy Court Chamberlain.)

4 Secondary Works

Bailey, Thomas A. *A Diplomatic History of the American People*. New York: Appleton-Century-Crofts, 1950.

**Becker, Otto. *Der Ferne Ostend und das Schicksal Europas, 1907–1918*. Leipzig: Koehler und Amslang, 1940. (Important for Germany's secret overtures to Japan.)

Benson, Edward Frederic. *The Kaiser and English Relations*. New York: Longmans, 1936.

Brenner, Anita, and Leighton, George. *The Wind That Swept Mexico; a History of the Mexican Revolution, 1910–1942, with 184 historical photographs*. New York and London: Harper, 1943.

Cline, Howard F. *The United States and Mexico*. Cambridge, Mass.: Harvard University Press, 1953.

Dennis, Alfred L. P. *Adventures in American Diplomacy, 1896–1906*. New York: Dutton, 1928.

*Gooch, G. P. *Recent Revelations of European Diplomacy*. London: Longmans, 1927.

Grattan, C. Hartley. *Why We Fought*. New York: Vanguard, 1929.

Jessup, Philip C. *Elihu Root*. 2 vols. New York: Dodd, Mead, 1938.

Kurenberg, Joachim von. *The Kaiser; a Life of Wilhelm II*. New York: Simon and Schuster, 1955.

*Link, Arthur Stanley. *Woodrow Wilson and the Progressive Era, 1910–1917*. New York: Harper, 1954.

Ludwig, Emil. *Wilhelm Hohenzollern, The Last of the Kaisers*. New York and London: Putnam, 1927.

Martin, Perry Alvin. *Latin America and the War*. Baltimore: Johns Hopkins Press, 1925.

Mowat, Robert Balmain. *A History of European Diplomacy, 1914–1925*. New York and London: Longmans, 1927.

Notter, Harley. *The Origins of the Foreign Policy of Woodrow Wilson*. Baltimore: Johns Hopkins Press, 1937.

Peterson, Horace Cornelius. *Propaganda for War*. Norman, Okla.: University of Oklahoma Press, 1939.

Pinchon, Edgcumb. *Viva Villa!* New York: Harcourt, Brace, 1933.

Pratt, Fletcher. *Secret and Urgent; the Story of Codes and Ciphers*. Indianapolis: Bobbs-Merrill, 1939.

Pringle, Henry F. *Theodore Roosevelt*. New York: Harcourt, Brace, 1931.

Reiners, Ludwig. *The Lamps Went Out in Europe*. New York: Pantheon, 1955.

Schieber, Clara Eve. *Transformation of American Sentiment toward Germany, 1870–1914*. Boston: Cornhill, 1923.

Spencer, Samuel R. *Decision for War, 1917*. Rindge, N. H.: Smith, 1953.

Stevens, Louis. *Here Comes Pancho Villa*. New York: Stokes, 1930.

Strode, Hudson. *Timeless Mexico*. New York: Harcourt, Brace, 1944.

*Sykes, Christopher. *Wassmus: "The German Lawrence."* New York: Longmans, 1936.

Tansill, Charles C. *America Goes to War*. Boston: Little, Brown, 1938.

Vagts, Alfred. *Mexico, Europa und Amerika*. Berlin: Rothschild, 1928.

Willson, Beckles. *America's Ambassadors to England, 1785–1929*. New York: Stokes, 1929.

Ybarra, Thomas R. *Hindenburg; The Man with Three Lives*. New York: Duffield and Green, 1932.

Notes

Chapter 1. A Telegram Waylaid

P. 1. Montgomery and de Grey: James, 136, names these two men as the decoders of the telegram. Facts of Montgomery's background supplied by R. D. Whitehorn, Principal, Westminster College, Cambridge. De Grey listed in *Who's Who*. Montgomery died in 1930, de Grey in 1951.

P. 3. 13042 a variant of 13040: A discrepancy exists that has never been explained. The telegram itself bears the code number 13042, and Ambassador Page twice referred, in telegrams to the State Department, to "thirteen thousand forty-two" as "indicating the number of the code used" (Hendrick, iii, 333 and 345). But Eckhardt, who received the telegram in Mexico, twice referred, in telegrams to Zimmermann, to 13040. He specifically stated that the telegram "was received here in code 13040" and, when trying to account for the betrayal, suggested "code 13040 is compromised" (Hendrick, iii, 357, and James, 152) Ambassador Page also told the State Department that the code "was never used straight, but only with a great number of variations which are known to only one or two experts here" (Hendrick, iii, 344), and it is possible that 13042 indicated the code key to one of these variations.

It has been suggested by several writers that the telegram was in an enciphered code, but this is disproved by the presence of repetitions in the code groups. There are eight cases of repetitions, and one group, 67893, the code group for "Mexico," is repeated three times, and there are several cases of code groups differing in only one digit. Such repetitions, or near repetitions, would not occur in an enciphered code.

Pp. 3–4. Text of the Telegram: German Documents, ii, 1337.

Pp. 6–7. Incomplete version of the decoded text: Hendrick, iii, 336–37, and James, 136.

P. 6. "Blinker" Hall: Certain of Admiral Hall's personal characteristics were told to me by Admiral James and Mrs. Hotblack; others were gathered from accounts of those who knew him, namely, Ewing, James, Sims, and others. The resemblance to Mr. Punch was noted in a London *Times* article reprinted in Sims.

P. 6. Not enough U-boats: Churchill, *Crisis, 1916–18,* i, 222. See also *Crisis, 1915,* chap. XIV, and *Crisis, 1916–18,* ii, chap.

XV. Bernstorff told the postwar German Investigating Committee that his arguments against the use of unrestricted submarine warfare had prevailed in the spring and summer of 1916 only because "of the obviously insufficient number of U-boats. We had on March 1 only 35 large U-boats ready for action." German Documents, i, 341.

Pp. 8–9. *Telconia:* Information supplied by Admiralty Archivist, Commander P. K. Kemp. See also Landau, 151–82.

P. 8. *German cables:* Bright.

P. 9. *Committee of Imperial Defense:* Information supplied by Admiralty Archivist.

P. 9. *Africa-Brazil cable cut by Eastern Telegraph:* From *A Great Seaman; the Life of Admiral Sir Henry Oliver* by Admiral Sir William James (London: Methuen, 1956).

P. 10. *Admiral Oliver summons Ewing:* This and subsequent facts about Ewing and the early history of Room 40 are from the life of Ewing by his son, A. W. Ewing.

P. 10. *Montgomery's translation:* Letter to *The Times* (London), October 1930, from Dr. F. C. Burkitt, Professor of Divinity, Cambridge.

P. 11. *Germans ignored possibility of enemy decoding:* Young.

P. 11. *Decoders read German messages more quickly than recipients:* Ibid.

Pp. 12–13. *Magdeburg signal book:* Corbett, i, 170; James, 29; Landau, Pratt.

Pp. 13–15. *Captain Hall:* His innovations, James, 16–17. His character and habits, James, Ewing, Hendrick, Sims.

P. 14. *Iron-bound sea chest:* James, 56–57.

Pp. 15–16. *Alexander Szek:* "The Mysterious Disappearance of Alexander Szek," unpublished manuscript by Wildon Lloyd. See also Landau, 155–58, and Pratt.

Pp. 17–19. *Wassmuss:* Sykes, 62–78; Landau, 158-59.

P. 17. *Anglo-Persian Pipeline:* Information supplied by British Petroleum Co., Ltd., formerly Anglo-Iranian Oil Co., Ltd., which states in a letter to the author, that although the tribesmen who cut the pipeline were instigated by enemy agents, "of whom there were several about, it cannot be said for certain that it was Wassmuss, nor were his capture, sometime later, and subsequent escape, connected with it."

P. 18. *"Lashed the tribesmen":* Sykes, 77.

P. 19. *Hall locates code book:* James, 69.

P. 19. *13040 one of two codes:* Hall's affidavit, Mixed Claims Commission, Ex. 320.

P. 20. *£5,500,000 a day:* Dearle.

P. 20. *Collapse of the allies would be a matter of months:* André Tardieu wrote in *France and America* that if the Federal Reserve decision had been maintained, "the defeat of the Allies would have been merely a question of months" (quoted in Grattan, 175). J. M. Keynes (273, n. 1) wrote that England's task would soon have become "entirely hopeless" without the assistance of the U.S. Treasury.

P. 21. *As Churchill was to say later:* "The action of the United States with its repercussions on the history of the world depended, during the awful period of Armageddon, upon the workings of this one man's mind and spirit to the exclusion of almost every other factor; . . . he played a part in the fate of nations incomparably more direct and personal than any other man." Churchill, *Crisis, 1916–18*, i, 234.

Chapter 2. The Clever Kaiser and the Yellow Peril

P. 23. *Die gelbe Gefahr:* According to the *Spectator,* December 11, 1897, the Kaiser was the first statesman to allude to the Yellow Peril in a public speech.

P. 23. *Kaiser grasped significance:* Writing to the Czar, September 26, 1895, the Kaiser says the danger of the Far East to Europe has been greatly on his mind, "and at last my thoughts developed in a certain form and this I sketched on paper. I worked it out with an Artist and had it engraved for public use." Willy-Nicky letters, 16–17.

P. 23. *"Christmas-tree candles . . .":* Ludwig, 252. Ludwig gives no date for this letter, and there appears to be some discrepancy, for the Kaiser has already described sketching the picture in his letter to the Czar of September 26, three months before Christmas.

P. 23. *Knackfuss:* Willy-Nicky letters, 20, n. 3.

P. 23. *Kaiser's picture:* The picture is reproduced in *Harper's Weekly,* January 22, 1898; also in Viereck, *The Kaiser on Trial,* facing 434.

P. 24. *"He wanted it always to be Sunday":* Zedlitz, xv.

P. 24. *Morning paper printed in gold:* Daisy, Princess of Pless, 265.

P. 24. *Kaiser on dynastic rulers:* Kaiser to Czar, October 25, 1895; Willy-Nicky letters, 21–26.

P. 25. *Kaiser's letters written in English:* Willy-Nicky letters, p. ix. *Errors in English spelling:* ibid., xi.

P. 25. *Kaiser and Santa Margarita Islands, Venezuela:* Thayer, W. R., *Life and Letters of John Hay* (Houghton Mifflin, 1915), ii, 284.

Pp. 25–26. *Kaiser's attempt to buy Magdalena Bay:* Ambassador Choate to Secretary Hay, undated [1902]. Hay Papers, Library of Congress.

P. 27. *God would choose Germany:* "And so the Creator has ever kept this nation in His sight—the nation elected by Him to bestow the gift of peace at last upon the world. . . . That God should choose a Prussian—that must mean great things!" The Kaiser, quoted by Ludwig, 309. The Kaiser generally referred to God as his "Great Ally," Ludwig, 317. See also chap. xviii, "Ich und Gott," in Viereck, *The Kaiser on Trial.*

P. 27. *"All Highest paid his respects to the Highest"*: Zedlitz.

P. 27. *"The Kaiser has had another fit . . ."*: Roosevelt to Hay, March 30, 1905; Schieber, 236.

P. 27. *"I ADORE the English!"*: Roosevelt to Trevelyan, October 1, 1911; Letters, Morison, vii, 396.

Pp. 27–28. *Kaiser's letters urging Czar to fight Japan:* Quotations are from letter of April 16, 1895, Willy-Nicky letters, 10. See also letters of July 10, 1895, ibid., 13; September 2, 1902, ibid., 86; and Memorandum to German Diplomats, August, 1904; "This will be the decisive battle between . . . Western civilization and Eastern semi-civilization . . . the battle which I prophetically drew in my painting . . ." Ludwig, 254.

P. 28. *10,000 Japanese in Mexico:* December 28, 1907, Willy-Nicky letters, 218–20.

P. 29. *Kaiser's remark to Balfour:* Dugdale, i, 214. The remark was made in 1899 during the Boer War on the occasion of the Kaiser's visit to the Queen at Windsor.

P. 29. *"Autocratic zig-zag"*: Pringle, 379.

P. 29. *"A great admirer of Your Majesty . . ."*: Dennis, 390.

P. 30. *Interview with Tower:* Tower to Roosevelt, January 28, 1908; Pringle, 403–404.

Pp. 30–31. *Interview with Hale:* Roosevelt to Elihu Root, August 8, 1908, Letters, Morison, vi, 1163–65; Roosevelt to Arthur H. Lee, October 17, 1908, ibid., 1292–94; Roosevelt to Whitelaw Reid, January 6, 1909, ibid., 1465–67.

P. 31. *In his "strongest manner":* Letter to Root, cited above.

P. 31. *"I wish he would not have brain storms"*: Roosevelt to Whitelaw Reid, December 4, 1908, Letters, Morison, vi, 1411.

P. 31. *"A tear fell on his cigar"*: Daisy, Princess of Pless. 256.

P. 31. *American Minister in Guatemala:* Archives, 712.94/27A.

P. 32. *Mexicans as racial brothers of the Japanese:* Pooley.

P. 32. *Admiral Yashiro's speech:* Reported by *La Campana* of Guatemala City, April 29, 1911, Archives, 712.94/1.

Pp. 32–33. *Goltz steals secret treaty:* This account of his exploit is Goltz's own, as contained in the memoirs he wrote in 1917 while awaiting trial as a wartime saboteur in the United States.

P. 33. *Ambassador Wilson's denial:* H. L. Wilson to Secretary of State Philander C. Knox, June 13, 1911, Archives, 712.94/2. Upon publication of von der Goltz's book in 1917, Wilson again wrote to former Secretary Knox: "That part of this story which relates to the Embassy in Mexico City and my action is pure invention. No such treaty was ever placed in my hands, nor to my knowledge in the hands of the Department of State during your administration of its affairs." Wilson to Knox, February 19, 1918, Archives, 712.94/26.

P. 33. *Ambassador Wilson scurried up to Washington:* H. L. Wilson, 207.

P. 33. *President Taft's mobilization:* U.S. Foreign Relations, 1911.

P. 33. *Major Herwarth von Bittenfeld:* N.Y. *Sun*, March 11, 1911.

P. 33. *Texas and border states in a ferment:* Ibid., March 23, 1911. Reports from Fort Sam Houston.

P. 34. *Foreign capitals buzzed:* Ibid., March 13, 1911. Reports from Paris and foreign press summary.

P. 34. *German press:* Ibid., March 18, 1911. Report from Berlin.

P. 34. *Ambassador Wilson's private report to State Department:* Henry Lane Wilson to Secretary Knox, June 13, 1911, Archives, 712.94/2.

P. 35. *Taft's mobilization inspired by Mexican revolt:* U.S. Foreign Relations, 1911, 422; see also Wilson, H. L., 208–11.

Chapter 3. "Seize the Customs House at Once!"

P. 36. *Madero on a white horse:* O'Shaughnessy, *Intimate Pages,* 173.

P. 36. *Madero as apostle and redeemer:* Ibid., 149–60.

P. 36. *Ten thousand dead:* The counter-revolution, called the *Dicena Tragica,* is described at first hand by Wilson, H. L., 252–88, and by O'Shaughnessy, *Intimate Pages,* 172–91.

P. 36. *Huerta's flat nose,* etc.: O'Shaughnessy, *Intimate Pages,* 191–93. A good portrait is in Moats, 112.

P. 37. *"Sneaking admiration":* Wilson to Mrs. Hulbert, February 1, 1914, Baker, iv, 305. *Huerta a "diverting brute":* Wilson to Mrs. Hulbert, August 24, 1913, ibid., 273.

P. 37. *"Puritan of the North":* Wilson, H. L., 295.

P. 37. *Wilson's "clear duty":* Memorandum to foreign governments, November 1, 1913, U.S. Foreign Relations, 1913, 856.

P. 38. *"Irony of fate . . .":* Wilson to E. G. Conklin, Baker, iv, 55.

P. 38. *"That scoundrel Huerta":* Wilson to Edith G. Reid, August 15, 1913, Baker, iv, 266.

P. 38. *Japan sold Huerta arms:* Archives, 894.20212 passim. See also Vagts, *Mexico, Europa und Amerika,* 191.

P. 38. *Señor de la Barra:* Pooley.

P. 39. *A fearful prospect:* U.S. Foreign Relations, 1913, 776.

P. 39. *President's scorn for Ambassador Wilson:* He regarded him with a "profound sense of distrust": Baker, iv, 238.

P. 39. *Refuses to communicate with Ambassador Wilson:* H. L. Wilson to Secretary Bryan, June 8, 1913, U.S. Foreign Relations, 1913, 807. In his memoirs Ambassador Wilson wrote that he never could obtain an answer or instructions from Bryan or Wilson so that he was without guidance as to American policy, "save by conjecture."

P. 39. *"The best thing that can happen . . .":* Bryce to Wilson, November 7, 1913, Baker, iv, 281.

P. 40. *"Morality is all right . . .":* Gerard to Bryan, December 20, 1913, Baker, iv, 300.

P. 40. *"That person who calls himself":* Baker, iv, 324.

P. 40. *Oil to British Navy:* Link, 116, n. 22.

P. 40. *Wilson's distaste for Cowdray and Carden:* This is fully documented in the exchange of letters between Ambassador Walter Hines Page and Colonel House on the Mexican problem, Hendrick, i, 201–31. See especially House to Page, December 12, 1913; "The President was delighted with what you had to say concerning Lord Cowdray. We do not love him for we think that between Cowdray and Carden a large part of our troubles in Mexico has been made," 218.

P. 40. *England recognizes Huerta:* Baker, iv, 243, n. 2.

Pp. 40–41. *Joint Board mobilizes fleet:* Daniels, Wilson Era, i, 163.

P. 41. *Wilson infuriated:* Ibid., 163.

P. 41. *Admirals "sat up nights . . .":* Ibid., 168.

P. 41. *"Bad taste":* Ibid.

P. 41. *Businessmen's memorandum:* Baker, iv, 248–49.

P. 41. *"That desperate brute":* Wilson to Mrs. Hulbert, November 2, 1913, ibid., 288.

Pp. 41–42. *Hale's report:* Ibid., 255.

P. 42. *Another confidential emissary:* This was Governor John Lind of Minnesota, who was as innocent of Mexican affairs and the Spanish language as Hale but was a friend of Secretary Bryan's: Houston, i, 72; Cline, 145.

P. 42. *"Seeking to counsel Mexico":* Baker, iv, 266.

P. 42. *"An act of bad faith":* Ibid., 277.

P. 42. *No appreciation in England:* Page to Wilson, October, 25, 1913, Hendrick, i, 184.

P. 42. *"Such means as may be necessary . . .":* U.S. Foreign Relations, 1913, 856.

P. 43. *Tyrrell's mission:* Hendrick, i, 202–204; Seymour, IP, i, 194–206.

P. 43. *"I am going to teach":* Hendrick, i, 204.

P. 43. *"Taking to their tents":* Page to House, November 26, 1913, ibid., 217.

P. 43. *Panama Canal tolls:* Ibid., chap. viii; Seymour, IP, i, 205.

P. 46. *Sir Edward Grey:* "I did not believe that morally there was much to choose between Huerta and his opponents": Grey, ii, 100.

P. 43. *Ypiranga, Bavaria, Cecilie:* Gerard to Bryan, May 5, 1914, reports *Cecilie* sailed from Hamburg on April 14, and *Bavaria* on April 17. Archives, 812.113/3167.

Pp. 43–44. *Dolphin:* U.S. Foreign Relations, 1914, 448–49.

P. 44. *Huerta asks why U.S. wants salute:* Baker, iv, 324.

P. 45. *One cabinet member:* Secretary of Agriculture David F. Houston, q.v., i, 116.

P. 45. *"Might take the nation into war":* Houston, ibid.

P. 45. *"In no conceivable circumstances . . .":* Ibid.

P. 45. *Wilson tells Congressional leaders:* Senator Lodge, who was one of the four, wrote a memorandum of the meeting which is reprinted in Baker, iv, 326. The mood of Congress is best conveyed in the daily reports of *The New York Times* (hereafter referred to as NYT) and other newspapers.

Pp. 46–47. *Midnight telephone conference:* Baker, iv, 329; Daniels, Woodrow Wilson, 182–83; Tumulty, 151–53.

P. 46. *"Ypiranga will arrive tomorrow":* Daniels, *Wilson Era*, i, 193.

P. 47. *Order to Admiral Fletcher:* U.S. Foreign Relations, 1914, 443–636, contains all the official dispatches connected with the Veracruz incident.

P. 47. *Wilson paced the floor:* Baker, iv, 330.

P. 47. *"Medieval points of punctilio":* Economist (London), April 18, 1914.

Pp. 47–48. *Veracruz action:* U.S. Foreign Relations, 1914, loc. cit.

P. 48. *"Four of our men killed":* Ibid.

P. 48. *"Preternaturally pale":* H. F. Forman quoted in Baker, iv, 330.

P. 48. *Bernstorff protests:* Daniels, *Wilson Era*, i, 200.

P. 48. *Bryan's apology:* NYT, report from Washington, April 23, 1914. *State Department Memorandum:* Daniels, ibid., 201.

P. 49. *Ypiranga delivers arms:* NYT, report from Washington, May 9, 13, 27, 1914.

P. 49. *"Mexico is a god-send to us":* Bernstorff, Memoirs, 122.

P. 49. *Kaiser's emissary to London:* Gerard to House, August 3, 1915: "Von Jagow confessed to me that they had tried to get England to interfere with them in Mexico," Seymour, IP, ii, 28. When Gerard's book, repeating this story, was published in 1917, a Chicago publisher, Mr. James Keeley, confirmed the incident in a statement carried by the NYT, August 21, 1917. Mr. Keeley said that during a recent visit to London a British official had told him that a German emissary, introduced by the German Ambassador as a personal friend and representative of the Kaiser, had come to see him just before the outbreak of war, to propose joint action in Mexico. The German emissary's quoted words are those quoted by Mr. Keeley as having been told him by the British official. The emissary was, in all probability, Albert Ballin, president of the Hamburg-Amerika Line and friend of the Kaiser, who was, in fact, sent by the Kaiser to London late in July, where he talked to Grey, Haldane, and Churchill in a last-minute effort to persuade England to stay out of the coming war. Hulderman, B. *Albert Ballin* (London, Cassell, 1922), 215.

P. 50. *"We have gone down to Mexico":* Address at Brooklyn Navy Yard, May 11, 1914, Baker, iv, 341.

P. 50. *"I am longing for an exit":* Wilson to Dr. Jacobus, April 29, 1914, ibid., 335.

P. 50. *Huerta aboard the Dresden:* NYT, July 18, 1914, report from Puerto Mexico.

Chapter 4. The Third Partner—Japan

P. 51. *"Disappeared around the corner"*: O'Shaughnessy, *Intimate Pages*, 252.

P. 52. *Germany believed Japan her natural ally*: Gerard, *Face to Face;* also Becker. After America was at war, Viscount Ishii told Secretary Lansing that "through various channels the German government had three times sought to persuade Japan to withdraw from the Allies . . ." U.S. Lansing Papers, ii, 435.

P. 52. *Von Hintze*: Portrait in O'Shaughnessy, *Diplomatic Days*, 74. Character and appearance, O'Shaughnessy, *Intimate Pages*, 249–53. His suggestion about Edith Cavell, Reinsch. Facts about his career, NYT, July 20, 1917 (when he was being considered as successor to Zimmermann) and NYT, July 12, 1918 (when he was appointed Foreign Minister). See also Diez, 111.

P. 53. *Hintze at Manila Bay*: NYT, July 12, 1918.

P. 53. *Huerta asks Japan*: NYT, April 30, 1914.

P. 54. *Disguised as steward*: China Press, Shanghai, quoted NYT, February 27, 1915. See also O'Shaughnessy and Reinsch.

P. 54. *"If you can do it once. . ."*: China Press, article cited.

P. 54. *Safe conduct for von Hintze*: Bernstorff to Bryan, October 7 and 31, 1914, Archives, 701.6293/3 and /4. Lansing to Chinda and to Spring-Rice, November 3, 1914, ibid.

P. 54. *Japan refuses safe-conduct*: Chinda to Lansing, November 9, 1914, and Bryan to Bernstorff, November 16, 1914, ibid., 701.6293/5.

P. 54. *Hintze cancels passage*: R. P. Schwerin of Pacific Mail Steamship Co. to Bryan, November 13, 1914, and Bryan to Schwerin, November 14, 1914, ibid., 701.6293/6 and /5a.

P. 55. *German visitors warn Gerard*: Gerard, *My Four Years*.

P. 55. *Baron von Schoen*: U.S. Lansing Papers, i, 76.

P. 55. *"Not only desirable but imperative . . ."*: Ibid.

P. 55. *Dr. Fuehr*: Senate, Propaganda; evidence of Captain Lester.

P. 55. *Geier*: Jones and Hollister, 52.

P. 55. *Ludwig Stein*: NY American, April 25, 1915.

Pp. 55–56. *Japanese commander visits Villa*: Scott, Hugh L., 512. Senate, Mexican Affairs, testimony of George Carothers, to whom Villa told it.

P. 56. *American General Staff's plans*: Times (London), March 2, 1917.

P. 56. *"Every European and Asiatic general staff . . ."*: Brigadier General Henry J. Reilly, quoted in Tompkins, chap. xxxv.

P. 57. *"Mr. V. Heintze"*: Consul Sammons at Shanghai to Ambassador Reinsch at Peking, January 18 and 20, 1915, enclosing articles from *North China Daily News* of January 18 and from *China Press* of January 20. Archives, 701.6293/7 and /8.

P. 57. *Yüan Shih-k'ai:* King-Hall, Stephen, *Western Civilization and the Far East* (London, Methuen, 1924), 160.

P. 57. *Japan notches up her price:* Japan's motives were well understood by her allies. Britain hoped, said Sir Edward Grey confidentially, to keep down the bill which they might present at the close of the war." Diary of Chandler P. Anderson, January 9, 1915.

P. 58. *Von Hintze's overtures to Japan:* Becker.

P. 58. *Overtures to Japanese Ambassador in Stockholm:* Becker.

P. 58. *Japan informs Russia:* Becker.

P. 58. *Russian Ambassador worried:* Becker.

P. 58. *Asama at Turtle Bay:* Archives, 894.20212, passim through April 1915. NYT, April 14–22, 1915.

P. 59. *Japanese blame Germany:* NYT, April 20, 1915.

P. 59. *German press:* Berlin *Post,* April 21, quoted, NYT April 22, 1915.

P. 59. *Spring-Rice:* Diary of Chandler P. Anderson, June 18, 1915. His being neurasthenic, etc.: Although Sir Cecil was a beloved companion of Theodore Roosevelt's during his early years in Washington, illness and worry over Wilson's policy toward the Allies disturbed his relations with the Wilson administration. In the index of House's *Intimate Papers* the name Spring-Rice has nine separate page references under the subhead, "his nervousness." Wilson called him that "highly excitable invalid," Link, 199, n. 8.

Pp. 59–60. *"It would be a serious day":* Diary, June 24, 1915, House papers, Yale.

P. 60. *"I think that if German militarism . . .":* Memorandum of July 11, 1915, Lansing papers, Library of Congress. This fear continued right up until the overthrow of the Czar. A few weeks before that event, another member of Wilson's Cabinet, Secretary of Interior Lane, wrote on February 9, 1917, of the "likelihood of a German-Russian-Japanese alliance as a natural thing at the end of the war." Lane, 234.

P. 60. *"Meticulous, metallic and mousy":* Daniels, *Wilson Era,* i, 441.

P. 60. *Triple alliance:* Becker gives a thorough analysis of the strategies and policies involved in Germany's attempts to bring this about. At one point it was feared that such an alliance had actually been concluded. Polk to House, October 19, 1916, Polk papers, Yale.

P. 60. *Von Hintze openly told:* This interview was given to the correspondent of the *Kokumin Shimbun* at Yokohama in April 1917, when von Hintze was on his way home after China joined the Allies, quoted in NYT, April 28, 1917. The fact that the Japanese sought out and published the views of an enemy ambassador is evidence of their desire to keep alive the Allied fear that Japan might change sides.

P. 60. *"I suspect the Germans and Japanese":* Gerard to Lansing, December 7, 1915, U.S. Lansing Papers.

P. 60. *New evidence about von Hintze:* Gerard to Lansing. December 14, 1915, ibid.

P. 60. *Hugo Stinnes:* Becker, 83 ff.

P. 61. *Hearst film:* Senate, Propaganda.

Chapter 5. "Von Rintelen Came Here . . ."

P. 63. *Huerta in Barcelona:* Archives, 812.0001 H. 27/6.

P. 63. *Rintelen in Barcelona: Current History,* April 1917. See also Jones and Hollister.

P. 64. *Rintelen sent by German High Command:* German Ministry of War to Captain Boy-Ed, April 4, 1915, Mixed Claims Commission, Exhibit 320. In interview given to NYT, January 3, 1940, Rintelen said he was sent on the direct orders of General von Falkenhayn and General Michaelis.

P. 64. *Rintelen's career and character:* Rintelen's career was fully documented in newspaper articles at the time of his first trial in April 1917 and again at the time of his release in November 1920; see especially NY *World,* May 2, 1917, and December 13 and 14, 1920; see also Jones and Hollister, Papen and Rintelen.

P. 64. *"Telling Wilson what's what":* NY *World,* May 2, 1917.

P. 65. *"Poor Mexico":* Quoted by Strode, 263.

P. 65. *"Starving and without a government":* Wilson, June 2, 1915. Baker, iii, 333.

P. 66. *German community in Mexico:* Report of House of Representatives Committee on Foreign Affairs, Congressional Record, 55, No. 4, 192–93; also Senate, Mexican Affairs, passim; see also Ackerman and Martin, P.A.

P. 66. *"Do something positive":* Papen to General von Falkenhayn, April 9, 1915, Mixed Claims Commission, Exhibit 192.

P. 67. *Boy-Ed equally resented Rintelen:* Papen, Memoirs.

P. 67. *"Most dangerous mind":* Wilson to Lansing, December 5, 1915, U.S. Lansing Papers, i, 90.

Pp. 67–68. *Bernstorff's character and career:* Bernstorff, Bernhard, Harris; *Current Opinion,* July 1915; also references in House, Lansing, and other memoirs of the period.

P. 68. *Willingness to be bored: Current Literature,* February 1909.

P. 68. *Rintelen meets Bernstorff:* German Documents, i, 255.

P. 68. *Private offices in New York:* Jones and Hollister.

P. 69. *Rintelen meets Huerta: Current History,* May 1917. Rintelen himself gives an elaborate account of this meeting, in which he pictures himself addressing Huerta "as a complete stranger" and the next moment "we came to terms" and completed arrangements for German financing of Huerta's counter-revolt in Mexico. In the precipitate manner in which he accomplishes incredible feats and the ease with which he vaults over difficulties, Rintelen's picture of himself is a replica of Baron Munchausen.

P. 69. *"I'm Voska":* Steed, ii, 43.

Pp. 69–70. *Voska's career:* Voska.

Pp. 70–72. *Voska's first coup, meets Gaunt, spy organization, plants dictaphone:* Voska.

P. 72. *Gaunt and Rathom:* For the role of Rathom, see Peterson; also Paxon, i, 263; also Rathom's articles in *World's Work*, December 1917 and February 1918.

P. 72. *Carranza and Villa demand Huerta's arrest:* NYT, April 9, 11, 13, 1915.

Pp. 72–73. *Rintelen's pseudonyms and sabotage:* NYT, October 23, 1915, October 1, 1916, January 3, 1940; see also Jones and Hollister.

P. 74. *Wilson orders watch on German and Austrian embassies:* McAdoo, Flynn, Senate, Propaganda.

P. 74. *"We rented an apartment . . .":* Flynn.

P. 74. *Wires tapped in New York:* Senate, Propaganda, evidence of Agent Bielaski and Gaston B. Means. When this testimony was given, Senator Overman interrupted, "Whatever the government did in tapping wires, we do not want to know anything about."

P. 75. *Hansen is really Rintelen:* Diary of Chandler P. Anderson, July 10, 1915. He writes that Ambassador Spring-Rice has told him that all information points to "a man named Hansen" as the head of the "German Secret Association" and Anderson finds this very interesting as a Miss Seward has just told him she recognized Hansen as her old acquaintance Rintelen. Two days later, July 12, Anderson notes that this is confirmed by a report of a Department of Justice agent.

P. 75. *Rintelen reports to Berlin on Huerta:* Rintelen.

P. 75. *Codes used between Bernstorff and Berlin:* Bernstorff to Ministry of War, December 10, 1915. Mixed Claims Commission, Exhibit 320.

P. 76. *Eight million rounds of ammunition and other details of plot:* NYT, August 14, November 23 and 24, December 5 and 8, 1915.

P. 76. *Papen goes down to Mexican border:* Providence Journal, August 4, 1915.

P. 76. *Boy-Ed carries on negotiations with Huerta:* Ibid.

P. 77. *Huerta boards train:* NYT, June 26, 1915.

P. 77. *Lansing told Huerta has changed trains:* Archives 812.001 H87. This is a special file on Huerta which contains all the documents concerning Huerta from the time of his arrival in New York to his death. For the events of his arrest and imprisonment, see also Lansing's desk diary, from June 28 through July, 1915.

P. 78. *Cobb's arrest of Huerta:* Archives, 812.001 H87.

P. 78. *Mayor of El Paso: Army invites Huerta to dinner:* U.S. Attorney in El Paso to Attorney General Gregory, June 29, 1915, Wilson Papers, Series 2, Library of Congress.

P. 79. *"I will leave this jail only . . .":* NYT, July 6, 1915.

P. 79. *"I have not had a drink . . .":* Ibid.

P. 79. *"Orozco gathering forces":* Archives, 812.001 H87.

P. 79. *"This solves the problem":* Ibid.

P. 79. *Huerta appeals to Bernstorff:* Ibid.

P. 79. *Bernstorff forwards message to Lansing; Wilson's comment:* Ibid.

P. 80. *Rintelen recalled; sails on Noordam:* James, 101.

P. 80. *Rintelen at Scotland Yard:* James, 101; see Rintelen.

P. 80. *Hall's role in recall of Rintelen:* NYT, October 4, 1939; a retrospective article on Rintelen's career, which states that his recall in 1915 was "the result of a trick message sent by the British Admiralty." Rintelen confirmed this in an interview given to the NYT, January 3, 1940.

P. 81. *Footnote; Rintelen's subsequent career:* NYT, November 25, 27, 28, 1920; October 14, 1939; January 3, May 24, 1940; November 6, 1945; May 30, 1949. See also *Forum,* February 1919; James, 102.

P. 82. *Purloined Briefcase:* McAdoo; also *Saturday Evening Post,* June 22 and August 17, 1929.

P. 83. *"Buried for the last ten days":* Diary of Chandler P. Anderson, August 21, 1915.

P. 83. *Archibald:* Great Britain, Foreign Office, Command 8012; see also James, 97–98; Grattan, Voska.

P. 84. *"A break may come":* House to Grey, September 13, 1915, Seymour, IP, ii, 45.

Chapter 6. Viva Villa!—Made in Germany

P. 85. *"I have never known a man . . .":* Wilson to Lansing, July 2, 1915, Link, 133, n. 54.

P. 85. *"The safest man to tie to":* O'Shaughnessy, *Intimate Pages,* 331.

P. 85. *Villa an "idealist":* Ibid.

P. 85. *Bryan's strong point not logic:* Lord Bryce once remarked that Bryan was "almost unable to think." Tansill, 165.

P. 86. *Lansing recommends support of Villa:* August 9, 1915, U.S. Lansing Papers, ii, 541 ff.

P. 86. *Lansing wrote it down:* Lansing Diary, October 10, 1915.

P. 86. *Americans made a deal:* Pinchon, 330.

P. 87. *"Obnoxious underlings":* House to Wilson, November 21, 1915, Seymour, ii, 47.

P. 87. *Department of Justice card file:* Strother.

Pp. 87–88. *"Convinced Rintelen was principal reason":* Bernstorff to Ministry of War, December 10, 1915, Mixed Claims Commission, Ex. 320.

P. 88. *Bernstorff's interview with Lansing:* U.S. Lansing Papers, i, 86.

P. 88. *"Utterly false":* Ibid., i. 91.

Pp. 88–89. *Huerta's illness and death:* NYT through November and December 1915 and January 1916; also O'Shaughnessy, *Intimate Pages.*

P. 89. *Thomas H. Holmes:* NYT, January 12, 1916.

P. 89. *"This foul and brutal murder":* Ibid.

P. 90. *Wilson, through shut teeth:* Baker, vi, 74–75.

P. 90. *Governor of Texas:* NYT, January 13, 1916.

P. 90. *Villa saw himself facing oblivion:* Cline.

P. 90. *Carranza's long white whiskers:* Stevens.

P. 90. *Edgar Held and Louis Hess:* Report of Agent Carothers, February 7, 1916, Archives, 812.00/17259.

P. 91. *"For the sole purpose . . .":* Baker, vi, 68.

P. 91. *Berlin press says Japanese back Villa:* Gerard to State Department, March 16, 1916, Archives, 763.72/2508.

P. 91. *"Villa's attacks made in Germany":* Gerard to Lansing, March 20, 1916, U.S. Lansing Papers.

P. 92. *Collier's correspondent:* James Hopper, *Collier's Weekly,* April 15, 1916.

P. 92. *Agent Cobb asks for extra operatives:* Archives, 862.20212/11.

Pp. 92–94. *Max Weber:* Report of General Funston, January 3, 1917, Archives, 862.20212.

P. 92. *Krakauer, Zork, and Moye:* Ibid.

P. 93. *"Fifty million Germans":* Gerard, *Face to Face.*

P. 93. *German agent offers thirty-two officers:* Archives, 812.20212/8 and /9.

P. 93. *General Funston troubled:* Funston to War Department, May 5, 1916, Archives, 812.00/10868.

P. 93. *Plan of San Diego:* Senate, Mexican Affairs, 1232 ff; see also Report of Vice-Consul at Monterey, June 9, 1916, Archives, 812.00/18068 and /20165.

P. 94. *Carranza's "impetuous generals":* Telegram of June 18, 1916. Archives, 862.20212.

P. 94. *German reserve officers:* Consul Canada, telegram of June 19, 1916, and report of Special Agent Rodgers, June 23, 1916, Archives, 862.20212/30.

P. 95. *Times warned:* NYT, editorial, June 23, 1916.

P. 95. *A Berlin paper: Tägliche Rundschau,* quoted NYT, July 12, 1916.

P. 95. *"Fate offers us":* Chicago Tribune, April 21, 1916.

P. 95. *"Perfectly silly of you Americans":* Bullitt, 32.

P. 95. *Carranza, truculent, etc.:* Lansing called him "obstinate and vain," Diary, October 10, 1915; see also Guzman, Strode, Martin.

P. 96. *Zubaran confers with Zimmermann:* Ackerman; *Fails to call on Gerard:* Gerard to Lansing, July 18, 1916, U.S. Lansing Papers, i, 690.

P. 96. *German infiltration in Mexico:* Report of Consul Canada, July 13, 1916, Archives, 862.20212/38; also Senate, Mexican Affairs; *World's Work,* "German Efforts in Mexico," December

1917; NYT, March 15, 1917; NY *World,* March 2, 1917; Acker-man; Martin.

P. 96. *Cia. Metallurgica:* Report of General Funston, January 3, 1917, Archives, 862.20212; also Cobb, January 11, 1917, ibid.

P. 96. *Eckhardt's, intimacy with Carranza:* Senate, Mexican Affairs, testimony of Charles E. Jones and Lathor Witzke.

P. 97. *No transmitter powerful enough:* A much disputed point. Reiterated reports of the existence of a secret German transmitter in Mexico were widely belived at the time but are refuted by the report of the American Military Attaché in Mexico City which stated, "There is no plant in the country capable of being used by Germany and none can be established without our knowing it." Archives, 812.74/60.

P. 97. *Señor Mario Mendez bribed:* Senate, Mexican Affairs, evidence of Lathor Witzke and Major Barnes.

P. 97. *Nauen and Sayville Wireless:* Scott, James Brown, Chapter iv, "Censorship of Communications"; Hendrick, iii, 337.

P. 98. *Germans circumvent Sayville:* Senate, Propaganda, testimony of Captain Lester of Military Intelligence Division of General Staff, 1769. See also German Documents, i, 328, 477 ff; ii, 728. See also Rathom, "Germany's Plots Exposed."

P. 98. *"We have traced nearly every route . . .":* James, 132–33.

P. 99. *Herr Cronholm; Eckhardt's letter to Bethmann:* James, 132–35.

P. 99. *"I now have nine decorations":* NYT, April 24, 1917, quoting Providence *Journal.*

P. 100. *Swedish roundabout:* Hendrick, iii, 338; James, 132.

P. 101. *"What do these compare . . .":* Grew to Lansing, November 22, 1916, U.S. Foreign Relations, 1916, 868.

P. 101. *"Carranza, . . . openly friendly":* James, 135.

P. 101. *Lansing warns Carranza:* Lansing to Carranza, October 27, 1916, U.S. Lansing Papers, i, 224.

P. 101. *Eckhardt informed by headquarters:* James, 135.

P. 102. *Reports of Japanese in Mexico:* Archives, 894.20212/102, /104, /105, /119, /126.

P. 102. *"Ostentatious display":* Parker, American Embassy, to State Department, Archives, 712.94/7.

P. 102. *Major Carpio:* Archives, 712.94/7–25.

P. 102. *German admirals and generals:* Holtzendorff to Hindenburg. December 22, 1916, German Documents, ii, 1262.

Chapter 7. Our Friend Zimmermann

P. 104. *"A very jolly large sort of German":* Gerard to House, November 4, 1913, Seymour, IP, i, 186.

P. 104. *Times fondly called:* NYT, November 22, 1916.

Pp. 104–105. *Bülow on Zimmermann:* Bülow, iii, 178.

P. 105. *Dutch Ambassador's story:* Hanssen, 70.

P. 106. *Chronically through 1916; debate on U-boat:* The military and civil arguments are fully documented in Hanssen and German Documents.

P. 106. *"Ugly mug":* Ludwig, 469.

P. 107. *"Our situation is such . . .":* Speech in Reichstag Committee, January 10, 1916, Hanssen, 121.

P. 107. *Bethmann like Abraham Lincoln:* Gerard to House, November 4, 1913, Seymour, IP, i, 186.

P. 107. *"Cause America to join our enemies":* Speech in Reichstag, March 28, 1916, Hanssen. See also Bethmann's Memorandum of February 29, 1916, German Documents, ii, 1140.

P. 108. *Bethmann's cigarettes and "personification of despair":* Hanssen, 141.

P. 108. *No replacement for Bethmann:* Hanssen, 126.

P. 108. *Bismarck's advice:* Reiners.

P. 108. *Jagow felt inadequate:* Bülow, iii, 176–77. A good portrait of Jagow is in this volume.

P. 108. *Zimmermann "always pro-U-boat":* Jagow to Bernstorff, September 2, 1919, Bernstorff, Memoirs, 165.

P. 109. *Zimmermann fancied himself expert on America:* Gerard, My Four Years.

P. 109. *Consul-General in New York:* German Documents, i, 442.

P. 109. *Zimmermann's hobby:* Ackerman; the hope of a German-American revolt "was one of Zimmermann's hobbies."

P. 109. *"In case of trouble":* Gerard to Wilson, January 24, 1915, Seymour, IP, i, 355.

P. 109. *Henry Morgenthau: Ambassador Morgenthau's Story* (New York: Doubleday Page, 1918), 404–405.

P. 110. *Zimmermann looked forward to war:* Hanssen, Ackerman.

P. 110. *Imponieren:* Gerard to House, August 30, 1916, Seymour, IP, ii, 331.

P. 110. *"Zimmermann hollered at the Colonel":* Gerard to Lansing, February 8, 1916.

P. 110. *"No use wasting words":* German Documents, i, 442.

P. 110. *"Feels and thinks English":* Zimmermann in Reichstag Committee, February 22, 1917, Hanssen, 173.

P. 111. *Kaiser bored by Bethmann:* Gerard to House, March 6, 1915, Seymour, IP, i, 392.

P. 111. *"Gasping in the reeds":* Helfferich in Reichstag, January 31, 1917, Hanssen, 165.

P. 111. *"Bread and peace!":* Hanssen, 152.

P. 111. *"Here in Germany":* Hanssen, 289.

P. 111. *New York Evening Post:* November 25, 1916.

P. 112. *House on Zimmermann:* House to Wilson, March 20 and 21, 1915; also Swope quoting House in NY *World*, November 8, 1916.

P. 112. *Gerard on Zimmermann:* Gerard to House, January 20, 1915, Seymour, IP, i, 347.

P. 112. *American Journalists on Zimmermann:* H. B. Swope in NY *World,* November 8 and 22, 1916; Karl von Wiegand in NY *World,* November 24, 1916; NYT, November 22 and 24, 1916.

P. 113. *Zimmermann conceives Mexican and Japanese Alliance:* Zimmermann in Reichstag, March 5, 1917, Hanssen, 178.

P. 113. *Flowery letter from Carranza:* Ibid.

P. 113. *"Help our submarines":* Telegram of November 8, 1916, Ibid.

P. 114. *Mexico and Japan would be tempted:* Ibid.; also Hazen, to whom Zimmermann explained his reasoning in an interview in 1933.

P. 114. *Mexican Ambassador absent:* Zimmermann in Reichstag, March 5, 1917, Hanssen, 177.

P. 114. *"Neither duplicity nor secrecy":* Hirsch.

P. 114. *"Knew nothing of . . . diplomacy":* Bülow, iii, 300.

Chapter 8. The Trap

P. 115. *"Developing very fast":* Wilson to House, December 3, 1916, Baker, vi, 391.

P. 115. *"Inevitably drift":* Wilson to House, November 13, 1916, Seymour, IP, ii, 390.

P. 115. *Bernstorff averted* Arabic *crisis:* "Without his patience, good sense and untiring effort, we would now be at war with Germany." House to Gerard, October 10, 1915, Seymour, IP, ii, 45.

P. 116. *Bernstorff pleaded:* German Documents, ii, 984.

P. 116. *Germany's rulers willing:* German Documents, i, 265–66.

P. 116. *No decision on land:* Falkenhayn to Bethmann-Hollweg, January 2, 1916, German Documents, ii, 1116. General Falkenhayn is said to have realized that the chances of complete victory vanished at the Marne; Gooch, 54.

P. 116. *Draft peace treaty:* Hanssen, 107.

P. 117. *Admiralty in feverish haste:* Grew to Phillips, October 3, 1916, Grew papers.

P. 117. *Jagow asked Gerard:* German Documents, ii, 987. Gerard's reception by Wilson, Baker, vi, 355–63.

P. 117. *Blustering memorandum:* German Documents, ii, 986–87.

P. 117. *"Jolly the Germans":* Grew Summary. After leaving Germany upon the rupture of relations, Grew, working from his diary and notes, wrote a recapitulation of his experiences at the Berlin Embassy (now deposited with his papers at Harvard), which is here and hereafter referred to as the "Grew Summary."

P. 118. *Did not think highly of Gerard:* Wilson "considers Gerard a reactionary of the worst sort and has but little confidence in his ability—too little, I think." House diary, September 18, 1914.

P. 118. *As if they were office boys:* Grew Summary.

P. 118. *Did not wish to be hurried:* Baker, vi, 353, 365.

P. 118. *Grew wired:* Grew to Lansing, November 7, 1916, Grew Papers.

P. 118. *"Broken in spirit":* Grew Summary.

P. 118. *"At first opportunity":* House to Wilson, November 20, 1916. House papers.

P. 118. *Peace "on the floor":* Ibid.

P. 118. *Lloyd George:* Interview given to Roy Howard for UP, September 28, 1916.

P. 119. *Briand:* Current History, November 1916, 285.

P. 119. *Northcliffe.* NYT, November 24, 1916.

P. 120. *Condescension:* "There was a condescension in this attitude that was offensive." Page diary, April 1, 1917, Hendrick, ii, 223.

P. 120. *"Men and women weep":* Baker, vi, 337.

P. 120. *"Make the U.S. a military nation":* Wilson speaking to House, August 30, 1914, Seymour, IP, i, 293. Wilson's recognition, at this time, of the evils of a German victory is also attested to by Ambassador Spring-Rice who reported to Sir Edward Grey on September 8, 1914 that the President had said "in the most solemn way that if that [the German] cause succeeded in the present struggle the United States would have to give up its present ideals and devote all its energies to defense, which would mean the end of its present system of Government." Spring-Rice, ii, 223.

P. 121. *"We cannot wait":* Stumm to Bernstorff, December 9, 1916, German Documents, ii, 987.

P. 121. *"Neither his accuracy nor his sincerity":* Wilson to House, August 31, 1915, House papers.

P. 121. *"Astute and unscrupulous":* Wilson to Lansing, Baker, vi, 353.

P. 121. *House admired Bernstorff:* Seymour, IP, ii, 334.

P. 121. *Lansing detested him:* House diary, January 11, 1917.

P. 121. *Bakmetieff "a reactionary":* Seymour, IP, i, 327.

Pp. 121–122. *Spring-Rice better off recalled:* House diary, September 20, 1916, and House to Wilson, December 3, 1916, Seymour, IP, ii, 397. Lansing also thought Spring-Rice should be replaced, Seymour, IP, ii, 397.

P. 122. *Bathing Beauty episode:* Thwaites and Flynn.

P. 122. *Hulsen-Haeseler:* Zedlitz. The episode is treated in every biography of the Kaiser.

P. 123. *Deliberately procrastinating:* German Documents, i, 442.

P. 123. *Compromise peace would mean revolution:* Rosenberg, Arthur, *Birth of the German Republic* (New York: Oxford, 1931).

P. 123. *Ludendorff:* Czarnin, 143.

P. 123. *Zimmermann to House:* House diary, March 24, 1915.

Pp. 123–124. *Eliminate Wilson as mediator:* German Documents, i, 133, 156, 244, 265–66. The motive behind the German peace proposal is discussed at length in the postwar German Parliamentary Investigation.

P. 124. *"Friedens Antrag":* Grew Summary.

P. 124. *Zimmermann press conference:* German Documents, i, 407.

P. 124. *"Absolute conquerors":* German Documents, i, 420–21, ii, 1072; NYT, December 16, 1916.

P. 125. *King George:* Page to House, Seymour, IP, ii, 407.

P. 125. *Bernstorff interview with House:* House to Wilson, December 27, 1916, House papers.

P. 126. *"The more we talk with Germany":* House to Wilson, December 28, 1916, House papers.

P. 126. *Answer was yes:* Ibid.

P. 126. *Permission to use State Department cable:* Hendrick, iii, 338–42. Lansing, 227. "Furthermore the American Government permitted me . . . to send telegrams in cipher without the contents of the same being made known to them." Bernstorff testimony, German Documents, i, 478.

P. 126. *Lansing shocked:* Bernstorff to House, December 30, 1916, January 10 and 11, 1917, House papers.

P. 127. *"In the hands of the liberals":* House to Wilson, January 18, 1917, House papers.

P. 127. *"Permission from our government":* House diary, September 18, 1914, Seymour, IP, i, 325.

P. 128. *"Moving in the right direction":* Seymour, IP, i, 271.

P. 128. *"Ugliest room":* Seymour, IP, i, 253.

P. 128. *"Most important world's work":* House to Wilson, February 23, 1915.

P. 128. *"God has given you":* House to Wilson, September 18, 1914.

P. 129. *Footnote:* See Edith Bolling Wilson, *My Memoir,* 246, who says that after her husband's first talk with House upon his return to Paris, the President looked as if he had aged ten years, and said to her, "House has given away everything I won before we left Paris. He has compromised on every side. . . ."

P. 129. *Bypassing State Department:* House to Phillips, June 18, 1915, House papers.

P. 129. *"Through us":* Grew to Phillips, October 10, 1916, Grew papers. Also German Documents, ii, 989.

P. 129. *Bethmann postwar testimony:* German Documents, i, 329.

P. 129. *Zimmermann testimony:* German Documents, i, 479.

P. 130. *Lansing diary entries:* January 21 and May 5, 1916.

P. 130. *Bernstorff complains of Lansing:* Bernstorff to House, December 30, 1916, and January 10, 1917, House papers.

P. 131. *Phillips telephoned:* House to Wilson, January 17, 1917. House papers.

P. 131. *"Unofficially through me":* Ibid.

P. 132. *"If we can tie up Germany":* House to Wilson, January 20, 1917, House papers.

P. 132. *House tells Lansing to see President:* House diary, January 23, 1917.

P. 132. *"We should know":* Spencer, 61.

P. 132. *"There will be no war":* Wilson speaking to House, January 4, 1917, Seymour, IP, ii, 412.

Chapter 9. The Telegram Is Sent

P. 133. *U-boat victory in six months:* Views of the German military leaders on use of the U-boat are fully documented in the testimony and correspondence of Generals Hindenburg, Ludendorff, and Falkenhayn, and Admirals Capelle, Holtzendorff, and Tirpitz in German Documents. Bethmann's testimony, beginning i, 340, presents the opposed point of view.

P. 133. *"Will amount to nothing":* German Documents, i, 525.

P. 134. *High command dialogue:* German Documents, ii, 1317–19.

P. 134. *Triumvirate:* Kurenberg, 313.

P. 135. *His Majesty was pale:* From von Valentini's notes of the occasion, Ybarra, 144.

Pp. 135–137. *Press conference of January 9:* Quoted remarks are all from German Documents: Holtzendorff's, ii, 1219–20, 1270; the Naval Memorandum, 1219–77; opinions of Albert, Haniel, Papen, et al., i, 148, ii, 868–76, 1183–99, 1307; concluding remarks of Bethmann, Holtzendorff, and Hindenberg, ii, 1320–21. See also Ludendorff's account in his memoirs, i, 380.

P. 136. *Kaiser's grunts:* from von Valentini's notes, Ybarra, 145.

P. 137. *"I Order . . . Wilhelm I R":* German Documents, ii, 1210.

P. 137. *Von Reischach:* Reischach, 283.

P. 137. *Von Valentini:* Gooch, 17; Ybarra, 145.

P. 138. *"If it is not trumps":* German Documents, i, 150.

P. 138. *Zimmermann on Western States:* Hanssen, 173.

P. 138. *Zimmermann on Yellow Peril:* Hanssen, 168.

P. 138. *Enticing Mexico:* Hanssen, 178; also Hazen.

P. 139. *Zimmermann to Austrian emissary:* Czarnin, 133–38.

P. 139. *"You must . . . be dilatory":* German Documents, ii, 1013.

P. 139. *Hotel Adlon dinner:* Gerard, *My Four Years*, 361–38.

P. 140. *"Our personal friendship":* Ibid. and Grew Summary.

P. 140. *"Running no risk":* Grew Summary.

P. 140. *Jollying them to the limit:* Ibid.

P. 140. *Deutschland canceled:* German Documents, ii, 1337, n. 1.

P. 141. *U-boat commander:* Nicholas Everitt, *British Secret Service During the War* (London: Hutchinson, 1920).

Pp. 141–142. *Text of Telegram:* German Documents, ii, 1337; text is also in Hendrick, James, Lansing, Sims; German text in Hendrick, 111, 345.

P. 142. *"The blundering Germans"*: Memorandum of January 28, 1917, Lansing, 208.

P. 142. *"Highly entertained"*: Ewing.

P. 143. *Wilson an honorable mediator*: German Documents, i, 283.

P. 143. *Zimmermann on Wilson*: Ibid.

P. 143. *"Absolutely no reliance"*: German Documents, i, 269.

P. 143. *"Any possible means"*: Ibid., ii, 1019.

P. 143. *Period of grace*: German Documents, ii, 1108, 1112.

P. 144. *U-boats already at sea*: Ibid., 876, 1113.

P. 144. *Bernstorff's last plea*: Ibid., 1047.

P. 144. *Jacob Noeggerath*: Maximilian of Baden.

P. 144. *January 29 meeting at Pless*: German Documents, ii, 876; Ludendorff, i, 379–81.

P. 144. *Washington taken by surprise*: Lansing, 213.

P. 145. *Bernstorff calls on Lansing*: Lansing 209–12.

P. 145. *"Finished with politics"*: NYT, February 4, 1917.

P. 145. *Danish journalist*: NYT, May 3, 1917, from Copenhagen, recalling interview with Zimmermann the previous February.

P. 145. *Zimmermann in Reichstag*: Hanssen, 168.

P. 145. *"Icebergs and fish"*: Brooklyn Eagle quoted by Bailey, 641.

P. 145. *Lansing's press conference*: Lansing, 215.

P. 145. *The President told House*: House diary, February 1, 1917.

P. 146. *Japan, Idaho, and Oregon*: NYT, February 2, 1917.

P. 146. *"What shall I propose?"*: Houston, i, 230.

P. 146. *"White race strong"*: Houston, i, 229.

P. 147. *"I refuse to believe"*: Baker, vi, 458.

P. 147. *Hall tells Page*: Hendrick, ii, 215.

P. 147. *After-theater supper*: Gerard, *My Four Years*, 375–76.

P. 147. *Zimmermann to newspapermen*: German Documents, i, 409; *his violent language and emotion*: Gerard, *My Four Years*, 377.

P. 147. *"Warmest way possible"*: Grew Summary.

P. 147. *Telegram of February 5*: Text in German Documents, ii, 1338; also in Hendrick, James, Sims.

P. 149. *Laredo, February 5*: Archives, 262.20212/56; *report from El Paso*, ibid., /58 and /59; *report from San Salvador*, ibid., /79.

P. 149. *"The schoolteacher"*: Ibid., /61.

P. 149. *Page diary*: April 1, 1917, Hendrick, ii, 223.

Chapter 10. "The Most Dramatic Moment in All My Life"

P. 150. *England's financial resources*: Lloyd George wrote in November 1916: "We are rapidly exhausting the securities negotiable in America. . . . The problem of finance is the problem of victory." Lloyd George, ii, 340.

Pp. 150–151. *Hall calls on Hardinge:* This, and subsequent facts about the handling of the telegram in this chapter, are based on Hendrick, iii, Chapter XII, and James, Chapter IX.

P. 151. *Hall's reasoning:* Hall's connection with the Zimmermann Telegram was not made public until the publication in *World's Work,* November 1925, of Hendrick's chapter, "The Zimmermann Telegram," from his *Life and Letters of Walter Hines Page,* published the same year. Hall was immediately besieged by reporters and finally consented to give a short interview to the *Daily Mail* (reprinted, *World's Work,* April 1926) in which he said, "If I had disclosed the actual wording of the telegram the Germans would have suspected something at once." He said the Germans' greatest mistake was that "they never gave us credit for any intelligence." Of course, he added, "our whole object was to prevent the Germans from giving credit for intelligence. . . . I am sure that if the position had been reversed the British would never have been so stupid as not to have suspected that the messages were being deciphered." See also James, 138.

P. 151. *Mr. H.:* The episode of the English printer is taken from James, 134–35.

P. 153. *Pelaez:* MacAdam.

P. 153. *Subsoil oil rights:* Martin.

P. 153. *"Embargo everything!"* The cartoon appeared in the Chicago *Tribune;* reprinted in the *Literary Digest,* March 3, 1917.

P. 154. *Two of German embassy personnel:* On February 23, 1917, Lansing informed the American embassy in Mexico that Richard Kunkel, Assistant Chancellor of the German embassy in Washington, had left suddenly for Mexico City on January 31, and that he believed Kunkel responsible for Carranza's embargo proposal. Archives, 862.20212 /76a. See also *Current Opinion,* April 1917.

P. 154. *Rafael Zubaran:* Spring-Rice to Balfour, February 16, 1917, Gwynn.

P. 154. *Balfour impatiently awaiting:* Dugdale, ii, 137.

P. 154. *Balfour and Japanese Ambassador:* This interview was reported to the State Department by Spring-Rice, Archives, 894.20212/120.

P. 155. *Completed decryptment:* James, 141.

P. 155. *Page's attitude:* The following paragraphs are based on a study of Page's own letters and diary in the Page Collection at Harvard, and those published in Hendrick.

P. 155. *Grey on Page:* Gooch, 198.

P. 156. *"Best I ever read":* B. Wilson, 456.

P. 156. *Bring Page home:* Wilson to House, July 23, 1916, House papers, and August 21, 1916, Baker, v, 371.

P. 156. *Wilson's tears:* Hendrick, ii, 188.

P. 156. *Cleveland H. Dodge:* House diary, January 3, 4, February 22, and March 5, 1917; also Wilson to Dodge, February 6, 1917, Wilson papers, Library of Congress.

P. 157. *Roosevelt: "I don't believe Wilson,"* Roosevelt-Lodge correspondence, ii, 495; *"If anyone kicks him . . . ,"* to Senator Johnson, February 17, 1917, Morison, viii, 1154; *"Trying his old tactics,"* to Lodge, February 20, 1917, Morison, viii, 1156; *"Yellow all through,"* ibid.; *If Germany won . . . ,* to George E. Miller, undated, Hagedorn, 65.

P. 157. *Elihu Root:* Jessup.

P. 157. *Lansing depressed:* Lansing, 236.

P. 157. *Bottle of champagne:* Spring-Rice to Balfour, February 23, 1917, Gwynn.

P. 159. *Footnote, "I almost wept":* Hendrick, ii, 403.

P. 159. *"Most delightful of men":* Lady Constance Battersea, *Reminiscences,* London, 1922; *"Most perfect of men":* Churchill, *Great Contemporaries,* 206.

P. 159. *"Seraphic equanimity":* Quoted by Malcolm, Ian, *Lord Balfour* (London: Macmillan, 1930).

P. 160. *"I cannot doubt":* Statement on Freedom of the Seas given to the American press, May 1916, reprinted in *Essays, Speculative and Political. "Those who think":* Note of January 13, 1917, reprinted ibid.

P. 161. *"Most dramatic moment":* Dugdale, ii, 138.

P. 161. *"In about three hours":* Hendrick, iii, 332.

P. 161. *Page's telegram to Wilson:* U.S. Foreign Relations, 1917, Supplement i, 140; also Hendrick, iii, 333.

P. 162. *"This would precipitate":* February 24, 1917.

Chapter 11. The Telegram in Washington

P. 163. *Polk receives telegram:* All the facts in this chapter about the handling and publication of the telegram by Wilson, Lansing, and Polk are, unless otherwise noted, from Lansing's memorandum of March 4, 1917, reprinted in his *War Memoirs,* 226–32. The time of arrival of Page's telegram—that is, 8:30 P.M.—is noted on the State Department copy, Hendrick, iii, 332.

P. 164. *"All evil counsel":* NYT, February 25, 1917.

P. 164. *"General paralysis":* Elihu Root; Jessup.

P. 164. *Stormy Cabinet:* Daniels, *Wilson Era,* 594.

P. 164. *Republican caucus:* This and following paragraph from La Follette, i, 608, and newspaper accounts.

P. 165. *"Alone and unbothered":* Franklin K. Lane to George Lane, February 25, 1917, Lane, 240.

P. 165. *Western Union:* Lansing. He said the company was "very unwilling to give it up" but that it was finally obtained after "using considerable pressure."

P. 166. *Cryptic comment "astounding":* Wilson to House, February 26, 1917, House papers.

P. 166. *Polk to Fletcher:* Polk papers.

P. 166. *Eckhardt to Zimmermann:* Hendrick, iii, 350.

P. 166. *"Cutaway of fashionable cut":* NYT, February 27, 1917.

P. 167. *"Good Lord!":* Lansing.

P. 167. *"Library lawyer":* Page to House, October 1914, Seymour, IP, i, 305.

P. 168. *Wilson thanks Balfour:* Lansing to Page, February 27, 1917, Archives, 862.20212/69.

P. 168. *Fletcher's answer:* Archives, 862.20212/70.

P. 168. *Aguilar:* Hendrick, iii, 351.

P. 169. *Senator Stone:* NYT, March 5, 1917.

P. 169. *Hitchcock pro-German:* NYT, February 28, 1917. Lansing's Memorandum of March 4 describes him as having "pro-German tendencies."

P. 169. *Hitchcock's reaction:* Lansing.

P. 170. *One reporter:* NYT, March 2, 1917.

P. 171. *"As soon as I saw it":* Lodge to Roosevelt, March 2, 1917.

P. 172. *Senate debate:* Congressional Record, 54, 4569–4605.

P. 173. *Lansing's telegram to Page:* Archives 862.20212/82A. Polk's penciled draft is in Polk papers, Drawer 73, filed under Britain, Embassy, January–June, 1917.

P. 175. *"We have tied the German note":* Lodge to Roosevelt, March 2, 1917.

P. 176. *Hearst instructs editors:* Senate, Propaganda.

P. 176. *Viereck's comment:* Lansing, 231.

P. 176. *Round Table Club:* Round Table Roster. *Gaunt's report:* James, 148–49.

P. 176. *Cabinet worried:* Lansing.

P. 176. *Bell's decryptment:* Archives, 862.20212/81 and /81½.

P. 177. *Villa left Parral:* Archives, 862.20212/77.

P. 177. *Aguilar's denial:* NYT, March 2, 1917; *Japanese denial,* NY Sun, same date. *Eckhardt's denial:* Ibid.

P. 178. *Hale's $15,000: Dictionary of American Biography;* also *Saturday Evening Post,* June 22, 1929; see also Senate, Propaganda, Bielaski evidence, citing copy of a telegram from Bernstorff to German Foreign Office, furnished by the State Department, in which Bernstorff said, "As Your Excellency knows, Hale has been since the beginning of the war a confidential agent of the Embassy and as such he has been bound by contract until June 23, 1918." This was in addition to his salaried post with Dernburg, the German propaganda chief in the United States.

P. 178. *"Of course Your Excellency":* Viereck, *Strangest Friendship,* 190.

P. 178. *"I cannot deny it":* Ibid; also NY *Evening Post,* March 3, 1917.

Chapter 12. Obliged to Believe It

P. 179. *Shattered indifference:* The Washington correspondent of *The Times* of London wrote that the Mexican revelations had aroused the public "more than anything else since the outbreak of war." He said it was "worth a dozen *Laconia* outrages," that the West had never been touched by the submarine issue but that the Mexican plot and Count Bernstorff's complicity "touched it and everybody else to the quick." *Times*, March 3, 1917.

P. 179. *Omaha World Herald:* This and all subsequent newspaper comments are, unless otherwise noted, from the *Literary Digest's* press summary on the Telegram, March 10 and 17, 1917.

P. 180. *Viereck: Strangest Friendship,* 190.

P. 181. *Staats-Zeitung:* And other German newspapers, summarized by NY *Sun*, March 2, 1917.

P. 182. *NY American:* March 2, 1917.

P. 182. *Roosevelt: comparison with Lexington and Bunker Hill,* speech to Union League Club, March 18, 1917. *"I shall skin him alive,"* letter to Lodge, March 13, 1917, Roosevelt-Lodge correspondence, ii, 503.

P. 182. *Alarming reports:* Spring-Rice to Balfour, March 1, 1917, Gwynn. After publication of the telegram, newspapers gave much space to reports of recent German intrigues in Latin America. *Guatemala:* NYT, April 2; *Herr Lehman and Central America:* NYT, April 24; *El Democrata:* NYT, April 27; *Monterey:* NYT, April 18; submarine bases: NYT, May 17, all 1917. *Junta at Córdoba;* Archives, 862.20212/114; *"My men on track":* ibid., /103; *secret meetings:* Consul Canada from Veracruz, March 7, Archives, 812.00/2066.

P. 183. *Fletcher sees Carranza:* Archives, 862.20212/89.

P. 183. *Zimmermann-Eckhardt exchange of telegrams:* All those quoted in this chapter from Hendrick, iii, 349–60.

P. 185. *Hilarity in Room 40:* Hendrick, iii, 356. Page, to whom the telegrams were shown as they came through, found them an "endless delight," ibid.

Pp. 185–188. *Bernstorff and' Swedish trunk:* Details of Bernstorff's departure, search of the *Frederick VIII*, Bernstorff's arrival in Norway and three days later in Berlin are from daily newspaper accounts in NYT from February 9 through March 15, 1917. See also Bernstorff's *My Three Years in America.*

P. 186. *Hall held up Frederick VIII:* James, 151.

P. 188. *Kaiser refused to see Bernstorff:* German Documents, i, 311.

P. 188. *Zimmermann questioned in Reichstag: Times* (London), March 12, 1917. *Current History,* April 1917.

P. 188. *Press scolded public: Times,* article cited.

P. 189. *Zimmermann to Reichstag, March 29:* NYT, March 31, 1917. *Current History,* April and May 1917.

P. 190. *"Alone with Wilson":* "Although I have not much faith in Congress we should be much safer here than we would be alone with Wilson for nine months." Lodge to Roosevelt, February 27, 1917.

P. 190. *Page's urgent message:* U.S. Foreign Relations, 1917, Supplement 2, i, 516–18.

P. 190. *Cabinet unanimous:* Lansing, 236; Seymour, IP, ii, 461.

P. 191. *Wilson to Frank Cobb: Cobb of "The World,"* ed. John Heaton (New York: Dutton, 1924), 269.

P. 192. *R. B. Mowat:* Mowat, 86.

P. 192. *Page's diary:* Page asked himself this question in April after the United States entered the war but wrote the note under an entry of the previous January 16, the day he had received an advance copy of the President's "peace without victory" speech.

P. 193. *Wilson to Baker:* Quoted in *Current Biography,* 1940, article "Baker."

P. 193. *Baker's judgment:* Baker, vi, 474.

P. 193. *Birkenhead:* F. E. Smith, Earl of Birkenhead, *Last Essays* (London, 1930).

P. 194. *Lansing's judgment:* Lansing, 232.

P. 195. *Churchill's remark: Great Contemporaries,* 151.

Index

ABOUT THE AUTHOR

BARBARA TUCHMAN was born in New York City and educated at the Walden School and Radcliffe College, of which she is now a trustee. She was on the staff of THE NATION and THE NEW STATESMAN and served on the Far Eastern desk of the Office of War Information 1943-45. Articles by Mrs. Tuchman have appeared in THE NATION and THE NEW REPUBLIC, FOREIGN AFFAIRS, AMERICAN HERITAGE, ESQUIRE, ATLANTIC MONTHLY and other magazines. The 1963 Pulitzer Prize in General Nonfiction was awarded to Mrs. Tuchman for *The Guns of August*. Her other books include *The Lost British Policy, Bible and Sword, THE ZIMMERMANN TELEGRAM,* and *Stilwell and the American Experience in China.*